THE STRUGGLE FOR NARMADA

Nandini Oza, writer, activist, chronicler and oral historian, has been a full-time Narmada Bachao Andolan activist for over twelve years. President of the Oral History Association of India (March 2020–March 2022), she is the author of *Whither Justice: Stories of Women in Prison* (2006), and *Ladha Narmadecha* (2017). She also maintains a website on the oral histories of the Narmada struggle: https://oralhistorynarmada.in/ and a blog: https://nandinikoza.blogspot.com.

Suhas Paranjape has been working on issues related to the participative management of eco-system resources for the last three decades and more. He retired from SOPPECOM (Society for Promoting Participative Ecosystem Management) as Senior Research Fellow. He is currently a trustee for the Shankar Brahme Samaj Vidynan Granthalaya, Pune.

Swatija Manorama has been an active member of the Forum Against Oppression of Women for the last thirty-five years. She has co-authored books on issues related to women's health, her main interest area, in both Hindi and English. She has also written and translated articles on women's rights, gender justice and environmental issues.

Indira Chowdhury is Founder-Director Centre for Public History, Srishti-Manipal Institute of Art, Design and Technology, Srishti, Bengaluru. She is an oral historian, and former President of the International Oral History Association and of the Oral History Association of India. She is the author of *The Frail Hero and Virile History: Gender and the Politics of Culture in Colonial Bengal* (1998), and *Growing the Tree of Science: Homi Bhabha and the Tata Institute of Fundamental Research* (2016).

THE STRUGGLE FOR NARMADA

An Oral History of the Narmada Bachao Andolan, by Adivasi Leaders Keshavbhau and Kevalsingh Vasave

NANDINI OZA

Translated from the original Marathi by

SUHAS PARANJAPE *and*
SWATIJA MANORAMA

With a Foreword by

INDIRA CHOWDHURY

Orient BlackSwan

THE STRUGGLE FOR NARMADA: AN ORAL HISTORY OF THE NARMADA BACHAO ANDOLAN, BY ADIVASI LEADERS KESHAVBHAU AND KEVALSINGH VASAVE

ORIENT BLACKSWAN PRIVATE LIMITED

Registered Office
3-6-752 Himayatnagar, Hyderabad 500 029, Telangana, India
e-mail: centraloffice@orientblackswan.com

Other Offices
Bengaluru, Chennai, Guwahati, Hyderabad, Kolkata, Mumbai, New Delhi, Noida, Patna

Originally published in Marathi as *Ladha Narmadecha* by Rajhans Prakashan (Pune, 2017).

Translated into English by Suhas Paranjape and Swatija Manorama, and published by arrangement with Orient Blackswan Private Limited.

First published by Orient Blackswan Private Limited 2022
Reprinted 2025

040933

ISBN 978-93-5442-297-3

Typeset in
Book Antiqua 10.5/12.6
by Le Studio Graphique, Gurgaon 122 007

Printed in India at
Replika Press Pvt. Ltd., Kundli Sonepat 131 028, Haryana

Published by
Orient Blackswan Private Limited
3-6-752 Himayatnagar, Hyderabad 500 029, Telangana, India
e-mail: info@orientblackswan.com

CONTENTS

FOREWORD

Listening to Voices from a Movement

Social movements define the times. In India, the 1980s have been defined by the active protests against the building of large dam projects across the Narmada river that flows through three Indian states—Gujarat, Madhya Pradesh and Maharashtra. While the Indian state saw the building of dams as a project that would aid development by providing electricity and irrigation, the Narmada Bachao Andolan (NBA) that began in 1985, saw this as large-scale displacement of people, destruction of livelihoods and grievous damage to the environment. The NBA comprising *adivasis*—the indigenous people, farmers, environmentalists and human rights activists campaigned against the project through rallies, hunger strikes and court actions. In popular perception the protest remained identified with Medha Patkar and Baba Amte. Indeed, both became household names associated with the movement. The adivasi people and their leaders who formed the core of this movement, and without whose participation the movement could not have gathered the strength it did, remained mostly in the background.

Nandini Oza, an active participant in the movement, has been a pathfinder in many ways. She has spent over a decade recording the voices of the affected people, indigenous as well as those belonging to other communities. My first meeting with her at an oral history conference was a memorable one; I recall that her talk brought home to me for the first time that the public understanding of the NBA as represented in the media was quite different from what had happened at the ground level. Those of us privileged to be there at that conference heard about the adivasi leaders, men and women who spoke movingly about all that they had lost—the land, of course, a way of life with its trees, medicinal plants, fish, their places of worship. We heard too about the community's relationship to the river and the pilgrimages around the river that communities undertook and also the kind of forestlands that they worked on. In this book, the two adivasi narrators recollect not only the landscape which now lies submerged but also the slogans and songs of the movement. Nandini's unique position within the movement and outside of it has enabled her to explore the interwoven nature of the land, language, movement and the strong sense of community. Nandini's oral history interviews with displaced communities raise questions about the meanings and the cultural, ecological and human costs of such projects.

By presenting us with voices of the adivasi participants of the NBA, Nandini Oza has sought to push the boundaries of social history beyond the predictable. While others have looked at this movement from the perspective of human rights, law, ecology and development, she has presented the hitherto unheard voices of those whose homes now lie under water and whose village is now submerged and they themselves dispersed into four resettlement sites. This book presents the oral history interviews of two adivasi leaders of the NBA, Keshavbhau Vasave and Kevalsingh Vasave in transcribed form. These interviews summon us not only to read, but to visualise and to understand what is remembered and to engage with the act of 'listening'. The invitation to 'listen' to a narrative (now given a written form and rendered visual), to the memories of a way of life and a political movement enables us to understand how narrators build their own historical narratives and articulate what the movement and their displacement meant for them.[1] Nandini's skillful conversation draws out her narrators, jogs their memory and shapes their mutual understanding of the movement. The oral historian is also, as Michael Frisch tells us, herself a protagonist in this encounter.[2] Nandini, as an insider/outsider, demonstrates lessons in 'shared authority' reminding us that the historian's collaborative relationship with the narrators disallows her sole interpretive authority.[3]

The larger theme of the loss of land and language is not unique to the Narmada movement. Indeed, it is faced by indigenous people all over the world. As G. N. Devy points out: 'Language, orality, identity, environment, gender, belief systems, performance traditions and rights are the issues relating to the struggles and the survival of the indigenous all over the world.'[4] As an oral historian working within the poly-vocal context of South Asia, Nandini is particularly sensitive to the loss of indigenous languages that large-scale displacement brings in its wake. She has conducted eighty-one interviews in seven languages and dialects, resulting in more than four hundred hours of oral recordings. Her attempt to preserve a language that is fast disappearing is, therefore, groundbreaking and inspiring. But her engagement is more than an act of preservation; she lets her interviewees tell their stories in their own words and on their own terms. The results of her interviews are oral histories that provide deep insights into the people's connectedness to the environment, the sense of loss they experienced when often a single village was dispersed across several rehabilitation sites, and their struggles to understand administrative mechanisms both within government and non-governmental bodies.

The interviews hold up before us several interrelated themes—education, land-ownership and the participatory politics of a movement. Keshavbhau Vasave traces his life story, tracing an earlier way of life and an earlier socio-political movement—the Bhoodan movement spearheaded by Vinoba Bhave. It was Vinoba's visit that led to the establishment of a school in their village. In Keshavbhau's narrative Vinoba's movement to redistribute land among the poor was connected to the establishment of the village school, and from there the thread of his narrative carries us through the trajectory of his incomplete education and his involvement with the NBA. Kevalsingh adds another layer to his recollection of village life, contrasting that peaceful life where burglary or theft was unknown with the harsh reality of the present where the educated have misappropriated and spoilt the ecosystem. The contrast of an idyllic past with a degraded present alerts us to the process of meaning-creation through recollection. For memory, as Alessandro Portelli has pointed out, is not a 'passive depository of facts, but an active process of creation of meaning.'[5] In this case, the past is lit up by values that the community held dear before they dispersed and the present darkened by a loss of values.

In the two oral history interviews in this book, the interviewees appear to speak for themselves; and yet these narrations should not be misrecognised as long, artificial monologues because they flow like natural conversations. The depth of the narrators' comfort and their familiar manner of speaking evokes the presence of Nandini, the interviewer. The narrators speak to her and with her throughout, invoking the intersubjective nature of the oral history interview, inter-meshing the role of the interviewer and narrator, even when the narrative is not presented in the conventional interview format.[6] It is her identity as an insider to the movement and as one who has also known the landscape that the narrators allude to in their narratives; without her presence their stories would not flow.

The two oral history interviews in this book enable us to see the narrations as presenting patterns of knowing that interrelate history with memory and legend with politics. Nandini's work in the field, as an active participant and as a recorder of historical memory, creates the context for the narrations. She is also one who shares the narrators' political understanding. Her role moves beyond that of the empathetic listener to one who shares a similar understanding of the movement even if she was not present at all the places and events recalled. Her understanding and experience mediate the emergence of the narratives for she understands their vulnerability and, as a participant in the movement, shares in it too.[7] It is this shared vulnerability that creates the space for Keshavbhau to speak fearlessly about the sense of betrayal people like him felt when educated middle-class leaders such as Medha Patkar turned their attention to other issues. At the same time, the sense of camaraderie that he felt with his interviewer enabled him to express the hope he still holds dear: 'And we won't rest until we build a new Andolan' (p. 129). The interviews presented in this book make us believe that listening to memory can be as much a political act as a transformational one.

Indira Chowdhury
Bengaluru, February 2022

NOTES

[1]For an elegant exploration of the complex relationship between memory and the visual imagination, see Luisa Passerini, *Conversations in Visual Memory* (Florence: European University Institute, 2018 [BABE]); Open Access: http://hdl.handle.net/1814/60164 (accessed 14 March 2022).

[2]Michael Frisch, *A Shared Authority: Essays on the Craft and Meaning of Oral History and Public History* (Albany, N.Y.: State University of New York Press, 1990).

[3]An interesting parallel can be seen in K. Lalita and Deepa Dhanraj's theorisations of oral history interviews with minority women survivors of collective violence. See K. Lalita and Deepa Dhanraj, *Rupture, Loss and Living: Minority Women Speak about Post-Conflict Life* (Hyderabad: Orient BlackSwan, 2016).

[4]G. N. Devy and Geoffrey V. Davis eds, *Language and Orality* (London: Routledge, 2021), pp. 2–3.

[5]Alessandro Portelli, 'What Makes Oral History Different?' in Robert Perks and Alistair Thomson eds, *The Oral History Reader* (London and New York: Routledge, 2nd edition, 2006), pp. 37–8.

[6]Indeed, intersubjectivity lies at the core of all oral history interviews. See Valerie Yow, '"Do I Like Them Too Much?" Effects of the Oral History Interview on the Interviewer and Vice-versa' in op. cit. Perks and Thomson, *The Oral History Reader*, p. 66.

[7]I would suggest that Martha Norkunas's concept of the vulnerable listener, elaborated in the context of family history, might also be applicable to oral historians of social and political movements who have been participants themselves. In Norkunas's words, 'Together narrator and listener negotiate what the narrator must tell, wants to tell, tries to shape into a coherent narrative and *cannot bear to tell*.' See Martha Norkunas, 'The Vulnerable Listener' in Anna Sheftel and Stacy Zembrzycki eds, *Oral History Off the Record: Toward an Ethnography of Practice* (New York: Palgraves, Macmillan, 2013), p. 81; emphasis added.

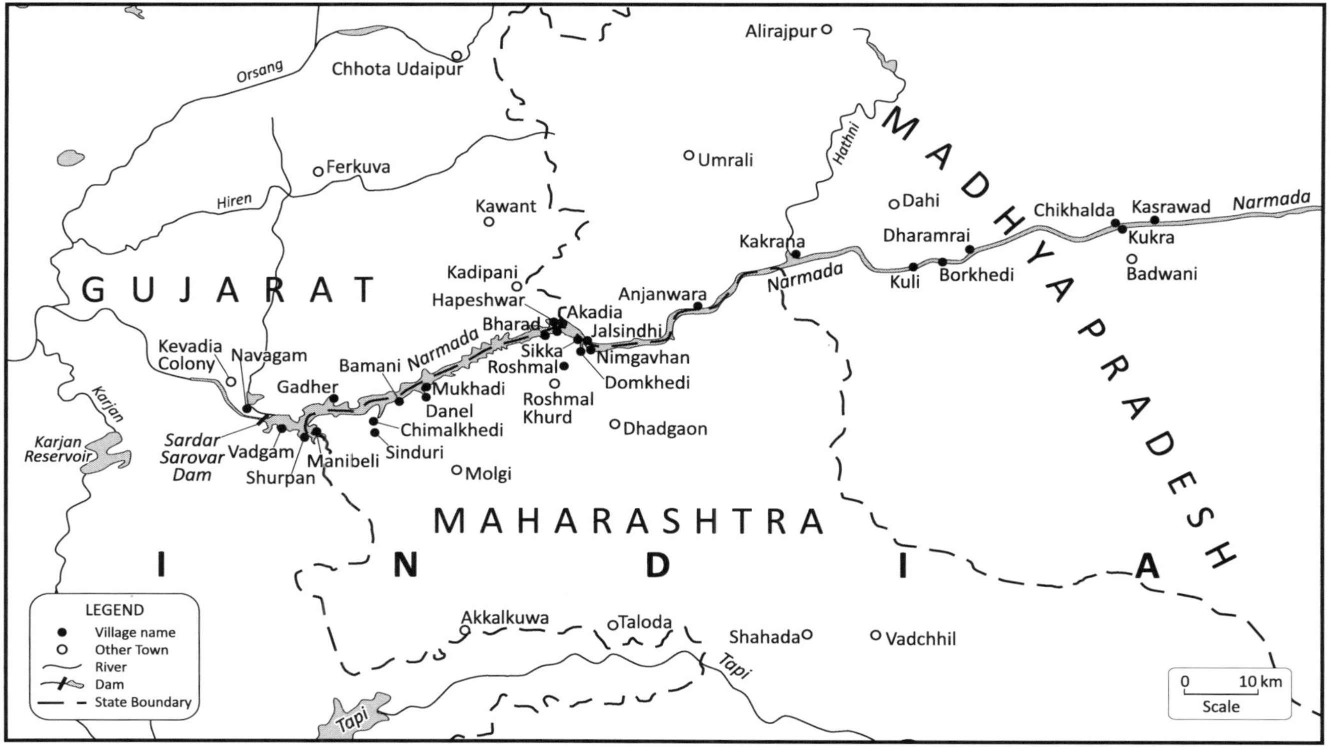
MADHYA PRADESH
GUJARAT
MAHARASHTRA
INDIA
Narmada
Orsang
Hiren
Hathni
Karjan
Karjan Reservoir
Tapi
Chhota Udaipur
Ferkuva
Kawant
Umrali
Alirajpur
Dahi
Dharamrai
Chikhalda
Kasrawad
Kukra
Badwani
Kakrana
Kuli
Borkhedi
Kadipani
Hapeshwar
Anjanwara
Akadia
Bharad
Jalsindhi
Sikka
Nimgavhan
Roshmal
Domkhedi
Roshmal Khurd
Dhadgaon
Kevadia Colony
Navagam
Bamani
Gadher
Mukhadi
Danel
Chimalkhedi
Sinduri
Sardar Sarovar Dam
Vadgam
Manibeli
Shurpan
Molgi
Akkalkuwa
Taloda
Shahada
Vadchhil
LEGEND
Village name
Other Town
River
Dam
State Boundary
0
10 km
Scale

ABBREVIATIONS

AKRSP	Aga Khan Rural Support Programme
ASS	Asargrast Sangharsh Samiti
BDO	Block Development Officer
CM	Chief Minister
DSP	Deputy Superintendent of Police
EL	elevation level
FRL	full reservoir level
GoG	Government of Gujarat
GoI	Government of India
GoM	Government of Maharashtra
GRA	Grievance Redressal Authority
KMCS	Khedut Mazdoor Chetna Sangath
MLA	Member of Legislative Assembly
M.P.	Madhya Pradesh
MPW	multi-purpose worker
MSL	mean sea level
NAPM	National Alliance of People's Movements
NBA	Narmada Bachao Andolan
NCA	Narmada Control Authority
NDS	Narmada Dharangrast Samiti
NGNS	Narmada Ghati Navnirman Samiti
NWDT	Narmada Water Disputes Tribunal
NVDP	Narmada Valley Development Plan
OECF	Overseas Economic Cooperation Fund
OSA	Official Secrets Act
PAFs	project-affected families
PAPs	project-affected persons
PM	Prime Minister

PSI	police sub-inspector
R&R	rehabilitation and resettlement
SC	Supreme Court
SETU	Centre for Social Knowledge and Action
SRP	Special Rehabilitation Package
SSD	Sardar Sarovar Dam
SSP	Sardar Sarovar Project

ACKNOWLEDGEMENTS

Oral history documentation of this kind is not possible without the conviction and faith in this work of all the people I interviewed. I am thankful to all those whose oral histories I have recorded not only for having shared with me honestly and transparently their lives, their work and the many intricacies of the Narmada struggle, but also for having hosted me. Special thanks to Keshavbhau Vasave and Kevalsingh Vasave for reposing faith in me and for having shared their oral histories in great detail and depth.

Two people without whom this work would not have taken off are Venu Madhav Govindu and Shripad Dharmadhikary. Their comprehensive inputs, right from the selection of equipment to methods of dissemination of the oral history, have helped in bringing the project this far. Shripad helped not only in conceptualising this work but also in conducting and recording some of the interviews as well as editing the text, all of which went into the making of the Marathi original, *Ladha Narmadecha*, of which this book is a translation.

Other friends whose inputs have been useful in taking this effort forward are Arundhati Roy, Neeta Deshpande, Nikku Nayar, Rahul Banerjee and Sanjay Kak. I especially wish to thank Dr Indira Chowdhury, one of the pioneers of the oral history discipline in India, for having been a source of encouragement to me in this task, and for writing the Foreword to this book.

Financial support, particularly during the initial years when it was uncertain if this work would see the light of day, from well-wishers and friends like Angana Chatterji, Anirban Hazra, Ashwin Gambhir, Deepak Malghan, Esha Shah, G. Gautama, G. V. Murthi, Hemant Badgandi, Manoj

Saranathan, Neeta Deshpande, Pradyumna Singh, Prasad Boddupalli, Rahul Banerjee, Shankar Krishnan, Shashi Enarth, Subramanya Sastry, Sumitra M. Gautama, Suresh, Venu Govindu, Vinod John and Vinay Kumar helped in keeping the work independent. In the later years, support was provided by the Global Greengrants Fund and Programme for Social Action.

Many activists of the Narmada Bachao Andolan and Khedut Mazdoor Chetna Sangath have helped me in different ways, including with travel to the inaccessible submergence areas in the Narmada Valley. The list is long. However, I would particularly like to mention Rajesh Khanna (Bacchu), Kemat Gawale and most of all, Rehmat.

The other friends who have extended support are Sunil Sawant, Narendra Damle, Ajit Gaunekar, Captain Vijay Prasada and Mrs Sheila Prasada.

Verbatim transcriptions and translations of these recordings have not been straightforward as the interviews are in different languages and dialects. I wish to acknowledge Alka Potnis and Sadhana Dadhich for their accurate transcriptions of the oral recordings of Keshavbhau and Kevalsingh. I am particularly thankful to Vandana Kulkarni for translating the English footnotes and preface into Marathi for *Ladha Narmadecha*. It was a proud moment for me to see *Ladha Narmadecha* published by Rajhans Prakashan in 2017. I am especially grateful to Dilip Majgaonkar Sir, chief editor of Rajhans, for helping me put the book together, and Vishakha Patil, without whose meticulous and painstaking editing the Marathi book would not have taken its current form.

I also wish to extend special thanks to Swatija Manorama and Suhas Paranjape for their excellent translation of *Ladha Narmadecha* from Marathi to English. Retaining the flavours of the Marathi spoken by Keshavbhau and Kevalsingh was not an easy task as they do not speak the 'chaste Marathi' that is spoken in some parts of Maharashtra—their mother tongue is Pawri, spoken by many of the Sardar Sarovar dam-affected adivasi people. The English translation matches the rhythm and flow of their speech and preserves its essence and spirit, which is essential for understanding the struggle of the adivasis of Narmada Valley against the current development paradigm—in the way that they wish to convey it to us—especially because these are oral histories.

For a writer, the most anxious moments are waiting for a positive response from the publisher. Publishing a subject which is not mainstream and which challenges the dominant development paradigm is risky. I am especially grateful to Orient BlackSwan for agreeing to publish the oral histories of two veteran adivasi leaders of one of the most important people's struggles of independent India. It has been a pleasure working with Orient BlackSwan's editorial team.

And lastly, I thank my family for supporting my voluntary work and taking care of my financial needs during large periods of this work. Without their support, I would not have been able to devote my time to the work of my choice and interest.

Nandini Oza

MY JOURNEY

From Being an Andolan Activist to an Oral Historian and This Book

I belong to a drought-prone area of Gujarat, the region of Saurashtra or Kathiawad as we like to call it. Water is a scarce resource for us all. As a young girl I have seen my maternal family in Jamnagar keeping awake at night when water tankers arrived to supply water in a severe drought year. During summer holidays when my father took us to the Velavadar Black Buck Sanctuary or the Gir National Park, we saw the forest guards using tankers to fill the artificial water holes for the wild animals. I have seen borewell water turn brackish in my home town, Bhavnagar, due to salinity ingress. News of the drying up of borewells and lakes, falling water levels in dams and other such information were exchanged during routine conversations whenever people met.

We grew up with stories about water. One lesson we were taught early through a popular saying was you may spill ghee but don't spill water! Another one was *Adi-Kadi Vav ane Navghan Kuwo je no jove, te jivto muvo*, which means, the one who has not seen the two stepwells Adi-Kadi and Navghan is as good as dead. These famous stepwells built in Junagadh in the fifteenth century were one of the first places that my father took us to see as children.

But it was the story of the Malav *talav* at Dholka, built by Rani Minaldevi of the Solanki dynasty of Gujarat in the eleventh century, which fascinated me the most. According to popular lore, when Rani Minaldevi was approached by a poor old woman to change the design of the magnificent lake Minaldevi was building and save her hut, Rani Minal conceded! The design of the lake was compromised and the perfectly round lake lost its glory to save the small hut of a poor woman. Even today one can see a small corner where the old woman's hut may have once stood, protruding into the otherwise perfectly round-shaped Malav talav.

Thus, water and water bodies have been integral parts of our lives, and water a very precious resource to us in Kathiawad. Coming from a family with socialist values, we were taught to look at the inequality and injustice prevailing in society. Therefore, from early on, I was quite clear in my mind that I wanted to work in the rural areas of our country that were deprived of the very basic amenities of life. Water being such a vital resource, I decided to work with communities that were deprived of water.

After completing a Master's in Social Work from Maharaja Sayajirao University, Vadodara, I took up a job with the Aga Khan Rural Support Programme (AKRSP) in Saurashtra. Here, our main thrust was to organise rural communities to conserve soil and water through decentralised watershed management programmes. But even while we were implementing these programmes, I believed these were only temporary measures to address the acute water scarcity of our region. I believed that only the mega Sardar Sarovar Project (SSP) being built by the government on the river Narmada would permanently solve all our water woes and turn the whole of Gujarat into *Nandanvan*—paradise.

The Government of Gujarat (GoG) had termed the SSP a mega dam-based multipurpose interstate scheme, one of the biggest projects being built on the Narmada, as Gujarat's lifeline. There are 245 villages—spread across the states of Gujarat, Maharashtra and Madhya Pradesh (M.P.)—which fall in the submergence zone of the Sardar Sarovar Dam (SSD). Additionally, about 250,000 people were to be affected by the project infrastructure, such as the canal network downstream of the dam, the project colony etc. The project benefits claimed by the government include irrigation, power generation and provision of drinking and domestic-use water to villages and towns in Gujarat. The GoG had promised that we had only to wait for a few more years for all our water problems to be solved permanently. Nobody had any reason to doubt what the government had said, and people of the drought-prone areas of Gujarat, including me, waited for the completion of the SSP with unusual faith and hopes.

After working in AKRSP for a year, I felt the need to understand the other problems our country was facing in different regions to broaden my understanding of issues. So I decided to travel and see for myself the challenges some of the other states were facing. As a part of this study tour, I visited several organisations and people working in remote parts of Bihar, West Bengal, Rajasthan, M.P. and Gujarat.

It was on this trip, while accompanying an activist group, that I came across a rally held in Bhopal by the adivasis and farmers living in the Narmada Valley. It was for the first time that I was seeing such a large gathering of thousands of adivasis and farmers together. What shocked me was that all of them, including women and children, were protesting angrily and fiercely demanding the scrapping of the SSP! So strong was their opposition to the dam that was to submerge their lands, villages, pastures and forests that they were courting arrest en masse. Large contingents of police were arresting people and forcing them into buses to be taken away to an unknown destination. And yet, the people continued to protest by defying the prohibitory orders and the police.

This incident left me shaken as I had never seen anything like this before. No one had told us back in Gujarat that the SSP—that we considered our *jeeva dori*, our very lifeline—was to cause the large-scale submergence and displacement of farmers and adivasis. My mind was filled with many questions. The protest seemed genuine and I wondered if we in the drought-prone areas of Gujarat could get water only at the cost of the thousands of families residing on the banks of the Narmada. I wondered if it was possible to get water without displacing so many people. To get answers, I returned to Gujarat and began studying the SSP as well as a few other dams built in the past. For the next six months, I studied irrigation projects by visiting government departments, meeting officials and reading official documents.

My tour and the subsequent study were an eye-opener that changed the course of my life and work. What I found from the government's own documents was that the SSP was not going to solve the water problems of the drought-prone areas of Gujarat. The government's claims were largely propaganda, a myth rather than fact. The waters from the SSP were mainly going to flow to the better-off and politically strong central Gujarat. Besides, the GoG was spending over 85 per cent of the state's entire irrigation budget on this single mega project. Therefore, most of the decentralised and small water and irrigation schemes of the drought-prone areas of Gujarat had little budgetary allocation left. Hence, despite being approved and cleared, none of these schemes were being implemented due to lack of funds. We were thus being deprived of our own water sources, which we could have conserved had there been sufficient financial allocation made for them. All this information came as a shock to me.

My study also revealed another reality behind large dam projects. The government reports that I studied concluded that the existing irrigation projects of Gujarat like the Ukai, Kadana, etc., were delivering only 45 per cent of their estimated benefits. Besides, these dams had displaced large numbers of villages and the people displaced had not been properly relocated. Among the displaced, the proportion of adivasis and farmers was large. The irrigation department I visited in Bhavnagar, my home town, could not tell me where the villages displaced by the nearby Shetrunji dam had been resettled!

With all these revelations and considering the large-scale displacement of over five lakh people by the SSP dam and its related works, the project was no longer making any sense to me. I began to see my earlier work at AKRSP in a new light. The decentralised soil and water conservation programmes that we were implementing were the true solutions to the water problem of Gujarat. These were cheaper, generated local employment, enriched the environment, did not displace people and had shorter gestation periods. I realised that only these decentralised schemes, if taken up on a large scale, could solve the water problem of the drought-prone areas of Gujarat.

It also became clear to me that efforts by the voluntary sector alone would not suffice to solve the state's water problems. At best, these efforts could help by setting examples and creating models. To address the acute problem of water and soil conservation, the intervention of the state government with its extensive machinery and funds was required.

But the government's energies and resources were locked up in building the SSP! Therefore, the need of the hour was to exert public pressure on the government to change its flawed water and development policies by targeting its emphasis on SSP. I was convinced that the best way for me to contribute in addressing the water problem of Gujarat was to help strengthen the people's movements working on these issues, questioning large dams in favour of genuine and sustainable alternative solutions.

That is how I joined the Narmada Bachao Andolan (NBA) in 1990 as a full-time activist. For the next twelve years, I was a part of this struggle, and I lived and worked along with the people of the Narmada Valley. As part of the NBA, I had numerous responsibilities, from mobilising people to organising and participating in programmes, protest actions, rallies, dharnas, sit-ins, to fundraising, research and documentation. But it was the time that I spent with the people of the Narmada Valley—as we fought against police repression and the rising waters of the dam flooding their villages and homes—which was most enriching of all. We fought together in extreme and difficult circumstances, and this resulted in a lasting bond between us.

Being an activist of the NBA was incredibly challenging, and yet it was one of the most exhilarating periods of my life. The strength and inspiration I received from the struggle was such a powerful experience that I greatly wished to share it widely with other people in the country. There is so much that the stories of the struggle can offer to others.

The SSP has been the target of people's struggles in the Narmada Valley right from the time the foundation stone of the project was laid by India's first prime minister, Jawaharlal Nehru, in 1961. Over the years, these struggles intensified, and have continued for over half a century now. Despite the many powerful forces that have been aggressively pushing for it, the SSP remains incomplete.[1] The struggle of the people of the Narmada Valley has gained extensive national and international support, and is one of the longest anti-big dam struggles of independent India. Importantly, the resistance of the people of the Narmada Valley, along with other similar struggles has contributed significantly to the development–environment debate in the country. Many of the important ideas that are a part of the discussion today, such as right to information, consent and participation of affected people, and environmental flows, find their roots in the early days of these struggles. The non-violent struggle against the SSP spanning many decades now has used several innovative strategies that demonstrate how a mass movement of the marginalised can translate into a powerful force against established and dominant interests.

The Real Strength of the Movement—People Power

The NBA could do all this primarily because of the collective power of the people. I have personally drawn immense courage from both adivasi and non-adivasi leaders of the Narmada Valley. It was awe-inspiring to be a part of a movement like the NBA which brought together and drew the support of thousands of people, groups, and organisations across the country and around the globe. It was humbling to see the indomitable spirit of the people of the villages that faced the swirling waters of the monstrous dam, who despite losing their homes, their lands and forest, continued to resist spiritedly with powerful slogans like, '*Koi Nahi Hatega, Bandh Nahi Banega*' and '*Doobenge Par Hatenge Nahi*'.

The stories of the people of the Narmada Valley and their personal and collective battles are both moving and motivating. To name just a few: the adivasi women of six villages displaced by the construction of the Kevadia Colony in Gujarat were so dreaded that the government officials and police dared not enter their villages unless they were in large contingents. These women stood firm against a state that had succeeded in projecting the SSP as an icon of modern development and progress. These six adivasi villages became the stronghold of the NBA right under the nose of the project conglomerate. The struggles of so many, like Bhula Moti of village Vadgam who let all his worldly possessions drown but did not budge from his village, may seem unbelievable but are true. The courage of 'Durgaben',[2] an adivasi woman who faced custodial rape for fighting the state against her forcible evacuation, is legendary. And of young Rehmal Vasave who resisted the forcible survey of his home and village, till the police shot him dead, and he became a martyr to the cause even before he was an adult.

Such was the determination and commitment of the people of the valley that it is my firm belief that had the government not flooded their villages and drowned their homes by filling up the dam, it would have been impossible for the state despite all its might to have physically captured the lands of the people residing on the banks of the mighty Narmada. How does one fight waters flooding homes and villages? And yet the people of Narmada continue to do so, and one of the largest projects of independent India remains incomplete.

I felt it was important for these tales of extraordinary courage and strength to be recorded in detail and reach others outside the struggle. The stories of the protest actions, the way the fight was waged, the strategies used, the thought processes behind the Andolan, and of course the moving sagas of determination, tenacity and persistence against overwhelming odds by the people of the Narmada Valley have much to offer people's struggles elsewhere.

Nature of Current Documentation

It is not as if there is nothing known about the NBA. On the contrary, being a contemporary movement, the Narmada struggle has been frequently reported in the media, and there is reasonable public knowledge about the movement and the issues it highlights and seeks to address. However, this information and the documentation of the movement in its various forms have several shortcomings.

One is that while much is known or written about the more recent developments of the movement, the history of its origin, evolution and early years is not fully known. Related to this is another issue. The Narmada struggle is seen as a large, well-organised movement that began around the mid-1980s and spread over the entire project-affected area. While this is certainly true, what is not so well known is that the earliest resistance dates to 1961 when the foundation stone of the project was laid by Pandit Nehru. From then onwards the Narmada Valley has seen a series of protests against the SSP, some spontaneous and unorganised, others more structured and organised. These struggles prepared the ground for the emergence of the subsequent movement in the form of the NBA. Indeed, several of them eventually became a part of the larger fabric of the NBA.

However, the most important shortcoming is that much of the media reportage and other documentation have focused on either the issues or major events or on the few prominent faces of the movement. The role, contribution and vision of the local leaders, activists and the common people, particularly the adivasis who have formed the backbone of the struggle, have hardly been recorded.

The Narmada struggle as a mass movement has seen the involvement of hundreds of key people, and this has been an essential characteristic of the struggle. It is primarily because of the collective power of the people that the struggle in the Narmada Valley against SSP has blossomed and been sustained for so long. However, there has not been adequate documentation of this collective strength, the many nuances and turns of the movement and the role and vision of all those who have been a part of it. For instance, all the village leaders who have never been written about and who are not in a position to record their own experiences but who have important stories to tell us and experiences to communicate.

An Oral History of the Andolan

I thus felt the urgent need to address these crucial gaps in the documentation of the NBA. Since many of those who played pivotal roles in the movement could not write their own stories or the history of the struggle, I felt that the best way to record their histories and share their perspectives would be through the voices of the people themselves, and hence thought that oral history was an appropriate way of recording this movement that began half a century ago.

In 2001, I relinquished my full-time work in the NBA and made Badwani, a town close to the Narmada and the headquarters of the NBA in M.P., my home for nine years. Residing in the Narmada Valley gave me the perfect opportunity to record detailed histories of the Andolan through the voices of some of its key players.

For the next ten years, I travelled across the three states of Gujarat, Maharashtra and M.P., collecting the oral histories of prominent NBA activists and key village leaders—adivasi as well as non-adivasi, women and men, and activists from within the valley and outside who played a significant role in the struggle. Some of the people I interviewed were Muljibhai Tadvi, Bawa Mahariya, Kemat Gawale, Pinjari(bai), Dedli(bai), Kamala (Kammujiji) Yadav, Rukmani (Kaki) Patidar, Girish(bhai) Patel, Anil(bhai) Trivedi. During this period, I completed 81 interviews with 409 hours of audio (digital) recording in seven languages and dialects of people spread across the three concerned states. The recordings were in Hindi, Marathi, Gujarati, English, Nimadi, Pawri and Bhilali. Some people were interviewed twice, and even thrice, over a decade to get a more comprehensive understanding of the Andolan's history and events over a wider timeline.

The oral histories I collected are records of a powerful people's movement, as well described by Professor Shiv Visvanathan in *The Hindu*, 29 March 2016:

> to me, the most important historical event of the last two decades has been the battle over the Narmada dam … [It] reflects a journey, a pilgrimage, and a recollection of 30 years of resistance … it demands a different kind of storytelling. This struggle is about a collective history of a people challenging the official history of a nation state. It is symbolic of all marginal struggles of the displaced, the landless, and that which is tribal.

These interviews chronicle the experiences and insights of this historic struggle as seen from within by its most active members but whose voices are rarely heard. An important feature of these oral histories is that the interviewer and most of the interviewees had worked together in the NBA for several years in challenging circumstances. Thus, there was a bond and a mutual trust between them. This was crucial for the free sharing of one's life and one's role in the NBA, the details of the struggle, its many highs and lows, and the personal views and motivations of those directly affected by the SSP.

Importantly, the key figures of the Narmada struggle felt in equal measure the need for such an archive, and so most of the interviewees have lain bare what they have wanted to say. The oral history that has emerged is therefore in the nature of candid conversations and, since the interviewees could talk in the comfort of their homes, in their mother tongue or in a language with which they were comfortable and with someone they knew and had worked with, what they have shared is special. And as a wide range of people, with different experiences, from three different states, with varied cultural, political and social backgrounds have been interviewed, the history so collected is extensive, rich and diverse.

I must also acknowledge here that such an oral history has its limitations, and I do recognise these. Some limitations are inherent to the methodology of oral history, like the fading memories of individuals over the years. Others are specific to this work. For example, adivasi people, even in these changing times, believe that talking of their own contribution to the struggle, however significant, is like blowing one's own trumpet and were therefore reluctant to talk about themselves, till I insisted, but were happy to talk about events, issues and the role of others as they saw it. Another problem was that while people freely shared many sensitive issues and a critical assessment of the struggle and its strategies, and much of this has been articulated well on record, other sensitive information concerning the movement was recounted off the record. Therefore, the narration of some important issues of the Narmada struggle remain only in my memory and in my private notes. Then, of course, my personal limitations of expertise or the lack of it must be accounted for.

However, every form of recording and documenting history has its own limitations, which by themselves do not detract from the importance of the history itself, so long as we recognise them. I have tried to be conscious of these limitations and attempted to address them wherever possible. I believe that the oral histories so recorded, even with the limitations outlined above, are inherently valuable as they represent the voices of people who have actually participated in *making* that history, voices that are powerful, diverse and authentic.

The recording of such an oral history is an ongoing process. But given the sheer volume of the collected records, publication would necessarily have to be done in parts, spread over time. As a first step therefore, this book documents the oral histories of two senior adivasi leaders of the NBA spearheading the struggle against the SSP since 1985.

Keshavbhau and Kevalsingh Vasave

It is my firm belief that the adivasi people living on the banks of the river Narmada and in the submergence zone of the SSP are the backbone of the NBA. I therefore felt it was important to know about their struggle and contribution first and in greater detail. I first interviewed Keshavbhau and Kevalsingh Vasave in 2007, soon after their displacement from their village, Nimgavhan, in Maharashtra.[3] I interviewed them again in 2012, several years after their displacement in their resettlement site, Vadchhil-Shobhanagar, to get a wider perspective on their life, struggle, displacement and rehabilitation.

Keshavbhau, a pillar of support for the NBA, and Kevalsingh, an all-round, all-weather NBA activist, have played a crucial role, both in the making of the Andolan as well as in sustaining it. Recording their work through their oral histories of the movement—one that has contributed immeasurably to the environment and development debate—therefore becomes important for several reasons.

The foremost is that the adivasis of Narmada Valley belong to a largely self-sustaining, remote and therefore isolated region of the country, with hardly any exposure to the world outside. This in itself put them at a disadvantage to fight forces with which they were unfamiliar. Even before they could get any exposure to the aggressive, for-profit development paradigm that existed outside of their world, it was being pushed to obliterate not only their lands and forests but their very life-world. Worse still, they were expected to sacrifice everything for that development model, which was fundamentally contrary to the concept of sustainable development that they believed in, lived by and adhered to against many odds. The battle of attrition in the name of development was an unequal battle from the very start. But, as the stories of Keshavbhau and Kevalsingh show, the adivasis and residents of the Narmada Valley rose up to challenge these unequal circumstances, and build a powerful and historic struggle.

Another reason for sharing the oral histories of Keshavbhau and Kevalsingh first is because their struggles against their individual and collective dispossession are still on. Attention needs to be drawn and support needs to be given to them in every possible way so that the pending issues of those already displaced by the SSP are taken towards some resolution.

Thirdly, while Dalit literature, biographies and auto-biographies are now becoming increasingly available, there is not nearly enough of such work as far as adivasis and their struggles in modern India are concerned. Hence it becomes important to bring to the fore adivasi history from which contemporary lessons can be drawn. Those who will benefit from such a history include all those involved in ongoing struggles of natural resource-based communities of India, as well as students of sociology, anthropology, environment science, ecological activism, civil activism, development studies, human rights and political science, to name but a few. This is particularly necessary when we as a nation march ahead with the slogan of 'Development'. The oral histories of Keshavbhau and Kevalsingh remind us what development means for the adivasi communities of our country and what, for them, constitutes development.

The life and work of Keshavbhau and Kevalsingh educate us and enable us to understand the Andolan, its making, its manifold outcomes, its current status and its future challenges. It gives us rich insights into issues of human rights, justice, equity, and ecological and economic sustainability, among others, as seen from their perspective. By sharing their enduring struggles against one of the biggest and most controversial projects of independent India, the two adivasi leaders help us become aware of all this and much more. It is with this in mind that I chose to share the oral histories of Keshavbhau and Kevalsingh first.

From the Oral to the Written

The oral medium being wholly distinct from the written one, I have had to make some considered adjustments in bringing the spoken to the written form.

When I interviewed Keshavbhau and Kevalsingh, I asked them the questions in Hindi, and they responded sometimes in the Marathi as spoken by them and at other times in Pawri, their mother tongue. As Marathi is not their mother tongue, the Marathi they speak is quite different from the mainstream 'chaste Marathi'. In *Ladha Narmadecha*, the recordings of their interviews were transcribed verbatim, but their articulations were not converted into 'proper' Marathi in transcription.

The transcriptions were edited to make for a more cohesive, broadly chronological narrative, avoiding undue repetition and overlap, and the sequence of narration was changed in a few places to knit together extensive discussions spread over the entire course of the interviews. To stay within the word/page limit of the book, parts of the interview were not included. But, care was taken not to embellish or change the content, substance and essence of their narrations in any way.

The same care has also been taken in the English translation, to ensure that the voices and the narratives of Keshavbhau and

Kevalsingh remain *theirs*, throughout, and it is their history in their own words that this book presents.

A Beginning

This is the first English publication in book form of the oral histories of the NBA that have been recorded so far. There are recordings of numerous other key players in the struggle; these too will be brought out in due course, I hope, through different mediums. Some of these interviews and oral histories—available on the website Oral History Narmada (https://oralhistorynarmada.in)—are particularly important for the future generations, especially for the children of those who have fought so bravely in the Narmada Valley, for the survival of Narmada *Maiya*, for all the animal and plant species that they share their life-world with, and ultimately for the survival of Mother Earth herself.

With this first book of the oral history of the Narmada struggle, I hope to ensure that the people of the Narmada Valley are acknowledged and accorded their due in the development history of our country in general, and in the history of the Narmada struggle in particular.

Nandini Oza

NOTES

[1]Due to its long and troubled history marked by interstate disputes and people's resistance, the SSD was completed only in 2017, submerging 245 villages across Gujarat, Maharashtra and M.P. However, the canal network, one of the main and costliest components of the project, still remains to be completed as this is being written in October 2021.

[2]Name changed; see note 76, p. 267.

[3]Keshavbhau and Kevalsingh continue to live in their resettlement site at Vadchhil-Shobhanagar, at the time of writing this in October 2021. Like most other PAPs, both face economic hardships and social and cultural difficulties at the site. Keshavbhau has had health issues and been wheelchair-bound after his legs were amputated. But despite all troubles, his spirits remain undeterred. Both continue to help other oustees as best as they can.

NARMADA BACHAO ANDOLAN

A Timeline

1948: The (erstwhile) Central Waterways Irrigation and Navigation Commission begins investigations for developing water resources and dams on the river Narmada.

1961: Foundation stone of the Navagam Dam (now Sardar Sarovar Project [SSP]) laid in Gujarat, with the proposed dam height (full reservoir level [FRL]) at 162 feet above the mean sea level (MSL). Spontaneous opposition by affected adivasi communities against the acquisition of their lands for Kevadia Colony, the project colony.

1965: Khosla Commission appointed in 1964 by Government of India (GoI) recommends the FRL height of the Navagam Dam to be 500 feet above MSL, against the backdrop of rising disputes between the riparian states of Madhya Pradesh (M.P.), Maharashtra and Gujarat over sharing of river waters and the dam height.

1969: Narmada Water Disputes Tribunal (NWDT) constituted to adjudicate on the dispute between the three riparian states. Rajasthan made a party to NWDT, although a non-riparian state.

August 1978: Final NWDT order and decision, setting the height of the SSP at FRL 455 feet above MSL, declared on 16 August.

1978: Nimad Bachao Andolan begins in Nimad, M.P., opposing the NWDT award and demanding lowering of the dam height.

December 1979: Final NWDT award published in gazette.

1979–1980: Nimad Bachao Andolan intensifies, but with the change of government in M.P. in 1980, it fizzles out.

1983: Kalpavriksh, a group of environmental activists, travels through Narmada Valley and releases a critique of the Narmada Projects, published in *Economic and Political Weekly* in 1984.

1984: Veteran Gandhians and leaders of the submergence villages in M.P. form the Narmada Ghati Navnirman Samiti (NGNS), questioning high dams on the Narmada, including the SSP. Leaders of the submergence villages of Maharashtra submit a charter of demands on resettlement to the collector of Dhule district.

1984–85: Arch-Vahini takes up issues of rehabilitation and resettlement of the submergence villages of Gujarat. Organisations like Rajpipla Social Service Society also take up issues of displacement by the SSP.

March 1985: The World Bank approves loan to the SSP.

1985–87: SETU: Centre for Social Knowledge and Action, Gujarat, begins work in the submergence villages of Maharashtra, culminating in the formation of the Narmada Dharangrast Samiti (NDS), an organisation of oustees of the 33 submergence villages of Maharashtra. The (Narmada) Asargrast Sangharsh Samiti (ASS), comprising oustees of 6 villages affected by the Kevadia Colony, is also formed.

April 1987: Work on the main dam of the SSP begins.

June 1987: The Ministry of Environment and Forests gives conditional clearance to the SSP.

1987–89: A global network of like-minded organisations working with oustees emerges, questioning the involvement of international financial institutions, like the Overseas Economic Cooperation Fund (OECF), Japan, and the World Bank, in the SSP.

July 1988: 'Anandvan Declaration' by eminent citizens appeals to the government to halt big dams, after detailed deliberations on how big dams have impacted the environment and people.

August 1988: NGNS, NDS and ASS declare their opposition to the SSP on 18 August. The Khedut Mazdoor Chetna Sangath

(KMCS), M.P., plays an important role in the process leading up to a joint struggle against the SSP.

January 1989: Imposition of the Official Secrets Act (OSA) on the dam site and surrounding villages opposed by thousands of people in Kevadia Colony, in which 18 people are arrested. Strike by SSP dam workers led by the Vadodara Kamdar Union, Gujarat, from 30 January, lasting 77 days. Leaders of the union are attacked.

September 1989: Some 250 organisations and thousands of people from across the country assemble at Harsud, M.P, calling for a halt to 'destructive development'.

1989–90: The conglomerate of NDS, NGNS and ASS, along with an extensive network of supporting individuals and organisations, begins to be known as the Narmada Bachao Andolan (NBA).[1]

March 1990: NBA blocks the Mumbai–Agra Highway at Khalghat, M.P., demanding a review of the SSP. Padma Vibhushan Baba Amte shifts to the submergence village Kasravad, M.P., to support and strengthen the NBA.

May 1990: The Japanese government announces withdrawal of its aid to the SSP.

December 1990–January 1991: The Sangharsh Yatra Long March moving towards the dam site is stopped at the Gujarat border at Ferkuva; 5000 people set up a *sangharsh gaon* for 22 days, with 7 people undertaking a fast and demanding a review of the SSP. Then chief minister (CM) of Gujarat Chimanbhai Patel pitches the police, veteran Gandhians and religious heads against the NBA at the border. The World Bank announces setting up of the independent Bradford Morse Commission to review the SSP.

1991: State repression intensifies in the affected villages as the anti-dam struggle goes on with a series of protest actions, fasts, *satyagraha*s and rallies.

June 1991: NBA launches monsoon satyagraha with the slogan, '*Koi Nahi Hatega, Bandh Nahi Banega*' (No One Shall Move, The Dam Shall Not Be Built), opposing illegal submergence in Manibeli in Maharashtra and Vadgam in Gujarat—the two villages near the Sardar Sarovar Dam (SSD).

December 1991: The Right Livelihood Award is conferred upon NBA, Medha Patkar and Baba Amte, and received by Keshavbhau Vasave and Medha Patkar in Stockholm.

1991–92: NBA intensifies its work in supposed SSP beneficiary areas of Gujarat, garnering widespread support in Gujarat. Vested interests, with government support, attack many of NBA's public programmes in the state.

March 1992: Oustees of Gujarat from Malu rehabilitation site return to their village Vadgam due to multiple problems, causing major embarrassment to the Government of Gujarat (GoG), which has claimed the 'best rehabilitation of oustees' in the world.

June 1992: The Morse Commission makes its report public, asks the World Bank to step back from the SSP.

July 1992: Resisting secondary displacement (displacement of people for rehabilitation of oustees from a project) due to the SSP, Dhaniben Padvi, an adivasi woman is killed in police firing at Taloda, Maharashtra.

January 1993: Repression continues in the Narmada Valley; police firing in the adivasi village of Anjanwara in M.P.; houses vandalised. People flee to the forests following a massive police crackdown. Activists of KMCS and NBA beaten in police custody.

March 1993: In an unprecedented move, the World Bank steps back from the SSP as national and international pressure against the project mounts.

April 1993: Senior adivasi leader of NBA, Durgaben,[2] raped during her midnight arrest from her submergence village in Gujarat and while in police custody; she is later kept in judicial custody at Vadodara Central Jail.

July 1993: Bhula Moti—the first person in the line of submergence to offer resistance with the slogan 'No One Shall Move, the Dam Shall Not Be Built' in village Vadgam—is arrested and evicted. Dam waters enter homes in Manibeli and

Vadgam. People remain steadfast in their resolve to not move, and are forcibly evicted and arrested by the police. The NBA declares *Jalsamarpan* (sacrifice by drowning) by the *Samarpit Dal* (sacrificial squad), demanding a complete halt of the dam construction and review of the SSP.

August 1993: The Ministry of Water Resources, GoI, forms the Jayant Patil Committee to review the SSP. Jalsamarpan called off as the Review Committee is set up; but the government refuses to halt the dam construction.

November 1993: Rehmal Punya Vasave, a young adivasi boy killed in police firing at Chichkhedi as people resist forcible surveys of their villages.

March 1994: NBA's office in Vadodara attacked, vandalised and sealed. NBA activists go underground. Nationwide outcry helps NBA restart office, but under police surveillance.

April 1994: NBA files a writ petition in the Supreme Court (SC) of India against the SSP.

July-September 1994: NBA's monsoon satyagraha moves upstream from Manibeli to Jalsindhi in M.P. and Domkhedi in Maharashtra as villages upstream also come under threat of submergence. As the dam height rises, there is unprecedented submergence and destruction of lands and homes in the Narmada Valley.

October 1994: Punarvasan Sangharsh Samiti is formed to look into issues of rehabilitation in Maharashtra.

December 1994: Indefinite sit-in and fast by the NBA in Bhopal, as a result of which the M.P. government calls for stoppage of dam construction.

May 1995: On the SC's direction, construction of the dam spillway blocks is halted at 80.3 metres.

July-September 1995: Monsoon satyagraha in the villages of Domkhedi and Jalsindhi.

1996-98: M.P. government begins construction on other dams on the Narmada as part of the Narmada Valley Development Plan (NVDP). A team of senior NBA members expand work and intensify struggles against the Maan, Veda, Goi,

Jobat, Maheshwar, Omkareshwar and Indira Sagar dams. During extensive hearings in the SC, the NBA successfully counters the government's arguments claiming compliance to rehabilitation and environmental conditionalities. SC orders a stay on construction of the SSD, while the struggle in the Valley continues.

1998: Over 200 leading artists of the country donate their paintings for fundraising in solidarity with the NBA.

January 1999: SC begins final hearings in the NBA matter.

February 1999: GoG appoints a Grievance Redressal Authority (GRA) headed by Justice P. D. Desai on the SC's direction. GRAs are also established in M.P. and Maharashtra later. In an interim order, the SC allows the dam height to be increased from 80 metres to 85 metres, and a further increase of 3 metres humps, before the final hearings conclude.

July 1999: Medha Patkar announces Jalsamarpan if the work on the dam is allowed to go beyond 88 metres.

August 1999: Writer Arundhati Roy gives a call for a 'Rally for the Valley' in support of the NBA, in which several hundred people from around the world congregate in the Narmada Valley.

September 1999: There is large-scale submergence and loss in the Narmada Valley as the dam height rises to 88 metres.

February 2000: The GRA, Gujarat, directs status quo to be maintained on the lands of the six villages of Kevadia Colony pending approval of a fresh rehabilitation package for the people whose lands were acquired in 1961. No such rehabilitation package has been approved as this is being written in January 2022, even as their lands get diverted for Statue of Unity-related tourism.

October 2000: In its final majority judgement, the SC allows dam construction to go ahead, but only *pari passu* with the rehabilitation of the people. The dissenting judgement of Justice S. P. Bharucha sets aside the earlier environmental clearance given to the project and states that the SSP needs a fresh clearance. The SC decision is criticised widely across the country and protests are held.

January 2001: NBA teams carry out relief work in Kutch, Gujarat, following the devastating earthquake in Kutch.

July–September 2001: Monsoon satyagraha starts further upstream in village Kasravad, near Baba Amte's residence in Nijbal, along with Jalsindhi and Domkhedi, as the dam height increases to 93 metres.

September 2001: Baba Amte and Sadhana Tai leave Kasravad on 7 September, to return to Anandvan after 11 years of residing in the Narmada Valley.

September–December 2001: M.P. government unleashes repression in villages opposing forcible surveys, and begins distribution of cash compensation instead of land for land.

March 2002: Communal riots and carnage in Gujarat and widespread planned attacks on minority communities as also in areas close to the villages that have been part of the NBA.

May 2002: In an emergency meeting held by the Narmada Control Authority (NCA), permission is given to increase the dam height to 95 metres plus 3 metres humps. The M.P. government cuts forests in villages in the submergence zone in Alirajpur district.

June 2002: Some 6,000 families in 38 submergence villages in M.P. receive eviction notices.

September 2002: Dam waters rise to 107 metres at the dam site, causing unprecedented submergence of villages and lands. People in Domkhedi thwart the Jalsamarpan of NBA activists, while police fail to arrest people standing in neck-deep waters.

May 2003: NCA gives permission to increase the dam height to 100 metres.

March 2004: NCA gives permission to increase the dam height to 110.64 metres.

April 2004: SC refuses to halt dam construction but rules that land-based rehabilitation is mandatory in M.P. and that cash compensation is not acceptable.

August 2004: Waters at SSD reach 113 metres, causing large-scale submergence and destruction in all the adivasi villages of

Gujarat and Maharashtra, without full and proper resettlement. Many adivasi villages of M.P. also face unprecedented submergence. The GoG puts pressure on the villages affected by Kevadia Colony to shift to allow for fresh tourism plans on their lands; people protest.

April 2005: SC states there is no distinction between temporary and permanent submergence; that adult sons of landholders should be considered as separate family for rehabilitation. Over 100 people are swept away downstream of the Indira Sagar Dam due to sudden release of dam waters.

January 2006: NBA exposes scam in disbursement of cash compensation, fake registry and violations in rehabilitation of project-affected families (PAFs) in M.P.

March 2006: NCA gives clearance to raise the dam height to 121.92 metres. This is the final height of the dam wall. Gates of 18.30 metres to be installed at this level to take the final height to 138.68 metres.

March–April 2006: Indefinite sit-in and fast at New Delhi by NBA against NCA's decision permitting increase in the dam height.

April 2006: Narendra Modi, then CM of Gujarat, undertakes a counter 51-hour fast in support of the dam construction.

December 2006: Dam height raised to 121.92 metres. Permission to install the dam gates does not come till June 2014; but other works like building of canals continue, and so does large-scale submergence in the Narmada Valley, without proper rehabilitation of oustees.

October 2007: NBA files a petition in the M.P. High Court concerning widespread corruption in resettlement-related works in the state.

November 2008: Commission of Inquiry set up under former High Court Judge S. S. Jha, as per the order of Jabalpur High Court, into extensive corruption in rehabilitation and fake registry in lands for rehabilitation.

2009–2013: Hearings before the Jha Commission and court hearings continue. Hearings in SC concerning non-rehabilitation of people and corruption in allotment of lands and cash compensation also go on.

August 2013: M.P. High Court puts a stop to cash compensation in lieu of land-based rehabilitation.

October 2013: Statue of Unity-related works pick up speed in Gujarat, in which more adivasi lands around Kevadia Colony get diverted for tourism purposes.

May 2014: Narendra Modi is sworn in as the Prime Minister (PM) of India on 26 May. Immediately thereafter, NCA gives approvals to install the 18.30-metres high dam gates in June 2014. Installation of dam gates takes three years.

February 2016: The Jha Commission submits its report on corruption in rehabilitation of SSP oustees in M.P.

January 2017: Indore High Court rules that those who have taken first installment of cash under the Special Rehabilitation Package (SRP) in M.P. will not lose their rights to land-based rehabilitation.

February 2017: SC goes against its own earlier decision and provisions laid by the NWDT for land-based rehabilitation, and orders GoG to pay Rs 60 lakhs or Rs 15 lakhs, depending on category, to those oustees not yet rehabilitated; with this payment, it ruled, they would be considered fully rehabilitated.

June 2017: NCA in its 89th emergency meeting on 16 June, grants permission for closing the dam gates and impounding water to FRL of 138.68 metres.

September 2017: PM Narendra Modi dedicates the dam to the nation on his birthday, 17 September, although the SSP canals remain incomplete, and so also the rehabilitation of its oustees.

October 2017: People repeatedly face the tragedy of submergence without resettlement as waters rise to 139 metres at the dam site.

October 2018: The Statue of Unity, the tallest statue in the world, inaugurated near the dam site as more and more lands of adivasis are diverted for tourism purposes in and around Kevadia Colony.

2021: The struggle for justice and proper rehabilitation continues in the Narmada Valley 60 years after the first protests started with the laying of the foundation stone of the dam at Navagam, Gujarat. The SSP canal construction also remains incomplete. Large quantities of waters of the Narmada from the SSP continue to be diverted to those projects and areas that are outside the official project plan and command area.

NOTES

[1]The NBA challenged the gigantic SSP on river Narmada. The dam alone was slated to displace 250,000 people from a total of 245 submergence villages across the states of Gujarat, Maharashtra and Madhya Pradesh. Another 250,000 were to be affected by project-related works like the massive canal network downstream of the dam and the SSP project colony called the Kevadia Colony. It is important to remember that the lands of six adivasi villages were first acquired in 1961 for the Kevadia Colony near the dam site in Gujarat. Back then, the adivasi inhabitants of these six villages were not rehabilitated, and only received meagre compensation for their standing crops. The oustees of Kevadia Colony continue to struggle for rehabilitation even now 60 years later, as this is being written in October 2021, as some of their lands that are no longer required for the dam after its completion in 2017 have been transferred to the Statue of Unity-related five-star tourism. (See: https://oralhistorynarmada.in/early-history-of-the-movement/muljibhai-tadvi-interview/ [accessed 24 November 2021].)

[2]See note 76, p. 267.

I

A CONVERSATION WITH **KESHAVBHAU VASAVE**

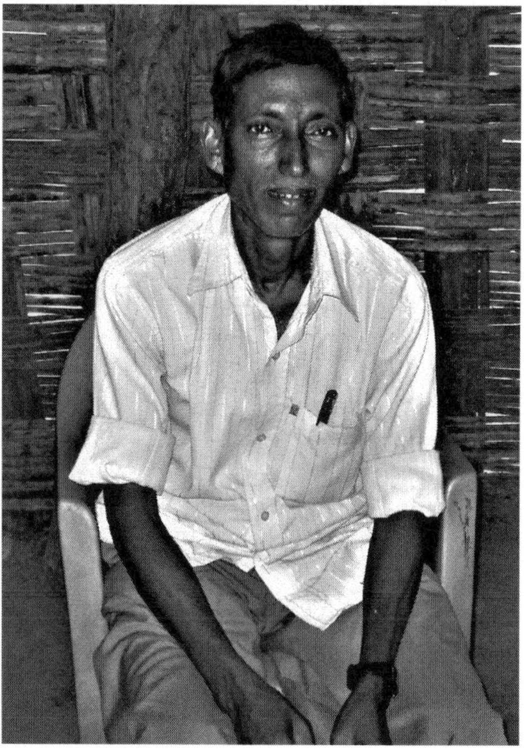

When schools were started in our villages, I was given the name Keshav Vasave on the rolls. But before that, in our Pawri language, I was called Keherya. Father's name, Sikka. Caste, Vasave. Village, Nimgavhan.[1] Tehsil, Dhadgaon (Akrani). District was then Dhule. That was my address.

In this region, schools existed only on paper. None of the schools could run—not even for a day. When Acharya Vinoba Bhave[2] first visited Akrani Tehsil, I must have been some eight or ten years old. Vinobaji reached Nimgavhan via Dhadgaon. Dashrath Tatya Patil[3] of Dhule was accompanying Vinobaji on his march.[4] One of Vinobaji's activists, Dagadu Sonavane used to stay in our village.

Many activists from many different villages had come to stay with Vinobaji, and several meetings were held over four or five days. There was also a discussion about starting *Bhoodan*[5] schools in Akrani Tehsil. During that discussion, Vinobaji asked, 'Who will take up the responsibility of a teacher in Nimgavhan?' Dagadu Sonu Sonavane raised his hand and said in assurance, 'I am ready to start a school in this village.' And so Dagadu Sonu Sonavane (Dagadu Maharaj) started the first school in Nimgavhan in 1958.

In those days, except for the one in Surwani, there was no other *ashramshala*[6] in Akrani Tehsil. In the beginning, there were only fifteen to twenty students in the Nimgavhan school, and the first student from the first batch was Ratansingh Satu Tadvi from our village. He is now a music teacher in Achalpur, Paratwada. He is still known as a teacher who studied in the Nimgavhan school!

In 1960 the school started regular teaching from the first standard onward. I was one of the students from that class. Villagers from the nearby villages started sending their children to this school. Then gradually it turned into an ashramshala. There used to be about 150 students on its rolls.

Our teacher was a follower of the *Varkari*[7] sect. He was keen on giving us a good education and so he managed to get us admission in the fourth standard in the school at Devachi Alandi[8] (Alandi, village of gods). From 1963–64 onward, I studied in this school, from the fourth to the seventh standard. During school hours I followed the school rules and studied. Outside school hours I would go around the houses asking for *madhukari*[9] to feed myself. In the evening we participated in *bhajan-kirtan*[10] and *Haripath*.[11]

We had very good support in Alandi. Madhukari was an organised practice that provided us with food. We hardly had to visit eight to ten houses and our plates would be full. In Alandi there is a big institution set up in the name of Jalarambaba, a saint. We, as adivasis and Rajput students, were provided with one free meal a day at the institution. The chairman of the Varkari educational institute gave us special attention and watched out for us. There were dharmashalas everywhere. Somewhere or the other, there would be a charitable or religious event taking place, and we would be served our meals there. We were always the first to be invited to these events.

The teaching in these schools was very good. That is why we used to outrank the brahmin students. Teachers used to consider us better than the others. We also got beaten up for that. But we became very well known. 'Nimgavhan has gone far ahead, way ahead…' That was the talk.

Our gram panchayat in Roshmal Khurd was a group panchayat that consisted of members from twenty villages. Right from the beginning it had a sarpanch, who used to be elected unopposed every five years. He was also an Akrani Tehsil leader. He realised that if we children succeeded and became well-educated, we would present a danger. He thought, 'Since these villages are very remote, I have to make sure no one from the twenty villages is better educated than me and my children. They should all live under my thumb.'

So one day, with the idea in mind that we twenty-two students should not study further, he came to Alandi with a truck, and lied to us. 'Your parents want all of you to come back immediately.'

He loaded us onto the truck, took us back and deposited us in our homes. He also threatened our parents. 'Do not send your kids to Alandi. They are not safe there, out of your sight. Someone may sell them off, and you wouldn't know a thing about it. They will get lost. It is such a big city.' He misguided our parents. And so, our parents opposed any further education for us. Our education stopped right there.

The Bhoodan school in our village ran for about eight to ten years. During that time many students studied there, and went on to study further. Then within the Bhoodan movement itself big differences arose. Due to that conflict the school could not run beyond 1966-67. Other schools in the Akrani villages of Dhadgaon Tehsil also closed down. The government began opening schools in different villages of Dhadgaon Tehsil.

According to the Bhoodan school records, my birth date is 15 November 1953. But in my estimate, I am older than that. I work on the assumption that I was born in 1950.

Nandini: Do you remember what happened at the time Vinobaji visited Nimgavhan?

Keshavbhau: Vinobaji stayed in Nimgavhan for four or five days. A number of activists from all over India came with him. He had come to see if the projects meant for the villages were truly reaching these remote areas of the country. For generations, the people from these villages did not speak languages such as Marathi, Hindi or Gujarati. They spoke either Pawri or Bhilori. They were also unaware of their own rights, the rights they had from village to tehsil level.

They also took up the work of building field bunds to prevent the fertile top soil from being washed away. They taught us that if the top soil is washed away, our land would be of no use. Field bunds were built in every field in our village.

Next was the question of the various departments at the tehsil. Which department had jurisdiction over the lands we tilled? They were in the name of the forest department. Even so, we now had possession. What is the forest department? What is the tehsildar's office, the block development office? What are the functions of the police stations? They explained all these things to us. We had heard that in Akrani Tehsil and in many states, Vinobaji has managed to get people to donate land for Bhoodan. Since ours was a forest village,[12] there was no land donated for Bhoodan. He told us, 'Work to improve the land you have in your possession. Not a single boy in any village should remain illiterate. And after they finish school, they should make their life and labour meaningful.'

There were large mango trees in the village, and the activists stayed in the shade of these trees. All of them had their own mattresses and covering sheets. They carried with them the necessaries to cook their own food. Some villagers also contributed. The village head was Satu Pisa Karbhari and the police *patil* was Nimba Banya Vasave. These two good people gave the visitors their full support. In Nimgavhan all of us got motivated by Vinobaji's meeting. And our village head, Satu Pisa Karbhari, who used to speak only Pawri, forgot his Pawri and started speaking Hindi, Marathi and Gujarati and became well-acquainted with Delhi and Bombay. He became a leading activist. He started spreading the message in other villages. He went to these villages and motivated the people. He told them, 'Join the Bhoodan movement. Without the movement we will not get the opportunity to be educated.'

Our teacher showed Nimba Banya and Satu Pisa Karbhari the two pilgrimage centres of Devachi Alandi and Pandharpur. After they had seen these two places, they realised how very remote our villages were. There they took an oath that they would wear the *maal*,[13] and that they would behave and live their lives like true human beings. And that henceforth they would not allow monstrous, savage behaviour in the villages. They took the oath and on their return to the village, they brought a ban on liquor. From that day onward, no one would brew liquor in the village and no one would drink. They tried this in earnest for many years. And they succeeded. They began to spread these teachings in other villages. Bhoodan taught us a lot and put us on the road to further progress. From that time, Nimgavhan became a leading light among the villages in Akrani Tehsil.

The school was held in a small room in the patil's house. There was no blackboard, but we had sliced off a rectangular wooden piece on which one could write numbers or the alphabet. After a few years, the Bhoodan people arranged for food for the students, and the school became an ashramshala. The villagers supported them and built eight or ten rooms where the students could stay. They arranged for a kitchen. The Bhoodan group helped open and run a small shop. A ration shop was also opened. The grain from the ration shop was bought at the regulated price by the group and supplied directly to the school. There was little need to buy grain from outside.

When we started our school, many activists from all over the country visited us. There were no roads back then. You had to walk 30–40 kilometres from Dhadgaon. There was thick forest. No one ventured to travel alone from one village to another.

In our village there are two lineages, one is that of the Tadvi and the other one is of the Vasavas. When I was young, I recall that the population of our village was something like sixty. Years ago, one person from the Tadvi lineage came to the village and began to live there. He was a good worker, and so, one of the villagers gave him his daughter in marriage and made him a resident son-in-law. That is how the two lineages in our village came into existence. Before that all our ancestors were Vasavas and ours was a Vasava village. That son-in-law was very smart and cunning. He had three or four wives. One of them was the daughter our ancestor had given to him in marriage. After that marriage he took two more wives. This way, with three wives, his property increased manifold. He also started snatching land from his father-in-law. He managed to get four big plots of forestland transferred on his name.

In this way, in my own lifetime the total number of people in our village increased from sixty to 4,000!

We led our lives the way our ancestors did. It was based on the land, the water and the forest. Since our population was small, if we sowed jowar and maize seeds on the *khashi*[14] on the banks of the Narmada, that was enough for us. We never felt the need to plough forestland. We reaped hundreds of quintals of maize. The Narmada provided us fish, and the forest provided us fruits and tubers. We had a very large number of mahua trees and brewing liquor from mahua flowers was an ancestral tradition, and every evening people would be high on the mahua liquor. Our teacher really had a hard time convincing people about his way. Since he was a Varkari, he used to turn to God Vitthala of Pandharpur in despair, 'Oh, Lord Vitthala, how long will this go on? Please make them stop.' Our Guru Maharaj would keep praying all the time!

Nandini: When you went to Alandi, it was the first time that you had stepped out of your village. What was that experience like?

Keshavbhau: Till that time, I had never heard the name of Lord Ram and had never gone to a temple. In Alandi, we had to get up at four in the morning, take a bath and a circumambulation of the village at five. That was the rule. Then we used to study for a couple of hours in the morning. Immediately after that we used to go out for madhukari. We had school from eleven to five. As soon as we reached home after five in the evening, we had to go out to make arrangements for our evening meal.

In the fourth standard we learned about all the saints and leaders in Maharashtra such as Jyotiba Phule and Shivaji Maharaj. They also taught us geography. There have been many saints, and we studied their biographies and their history. Dnyaneshwar wrote his treatise *Dnyaneshwari* at the age of sixteen. Why should we remain behind? That was the question that motivated us to study at the school.

There were differences in language too. We spoke Pawri at home, but it was the Marathi of Pune that was considered pure. That was the language we had to speak. At Alandi we were taught Sanskrit along with Sanskrit shlokas and shlokas from the *Gita*. I had memorised the ninth, twelfth and fifteenth chapters of the *Gita*.

We used to spend between one to two hours in the morning and evening in the bhajan-kirtan of Dnyaneshwar, Tukaram and other saints. Another thing—something we do not do over here—as soon as we got up in the morning, we watered all the trees and tulsi plants around the dharmashalas. Wherever prayers and kirtans were held, we would attend them without fail.

The kirtans would describe how we should retain the good things and leave the bad things behind. I am not sure how many among the twenty-two of us kept the lessons in their minds, but I have certainly kept them in my head. I was very keen on pursuing my education further, but that was strongly opposed and I could not study any more.

All twenty-two of us had to come back. I was crying and shedding tears for a long time. I had to leave school in 1966. I was crying all through 1967 and 1968, asking myself why I could not study further. My teachers wrote me letters. I had scored 95 per cent, and it was all wasted. My teachers tried to persuade me. 'If you don't have the money, do not worry. We will send you a money order. Come and join immediately.' But my parents were ignorant, so they did not let me go. And I could not continue my studies.

After two years it was time for marriage! In 1968 I got married. After marriage there was no question of studying further. And so, I turned to the farm and started looking after it.

Our Dagadu Maharaj too was forced to leave by the Roshmal Sarpanch. He was threatened with death. 'Are you bent on staying here? We will kill you.' When he received that threat, Maharaj left for his own village. And in this way even the Bhoodan School closed down.

A number of years passed before Maharaj left his Narmada *parikrama*[15] and came back to my house in 1972. We started another school. Because the (government) school existed only on paper. He used to have his meals at my place and once again we started teaching the children. Many children learnt to read and write. But whenever we demanded a school in the village, the Block Development Officer (BDO) and the Collector Sahib, would say, 'There is already a school in your village. What more do you want?' But in reality, the school did not function. After dealing with a lot of this, our Guruji said, 'The government is not listening. We want to spread knowledge. Let us begin our journey chanting the name of God, *Hare Ram, Hare Ram*. And we will travel in the form of a *Dindi*[16] and visit the villages one by one.' Finally, from 1973 for two months every year we went from village to village chanting *Hare Ram, Hare Ram, Hare Krishna, Hare Krishna*. Forty or fifty children used to accompany us. And there were many people who were willing to give. Some gave in the form of grain.

There are hundreds of thousands of people who take up the Narmada parikrama every year. But in the Shoolpaneshwar forest nobody provides them with food.[17] We then took a decision that we should start serving them meals. I was the first to start this practice.

The people who started their parikrama of the Narmada from Rajghat[18] arrived here after four or five days, hungry and tired. And they found rest and peace at my place. I did not have enough grain and did not have all the necessary equipment; I also fell short of spices. But never did I allow anyone to go hungry. We continued this practice from 1973 right up to the year 2004.[19]

From 1973 onwards a large number of people have arrived in the village for the Narmada parikrama. And we have served them food, not for two or three but for more than twenty years. As the height of the Narmada dam increased, the number of people who took up the parikrama dwindled. Today, after the construction of the Sardar Sarovar Dam (SSD) has been completed, the practice of the parikramas has all but stopped! Those who take it up now start the parikrama from a point in Shahada Tehsil on the Ankaleshwar–Burhanpur Road, and those on the other side of the Narmada start from Rajpipla.

Nandini: It must have taken a lot of work to feed the *parikramavasis*.

Keshavbhau: Our Dagadu Maharaj would collect 10–20 quintals of grain from three tehsils namely, Taloda, Shahada and Akkalkuwa. The grain was loaded onto donkeys and carried here.[20] My wife would grind the grain between the grindstones. I would fetch water from the Narmada and firewood from the forest. During the winter, we would pile up the firewood and light fires, and the pilgrims would sit around the fire in the evenings warming themselves. We served them cooked meals. For those who observed caste restrictions we gave them uncooked grain and other necessaries. Later on, Dongare Maharaj from Gujarat heard about us. 'In the Shoolpaneshwar forest there is this brother who is doing very good work. We must invite him.'

He called me to Malsar. I also took Dagadu Maharaj with me. I tried to bow down in front of Dongare Maharaj,[21] but he did not allow me to do so. Instead, it was he who touched our feet. He said, 'I am aware of your reputation. You are doing a great job. I have called you over to speed up your work. We would like you to continue providing meals on our behalf. We are providing you with some assistance. It will be sufficient for a few days. Once you are made a trustee,[22] the amount will be automatically sent to you on a regular basis. And this will help you continue your work smoothly.' We took on the responsibility of running three centres. I was to manage the Nimgavhan centre. The Bhusha centre was run by Murlidhar[23] and Dagadu Maharaj was given the Zharkal centre. The other two could not continue, but Nimgavhan continued to provide meals.

I fed them whatever I had grown myself. Because, you know, by now I knew that in our country there were many saints and sadhus. I had read their biographies. I realised that feeding someone should not be a problem. We had only a small piece of land, and most of the guests would stay with me, but we never fell short.

Now let me tell you about something that happened in later years. I got married in 1968. In 1970[24] there was a very severe drought. That year, the Narmada also had big floods. Many crops sown on the banks of the Narmada were washed away. Today, if there is ever a flood of that magnitude it will simply destroy the Sardar Sarovar! So, there was this big drought. Grain was scarce. A full week would go by before we could eat jowar rotis again. In March and April, we somehow survived on mahua flowers and that kind of stuff. But by September and October the situation became extremely bad. I was repenting and crying all the while, thinking that if only I had pursued my education and taken up a job, it would have been so much better. Towards the end we dug tubers and roots from the forest and ate the leaves of trees and managed to survive. We did not even have chilli to garnish that stuff.

And look, if there are rains in September and October, we get a good jowar crop. But if there are no rains in September and October, then we are in for a big drought. At that time, we grew the traditional tall jowar. And that does not ripen till very late. Hybrid jowar came later. I was the one who brought hybrid jowar to the village. I was the first to sow it in my fields. People were scared. They were like, 'Oh, my God! From where has such a big cob come? Come, let us go and see.' It was only after they saw my crop that everyone started to grow hybrid jowar. You may have only a small piece of land, but if you put in the effort to tend it well, you will get a good crop even in that small piece of land. If you do not weed it, then you will harvest very little and you may get small cobs. But if you look after it and put in labour, it will give big healthy cobs. We had no training in agriculture. Acharya Vinobaji had said at that time that if you do good farming, you get good produce. But our people, they were not willing to abandon the tall jowar, were they? Only after they stopped sowing the tall jowar could they progress. The tall variety of jowar needed water right up till the end of October to get a good crop.

Nandini: By tall jowar you mean the local *desi* variety?

Keshavbhau: Yes, the *desi* variety. It takes up to four or five months before it is ready to be harvested.

Nandini: There was a thick forest in Nimgavhan. There were mahua trees. The Narmada had fish.Then why did the people face difficulties and scarcity despite all these?

Keshavbhau: Look, mahua has been there in Nimgavhan for a very long time. All over Akrani you get mahua. But how can you eat mahua every day? You can eat it once, you can eat it twice maybe. But mahua every day?

Nandini: Was it not possible to sell mahua and carry on for a few days?

Keshavbhau: Earlier mahua flowers were not sold. It is only nowadays that you can sell it and get twenty or thirty rupees a kilo! Another issue was that of the mahua fruit—*tadambi*. We used to get a large amount of oil from it. In those days we never sold anything. Buying and selling started sometime after 1980. Now you won't get any fruit in the forest. All of it is sold. *Puhadia* seeds are sold at eight to ten rupees a kilo. *Ambadi* seeds will fetch eight to ten rupees a kilo. *Behada* also fetches some money.

Nandini: In Alandi, was there any caste discrimination?

Keshavbhau: A lot! Quite a lot. In Alandi we were not allowed to touch brahmins. They subjected me to a lot of injustice. I got 95 per cent marks, so they threw stones at me. They would say things like, 'You practitioner of black magic! You want to get ahead of us? *Chya Maychya*! We will kill you and throw away your body.'

Those are the kind of bad words they used. I said, '*Arre baba*, you too get educated! I have not brought any undue influence to bear, have I? Whatever my teachers taught me, I wrote down on the basis of my own experience. And I am not the one who has written this report card!' But they were not prepared to listen to me.

In Alandi, the Varkari sect is the foundation of the society. It is based on the Hindu religion. In those days, I listened to the sadhus and saints and followed their preaching. I used to say, he is Muslim, he is Christian, and he is something else, and so on. But after I became an activist in the Andolan I saw that there were many people belonging to many different religions and castes who worked together with all of us. Here we were all people who were poor and who faced injustice in society. That is why I state very clearly that to say he is a Muslim, he is a Hindu, is all politics. All I say is that I am an adivasi human being. And that is the right thing to believe.

There was only one kind of worship in Alandi. We worshipped Vitthal, Rakhmai and Dnyaneshwar. There was no dispute over it. There existed no other sect. All were brahmins. The town was a brahmin town.[25] While we recited *Raghupati Raghav Rajaram, Patitpawan Sitaram,* I also used to remember *Ishwar, Allah tero naam, sabko sanmati de bhagwan; Ram, Rahim hai tere naam sabko sanmati de bhagwan.*[26] At one level we are Hindu, then why this verse? I got an explanation for it after I joined the Andolan. At my young age it was not fully clear to me. Arre, he is Muslim, and he is Christian; how can I eat food cooked by him was what I thought.

Anandibai is my wife. She is the daughter of a Christian. My elders opposed our marriage. Her father had joined the Pawra tribe. Anandibai, she was a Pawra.

Assume you are my sister, but I became a Pawra and you remain Christian. Won't I come to your house as a visitor? But then I would not eat food cooked by you. You would give me the grain and I would cook it myself. Such was the situation! I have seen it with my own eyes! (*Laughs.*)

Many people would blame me. 'How come you married a Christian girl?' I would say, 'No, no. Come on, she is also a human being. What else do you need?' (*Laughs.*)

Nandini: Was it a practice that some adivasis would choose to become Christians and some to become Hindu?

Keshavbhau: Not in this region. But in Mundalwad there are a lot of them. Many of my father-in-law's relatives became Christian. They greet me very courteously because I do not believe in caste, do I?

But the effect is that no adivasi—neither a Pawra nor a Bhil will eat food touched or prepared by a Christian. They call him a *padrya*! But nowadays people eat at a Muslim's house and also at a Christian's house. Everything has changed completely. When Medha Patkar[27] was here, there was a large gathering at an event that had been organised in Dhadgaon. There were speeches given to say that people who treated lower caste people as separate should go and eat at their house. I had said, 'You may belong to any caste; my only concern is that the utensils should be properly cleaned. If it is cooked with the utmost care for cleanliness, then I will eat food prepared by anyone.'

Then slowly these things started to change a little. Otherwise, we had a lot of problems when Didi used to visit us. Because in Bhusha and Sikka they were all Pawras. They used to look down on others saying that he is Bhil and we are Pawra. We belong to a higher caste. Bhils would say we are the higher caste. This kind of discrimination was quite common.

But look at those Pawras who used to claim that they belong to the higher caste. The Bhils have climbed even higher these days. That is why there is not much caste discrimination now. All that 'he is Pawra, he is a Bhil' talk is gone now. Nowadays Bhils and Pawras have even started intermarrying.

But in Akkalkuwa there are many schools run by Muslims. They have a large population there. There adivasis are getting converted to Islam. This should not happen. They should remain adivasis and should not become Hindus, or Christians, or Muslims. We are adivasis and should remain adivasis.

Now, we have come to Taloda and Shahada tehsils.[28] In our old village we used particular stones to represent our gods. We did not bring them here. But we have managed to install our gods on the hills over here. We have named each of the different gods and we worship them every year. Which other god should we worship? It is better to worship our own gods, isn't it? Our own traditional gods, and not any others.

We pray to Nilpideo as soon as it starts to rain. During the rainy season, we have to walk about in thick grass in the day and even at night. So, this is the way we worship, 'Nilpideo, wherever we may go, in thick forest, in our farms, at any time of day or night, in the streams, in ravines or pools, let us not get bitten by a scorpion or snake or such creatures even by mistake.' And if by chance someone gets bitten, we ask that the person should not be harmed. We worship Vaghdeo once a year. We tell him, 'Dear God, you are the god of our village, you must protect all of us in the village. In the night, let no tiger or leopard enter our village. Nor should a thief enter and nor should vices.' Every year during Holi those who don't have children pray, 'Oh, Mother Holi, three or four years have passed but I have not had a child. Please give me a child.'

Once the son is born, they have to make a promise to God. They have to offer to place a certain amount of grain in front of Goddess Holi. If a child gets ill often, then too we pray to Holi and promise her something. Or we ask: 'Let there be prosperity in my house.' Or that 'No illness should enter my house.' People promise offerings to Holi. 'As soon as I have a child, I will certainly give offerings to Indaldeo.' And so on.

It is only educated people who have been to school who give less importance to religion. The old people insist that whatever culture we inherited generations ago, we must retain. If you go to Shahada Tehsil or anywhere in the area, it is the same tradition of sacrificing goats, chickens, etc. Others like Hindus may not like it, but because it is our adivasi tradition, the sacrificing of goats continues and is regularly done every year. Doesn't the sacrifice of the goat bring all the villagers together? Villagers eat it as *prasad*—a gift from the gods. When they do cut goats, they do so in the name of God. The other communities around this area like the Patels and the Gujars, they sacrifice goats to the Goddess in very large numbers. We pray and offer them only to our traditional gods.

Nandini: What was the situation like in the region before the dam was built?

Keshavbhau: In 1975, the situation was such that we had land given by the forest department, which we had tilled for generations, but we were finding it difficult to get two full meals a day. Between the villages there was thick forest. It was very difficult to travel from one village to another. There were thousands of wild animals like tigers and bears all along the way. Travelling alone from one village to another was out of the question.

In such a situation, slowly, little by little, encroachment began to increase. As soon as the forest department people came to know of it, they would land up there. From around

1972 they set up a system of extraction of fine we called *fala* or 'contribution.' The department people had to be paid in June every year. In our village we had to pay a much smaller amount, but in other villages people paid very large amounts. We used to pay 500 rupees a year. Those 500 rupees we would collect through contribution for each pair of bullocks. The collective village fine for another village could be anything between 3,000 to 6,000 rupees. But in spite of paying regularly, there was no record in our names of having paid it![29]

From 1972 onwards the situation was such that when police came to visit the village, they would ask for liquor for themselves, but if they happened to come across someone brewing liquor, they would beat him up badly and extract a fine or *fala* from him! For generations, the house tax was a very small amount. A year's tax for a house could be fifty paise, seventy-five paise or a rupee. But the *gramsevak*[30] would collect ten rupees from each house as house tax. We never got just treatment. For us, the government was the officers we would meet. That's all we knew! This was the situation we were in from 1980 to 1985.

Between 1980 and 1985, there was this big hustle and bustle among all the government officers. Our teacher Dagadu Sonu Sonavane and all of us had heard this news. 'Look, a very big dam is going to be built in Gujarat. Your entire village is going to be submerged by the dam. This is going to be your biggest stroke of luck. Here you are living inside this forest. You have no drinking water. You have no electricity in the village. You have no roads. But now we are going to change all this. In exchange, you will now get good land in the plains. The government will build you good houses. They will bring you electricity and roads, and you are going to get the best possible rehabilitation package ever!' Listening to them we felt so very happy. (*Laughs.*) There was going to be this great big change! And we couldn't wait for it to happen. We would say, let it happen as soon as possible!

Oh, yes, the *surveywalas*, they used to come to our village. From 1980 all of a sudden, they started coming. They never conducted meetings. They used to talk to us as they walked around, saying, 'You see, this land is in the name of the forest department, and to transfer it on your names we need to measure the land. How much land is getting submerged? How many trees are going to get submerged? How many houses are going to get submerged? All this needs to be surveyed.'

At the same time, they started showing us the land for rehabilitation. On the orders of our local MLA (Member of Legislative Assembly) from Akrani Tehsil, the collector said that they needed to show us the land at Parveta[31] village in Gujarat. Two people were chosen from each village—the police patil and the *karbhari* (village head). People were loaded into trucks and taken there. There were people from Madhya Pradesh, Maharashtra and Gujarat. All the people from all the submergence areas were taken to that one place.[32] 'See, we are going to give you land in this place. Just inspect the land. Say whether you agree or not. Look closely at the boundaries of your land.'

The police patil of our village was naive, but he gave a good answer. 'Fine, but are you going to give land to all these other people also in this same place?'

'Yes, you are right.'

'The land seems to be good. But is it going to suffice for all the people?'

What they said in response was, 'You don't even need to ask this. It is the responsibility of the government.' Our MLA from Akrani Tehsil—today he is an old man—his advice was, 'The government is not going to show you land again and again. Select your land right now.'

At that time, we all thought, 'Who knows what the villagers back home will say?' So we told them, 'We will go home and let you know.' We had a narrow escape.

The issue was, Parveta did not have enough land to rehabilitate even one village—and they were showing it to all the people from the three states! (*Laughs.*) They just wanted to mislead the people. What we said in our Pawri language was, '*Aamdokha duhari jage jane aamri tayari nimbe. Maharashtra ma aple tari theek aahe. Nahi tar ithech marijanya. Pan nahi janya.*' (We are not prepared to go to some other place. If you give us land in Maharashtra, well and good. Otherwise we will die here, but we won't go to any other place.) People used strong words and came back. They even brought back soil samples.

The MLA kept telling us, 'Say yes while I am the MLA. Later no one will listen to you.' The situation was really bad. No one could say anything to the MLA's face.

From 1980 to 1985, there was the Narmada Development Department which did the surveys. They began to measure the lands. They calculated how much of the forestland would get submerged. In 1984, along with our Dagadu Maharaj and the police patils from two to four other villages we came together and put up our demands. I, Dadala Karbhari, Jirya Karbhari, Batu Patil from Bharad, Khabadya Karbhari and Pankya Karbhari from Surung went in a group to Dhule.

After we reached Dhule, we prepared a statement with the help of a lawyer and submitted it to the collector. 'Sahib,' we wrote, 'We have been citizens of the state of Maharashtra all along. So, we must be allowed to stay here, in Maharashtra. And we should be given land in the forest areas of the three tehsils namely, Taloda, Shahada, and Akkalkuwa. And in no other place in Maharashtra. Only then can we survive. Each of us should get 5 acres of forestland. We must also get a well, equipped with an electric motor pump. Our homes should be transferred to the new place.' After submitting this statement that had some fifteen or twenty of these demands, we also gave it out to the newspapers.

Within eight days, we got a directive from the collector that said, 'Okay, take statements from these people.' We were then called to Roshmal. The person who came to meet us was an assistant collector, lower than the deputy collector. He read out all our points one by one.

This happened in 1984. We had gone to Parveta twice. Once in 1982 and then in 1984.

Earlier we didn't even know how many dams were going to be built in the Narmada Valley. The dam sites were not yet fixed. Four sites were being discussed—Nimgavhan, Surung, Jalsindhi and Sikka, of which two were being actively considered. Would the dam be constructed upstream of

Surung or towards Sikka?[33] Crores of rupees were spent on constructing the road to bring in the machinery, and the road was rapidly laid using bulldozers, and all the machinery and material were transported to the site opposite Sikka. Machinery worth crores of rupees was piled up. Boreholes were dug all over the place at that point on the river bank. This happened sometime after 1970. Then they started the survey work.

I was a young boy. No one of my age got a job on the site. Women got one rupee fifty paise and men two rupees as daily wage. Sahib was paying me one rupee. I was sent to the place where the sahibs carried out the survey. I had to hold the flag and run wherever the sahibs told me. They would say, 'Go take it to this hill, go take it to that hill.' At that time, I was one of those who understood Marathi well and so this work was entrusted to me. No, wait, Nandinibai, I am wrong. I think this whole thing must have taken place much earlier, in 1963. In 1964, I was in Alandi. In 1963, I spent the entire year earning wages.

All that machinery costing crores of rupees! The work provided wages for a very large number of people. The machinery was used there for five to six years. In 1970, out of the two sites they decided upon one. That was the Jalsindhi dam site near Sikka.[34] We were told that a helicopter was going to land there. In the first year, helicopters belonging to all three states landed there. They made their observations and a final decision was taken about the dam site. All these things happened between 1963-1965 and 1970-1971.

The chief ministers of Maharashtra, Gujarat and M.P. came—they may have been chief ministers or secretaries—but three helicopters from three states landed there. Who knows what they discussed among themselves! But after the helicopters left the work was suspended. Next year the pace of work increased. After a year whatever was constructed got drowned and washed away. Next year they started constructing a helipad again. We also latched on to that work. One day they kept saying the helicopter would come. But on that particular day the helicopter did not come.

The first year three helicopters had landed; the next year only two landed. And it seemed that a dispute had begun.[35] Maybe the dispute was: would a single dam be built on the Narmada at Bargi, or would there be thirty big dams on the Narmada?[36] But according to what these people said, the Jalsindhi dam was to be constructed within the boundaries of all three states. Perhaps there was a dispute over the distribution of water. Because of all this, the same year in Gujarat, this person…who was that chief minister (CM) of Gujarat? That big leader? That minister in Delhi? Oh yes! Morarji Desai. He got elected. Wasn't he the prime minister (PM) then? Yes, Morarji Desai got elected the same year. In the end, he cancelled the dam site over here and announced that the dam would be built near Navagam. He said, 'This site will not do. All of Gujarat is affected by drought. We can bring water to this drought-affected area only from Navagam. It cannot be done from any other place.' And then he also managed to get it approved, and so the dam here got cancelled.[37]

Who knows where all that machinery worth crores of rupees has gone! No one has any idea! The work on the dam over here had been going on for ten to fifteen years. It was completely abandoned. Many, many crores of rupees must have been spent in the name of building a dam here for us!

Once they managed to get the dam site here cancelled and the Sardar Sarovar approved, the work over here came to a halt. But those days, we too were hopeful. On the one hand, we felt that the government would look after us, and once the government gave us land on the plains, we would lead a very happy life. On the other hand, we thought it would not be possible to dam a big river like the Narmada. That too was an issue.

So this is the story, from 1963 to say 1972, 1973. After this the Jalsindhi site was abandoned and the work on the Sardar Sarovar in Gujarat began to pick up speed.

Now let us come to the meeting that was held in response to our application—the one in 1984. An officer lower than the deputy collector of Dhule district, the assistant district collector was sent.

All the people from the villages on the banks of the Narmada had been called to the house of the sarpanch of Roshmal Khurd.[38] He started asking us questions:

'Look here, do you all know that the Sardar Sarovar Dam is going to be constructed in Gujarat?'

'We don't know whether it will come up or not, but yes we do know about it.' That is what we said.

'All your villages are going to be submerged by the backwaters of this dam. Even this Roshmal will be submerged. So, all of you will be given land around Parveta in Gujarat. You better tell them that you accept the land there. Get the process started as soon as possible.' That was what he said.

And we kept saying, 'No, Sahib, we have been citizens of Maharashtra all along. Why are you driving us out of Maharashtra?'

'No, no, it's nothing like that. Do you know how many states there are in India?'

That sahib was saying, 'Maharashtra is one of the constituent states of India—M.P., Gujarat, Rajasthan, all these states together make our country, India. If you go to Gujarat or anywhere else, you are still in your own country, right? Are we driving you out to some other country?'

We kept saying, 'No, no, no, Sahib, we do not understand that Gujarati language. We also don't approve of the way they do things.'

They said, 'Come, come, raise your hand. Who all want to go to Gujarat?'

Batu Patil from Bharad was rather silly. He raised his hand!

'Patil, stand up! Are you ready to go to Gujarat?'

'Yes Sahib, we have relatives there.'

'Okay. Who all are willing to go with him?'

No one agreed! Just him alone! Then he changed his mind, 'If Keshav and all the others are not going, then I will also not go. If they are going, then I will go too.'

'If you want to go, go. We will stay here and die, but we will not go. We would rather become beggars here, but we will not leave.' That is what all of us said.

'Okay, let us take up the next point.'

'We will not leave Maharashtra, Sahib. Just keep that in mind, okay?' All the villages took a firm decision.[39] 'And another thing: each and every family must be given 5 acres of land along with a dug well equipped with an electric motor pump.'

'What? Who has written this?' he asked.

We said, 'Sahib, we wrote it.'

'What? Each of you is to be given a dug well in your land, and it is to be fitted with a pipe? What for? To wash your arse?' That is what he said.

'Not to wash my arse, Sahib, but for irrigation,' I said.

'Do you think you are ever going to get what you have asked for?'

'No, but isn't it the duty of the government, Sahib? Why do you say these things?' That is what I kept on saying. Those were early times, so I was a little afraid.

There were other points. 'Whichever place we will be rehabilitated in…where we will be given land, our houses should be transported there intact and we should be given a bungalow there.'

'Is the government your slave? Is it sitting idle waiting to serve you?' (*Laughs.*) He was really angry.

'Sahib, give it to us if you can, otherwise we are going back. It is your need, Sahib. What is it to us? Haven't we been living here for generations? Here we do not beg anyone for our meals,' I said.

In the end one thing was very clear—submitting that application was the most important thing we had done. It provided us with a foundation.[40]

Later on, this sahib asked us, 'Suppose you get land near Solapur, will you go?'

'No, Sahib, how can we go to Solapur?'

'Okay, in that case, will you go to Gadchiroli?'

'We cannot go to Gadchiroli either, Sahib.'

'There is some land near Navapur. Will you go? There is some land in Thane district, will you go?'

I was angry. Because others were not so well informed, I told him bluntly in just one sentence, 'If you give us land in the forest area of these three tehsils, Taloda, Shahada or Akkalkuwa, fine.[41] Otherwise what is the point in wandering here and there, Sahib?'

'Okay, then.' But he did write that point down. The proposal he forwarded said that forestland from these three tehsils Taloda, Shahada and Akkalkuwa needs to be allocated. But as it is, that point was sidelined. At that juncture, the difference of opinion started. Batu Patil declared that he would go to Gujarat. We said, '*Batu Patil, tu janar tari jaajhe, baki amu marijanar pan nahi janyar* (If you have decided to go, then go, but we will die over here but we will not leave),' we told him firmly in our Pawri language and returned to our villages.

People from the villages of Bharad, Sikka, Domkhedi, Nimgavhan and Surung[42] came together, took a decision and had written this application. The important people from these five villages had a meeting. We decided that we must put forward our position. We felt that even if the five villages were rehabilitated together, that was good enough, and that is what we had demanded. We prepared a draft, and at Dhule, Kisan Pawar, a journalist, corrected the draft. That was the first application.

We wrote giving the number of people of all the five villages and requested that we did not want resettlement in different villages. We were ready to settle in a single village. We wanted to settle in the forestland of one of the three tehsils. We did not want land that was under dispute. In Maharashtra, there is lot of barren land without any forest or trees. Another demand was that they should transfer our houses and our belongings to the new place. We should get compensation for whatever damage might be incurred in the process of transfer. We must get plots of land for our houses. We had put down all these demands in the application. Because if later there was a dispute, what would we do?

People from all the thirty-three submergence villages in Maharashtra were invited to this meeting. Perhaps those in Akkalkuwa had been invited to a separate meeting. But people from Poula to Bhusha had all come. People from Bharad, Sikka, Domkhedi, Nimgavhan, Surung, Bhusha, Shelda, Junana and even Bilgaon, and from the other side, Keli-Thuvani, Atthi, and Pipalchop and Poula, they had all come. In all somewhere around 150 people were present.

Nandini: Before you submitted your application, had no official conducted any meeting in the village?

Keshavbhau: No, absolutely not. None of the officers except those from the Narmada Development came to us. The Narmada Development people visited many times for survey work. After this meeting, the survey started taking place again. Fifty officers were already appointed. The work they had to do was like this: those who were not registered for the house tax had to be immediately registered; for those who had land, they immediately had to partition that land amongst the heirs.

There is a village, Poula, in Akrani Tehsil on the border of Akkalkuwa Tehsil. They had started their work from there. Two peons used to go ahead to the village to inform the villagers. 'Many officers are coming. They are going to conduct the survey in your village. This is for your benefit.' They used to come eight days before the officers to make sure all arrangements for them were in place. They used to tell us, 'See, fifty people are coming. They will need two big pitchers of liquor. And one chicken will not be enough; they will need ten chickens. Keep chilli, salt, masala—everything ready, and see that there is milk for their tea.'

The survey started from village Poula. To record one tree, the price was fifty rupees.

'Come on, hand me fifty rupees.'

'Listen Sahib, I do not have so many trees.'

It didn't matter how many trees you had, you had to pay fifty rupees. If land was to be recorded, fifty rupees. If the house was to be recorded, fifty rupees. Get this clear, every person had to pay at least 150 rupees.

'Sahib, I have five mango trees, and I have mahua trees.' They were forced to pay fifty rupees each.

Even if they collected only 150 rupees from a person, with so many people, imagine how much money they must have made! This is the work they did! And then their stay and lunch and afternoon snacks, two pitchers of liquor, ten chickens, mutton and bread and tea and so on. The forest department people also came along with them. If they found some fresh cut wood, you were fined right away. And in this way, they all travelled, from Poula to Pimpalchop, Pimpalchop to Atthi, Atthi to Keli-Thuwani, and from Keli-Thuwani they came to Bharad. From Bharad they went to Sikka.

My only worry was that I did not have a single paisa with me, so how was I to pay the surveywalas? Our police patil was running around, worrying about where to get so many chickens? He wanted everyone to contribute one chicken. The night the surveywalas left for Sikka, the same night Vasudha Dhagamwar[43] and Medha Patkar[44] came to our house. We did not have much information. She told us she stayed in Delhi and worked for an organisation named MARG. Vasudha Dhagamwar had come once before this, but had not given us any detailed information. The second time was that day, when she came along with Medha Patkar.

Earlier she had come all alone. She stayed the night and left in the morning. Lotan, the sarpanch, had tried to dissuade her, 'These monsters will kill you and throw your body into the Narmada. Do not go there.' But she had replied that she had to go, and in her first visit she had approached Jirya the karbhari of Domkhedi. He couldn't understand her language, and so he had brought her to my house.

'Do you understand Marathi?'

'Yes, yes, Tai, I do, I do,' I told her. In 1985 there were very few people who had knowledge of Hindi, Marathi and Gujarati. I was the only one there who knew both Marathi and Hindi.

After she got the information she needed, she told me, 'Keshavbhau, I will tell you the truth. Lotan, the sarpanch, told me not to come here. He told us that the people on the banks of the Narmada were monsters, and they would kill me and throw my body into the Narmada. But you are all very good people. I was going to touch Hapeshwar on my way, and so I thought I would come visit the village.'

My mother was ill so Vasudhatai gave her some medication. Her name was Dr Vasudha Dhagamwar, wasn't it? But she did not give us even a hint of who she was at that time. 'I am going to come again, Keshavbhau. When I come again, I will give you information. Right now, I have just dropped by to see the village,' she said. She stayed the night, had her tea in the morning and left.

When Vasudhatai came along the next time with Medhatai, that was the first time a meeting was held in our village where many different types of questions were asked.

'Are you aware that there is going to be a dam constructed in Gujarat?' Only the main people like the patel and the karbhari knew about it. The others did not know.

'The dam is being built in Gujarat; how will the water reach here? It won't.' They were expressing what they believed. 'We are leading quite a good life here; why should we go anywhere else?'

'Do you think you will get land in exchange for your land?'

We spoke out. 'The government is saying that they will give us land in Gujarat, but the government cannot be trusted.'

'What are the difficulties you are facing today?'

'Look here, there have been no schemes for us since Independence. The school in the village is in name only. The schoolteacher does not stay in the village; there are no doctors, no roads. No development work has taken place here. The ration shop in our village is supposed to be running, but we don't even know who runs it. This is the sorry state of affairs. Every year 2,000 to 4,000 rupees are taken away as contribution by the forest department people. If we fell short of land, we used to till some land in the forest. If we didn't have a good crop that year, we used to eat fruits, leaves, roots and shoots of the trees and managed to keep body and soul together. We had no give and take with anyone,' we said.

In the next round of their visits, when both Medha Patkar and Vasudha Dhagamwar had come to Nimgavhan, about fifty people who had come for the survey were camping in Sikka village. So, we did not have the opportunity to have a detailed talk. That day too, the interview could not be completed.

We didn't even know that she was Medha Patkar. She was accompanied by Dnyaneshwar Patil[45] and two or three girls. In all, there were about five people.

They had walked from Bilgaon to Mal, to Junana, to Selakda, to Surung, and then they reached Nimgavhan. I started making arrangements for their meals. Medhatai kept on telling me, 'No, don't trouble yourself so much.' But then, we were not even aware that she was Medhatai, were we? Still I insisted and fed them with a lot of affection.

'Okay. Do any officials ever come and visit you here?' These were the kind of questions they asked.

'None of the officers come and visit us but every year the forest department people take fala from us. Every year from our village we do not pay much, but from other villages they take 3,000–4,000 rupees each. In our village we give only 500 rupees every year.'

'So, does the *talathi*[46] make any visits?'

'We don't even know who the talathi is, but the gramsevak does visit. If the house tax is one rupee, he collects ten rupees.'

'Do the police visit?'

'Sometimes they do. They themselves drink liquor, but if they happen to notice someone brewing liquor, they beat them up badly with lathis. If the forest department people see some freshly cut wood being used, they too beat us up, and very badly too.'

'Okay. And what else?'

'Nothing else, Tai. A large force has already reached Sikka. We are very worried about them. We don't know how we are going to feed them tomorrow. Where do we get the liquor?'

'Why liquor?'

'Tai, there are some fifty of them in the group. They say, somewhere in Gujarat a dam is being built and our village is going to be submerged. They say they are going to give us good land in Gujarat. So they say.

The survey is going on. If you own a tree and want it recorded, you have to pay fifty rupees. If you own farmland, another fifty rupees. For your own house, fifty more. Every person has to pay at least 150 rupees. Tai, from where do we get

150 rupees? Plus they want two gallons of liquor, ten chickens in every meal and more. There's no town nearby where we can buy all this stuff. Things are really very bleak.

They really listened to us, you know! They gave us no advice, one way or the other. They were in a hurry. 'Keshavbhau,' they told me, 'we will definitely visit you again in the next eight to fifteen days.'

'Which way are you going?' I asked them.

'We are going via Hapeshwar and Kadipani,' they said and left in the morning without even having tea.

All the fifty surveywalas were sitting drunk and half naked in their underpants in Sikka. Medha Patkar and Vasudhatai took out their cameras and started taking pictures. The surveywalas started running about in their underpants. 'Who are these people? Where are they from?' they kept asking. (*Laughs.*)

After Sikka that survey was over. It never got completed. (*Laughs.*) They never even visited the place again. In their heart of hearts, they were frightened. (*Laughs.*) 'Where is this woman from? Where are these people from?' Oh, they were very scared!

After a few days, people's minds began working again, especially those who had seen Medha Patkar and Vasudhatai. 'Who is this young woman? What work brings her here?' Then a few days later, Medha Patkar came back for her next visit.

On the same day one of the district rehabilitation officers had reached there via Bilgaon. He was sitting in his Jeep and was asking, 'You Sukhlal, will you go to Gujarat or not?'

'I will die, but I will not look at Gujarat. I do not even understand the Gujarati language. I will not go to Gujarat.' That is what Sukhlal said.

The rehabilitation officer was threatening him, 'One way or another, we will bodily lift you and dump you in Gujarat.' Just at that time Medha Patkar reached the place. She heard him, and then she had a talk with the officer.

Dnyaneshwar Patil was there too and also the other girls. They lost a lot of time in Bilgaon so they stayed in Selakda. Next morning they reached my house.

They began their interview immediately. There weren't too many people. Murlidhar and a few of us had come together.

'A dam named Sardar Sarovar is being built in Gujarat. So, what do you think? Do you think the dam will be built?'

We said, 'Tai, if the dam is being built down there in Gujarat, why would the water come here?'

'Suppose it does, then what would you do?'

'Even if it comes, it is better for us here. The village is so much better.'

'No, but you will be rehabilitated. What do you feel about that?'

'If they do so, that would be good, but what we get must be good.' That is what I said.

'What is going on over here now?'

'Nothing. The Narmada Development Authority people are carrying out a survey.'

'Why are they doing that?'

'They are going to convert our land to revenue land, so they tell us.'

They wrote down all these points, the big and the small. 'When the talathi comes, what does he tell you? What do the gramsevaks and the *forestwala*s (forest officers) tell you? Are there any other development schemes being taken up here?' After noting down all this information, they told us, 'We will definitely organise another meeting,' and then they left for Sikka. Later they managed to catch a forestwala in Bharad. This fellow was terrorising a family and was eating mutton at their house. And at that time, they clicked just one photograph. And away he ran into the forest with his plate! (*Laughs.*)

'Our next meeting is being held in Nimgavhan on such and such a date; everyone should attend,' they said. We passed on the message to all the villages from Manibeli[47] to Bhadal.[48] The next meeting was held in Nimgavhan. It was towards the end of the year in 1985, probably sometime in November or December.

In Nimgavhan, Bhamtakarbhari has a very big house. It was packed full with people!

She (Medha Patkar) explained each and every point to us in detail, and then people realised the truth. If she had not come and met us and talked to us, we would have been completely fooled.

So, the first big meeting was in Nimgavhan. There was no one from the other states. This meeting was organised with Dnyaneshwar Patil's cooperation. In that meeting it was felt that we needed more representation, and so another meeting was called in Molgi. The Molgi meeting was attended by representatives from all the thirty-three villages in Maharashtra. In Molgi, the Narmada Dharangrast Samiti (NDS) was formed.[49] A decision was taken in Molgi to look for supporters.[50] We did not get any. We also explored the possibility in Dhadgaon. There we got cooperation from a young activist, Baba, but he was too young. We got some cooperation from Janardan Maharaj. He was an ex-MLA and he ran many hostels.

After the formation of the NDS in Molgi, in the same meeting it was decided who should go to Dhule to tell the people there that such a samiti had been formed, and that we were looking for supporters in Dhule to form a Narmada Dharangrast Sahayak Samiti in Dhule. The first name selected was mine; it was a unanimous decision. The second name was that of Batu Patil, the third was of Dadala Patil, then Khaja Karbhari, then Ukhadbhai from Manibeli, Ambalal Nama from Chimalkhedi, Noorjibhai[51] who came much later and Narayanbhai from Sinduri were also there.

So, only a few of us who were members of the NDS reached Dhule and we were to form a support committee, and then the next day we were to go to the collector and submit our report. The support committee, Narmada Dharangrast Sahayak Samiti was formed under the chairmanship of Bhai Madane with P. D. Dalal, Dashrath Tatya, Dr Chaudhari (President), Mubarak Shah and Khairnar Sir and another ten to fifteen members. The meeting was called and presided over by Dr Chaudhari.[52] There was a lot of discussion at the meeting. We and the support committee members then sat together and prepared the report which was to be submitted to the collector.[53] We had put forward thirty-five demands. The first demand said that today we have formed the NDS and we declare that from today, there shall be no corruption. In our region no official should demand any money from any adivasi person. If they do so, they shall not be spared. I still have that charter of demands with me.

The next thing was, why were we being told all the time, 'Go to Gujarat, Go to Gujarat'? We are citizens of Maharashtra, and those interested in going to Gujarat can go there. But as part of our rights, as people who have been living in Maharashtra all along, we wanted to be given land only in Maharashtra. We also demanded that we should get forestland. We demanded that their monthly committee meeting should include our members as participants. All our demands were accepted. We submitted our charter of demands in the presence of press reporters. That process helped the campaign to progress further.

But, apart from a couple of points none of the other issues was getting resolved. And so, three years passed, and we said, 'Okay, fine. Why are we so bothered? We have a beautiful village. We have beautiful trees in our villages. We have a beautiful river. We have beautiful lands. Why should we give them away? Isn't it better not to have this dam?' And so, all of us took the decision, 'We do not want the dam'.

For three years we constantly followed up our charter of demands. Every three months we participated as members in the meeting of the district committee. We put forward our point of view. If you do not have the land for rehabilitation, then why build the dam? The 'No Dam' slogan opposing the dam was emerging. Someone would come and tell us, go to Gujarat; someone else would say, go to that place; they were constantly at us. Then we warned the officials, 'Do not even take the name of Gujarat from now on! If anyone wants to go, they will ask you themselves. But we will not go there, so why do you want to send us?'

They said, 'It is not in our hands to give you forestland. That falls under the purview of the central government and so we cannot decide on it. Yes, but if you go and get it sanctioned then we will have no problem giving it to you.' And they went on and on in this manner.[54] Because of this people were divided. Half of them felt, 'If only we could get the land, it would be very good.' The other half felt, 'Whether we get land or not, we won't leave here. We will continue to live here. We will not go anywhere.'

People were under a lot of pressure. The foundation of the dam was being completed. By 1985 the foundation had been laid, filled and completed. At that time Sharad Pawar was the CM. We held a large protest march in Mumbai. Before the march we called a conference in Dhadgaon to finalise our demands and issue our statement. During 1980–85 a survey was undertaken by the Narmada Development Authority to determine whose land was forestland and whose land was revenue land and whether it fell under any other department. When that survey was conducted, Medhatai was not on the scene. After the NDS was formed, Medhatai put forward the demand before the collector and the CM that the survey should be re-done. She forced them to unroll the old survey record which had been rolled tight and put away. So, the old record had to be re-opened! This by itself benefited thousands of people. Thousands became landholders. This demand was on top of the charter of demands finalised in the Dhadgaon conference.

Nandini: When the NDS was formed, the *Karbhar Samiti* (executive committee) was also formed. Will you please tell us about it?

Keshavbhau: People did not understand the English calendar and its dates.[55] So we scheduled the meeting of people from the *padas*[56] (hamlets) with their representative for every full moon night. And on every new moon night, a meeting of the representatives of every hamlet in Dhadgaon. We called this the executive committee, which comprised at least one representative from every hamlet—two from this one, one from that one, and so on—and they would all come to Dhadgaon every new moon night, and the meeting would take place. There they would talk about every village, like, what is happening in Nimgavhan? And they would put forward and discuss whatever be the issues of any hamlet. There was a big conference in Dhadgaon. A to Z, all the information was shared in this conference. Between 8,000–10,000 people attended it. It forced the reopening of old records and made it necessary for resurveying to be done. *Shibir*s (workshops) were organised. And in this way we took up issues big and small, bit by small bit.

Nandini: Who organised the people? Who did all such work?

Keshavbhau: It was I who did most of the work in Akrani Tehsil—from Surung in the east to Domkhedi in the west. In fact, I did not know much about Surung or Domkhedi at the time. But after I joined the Andolan as an activist, I started visiting each and every village in the tehsil. In each village, I would begin with an introduction of Medhatai.

I would tell them: we now have support from a woman who will not be intimidated by the collector, who will not be scared of any officer. She has given us full support, and she is always going to be with us. I have come here as one of her activists to give you information. We will have to unite. And in this way, I took the meetings from house to house and hamlet to hamlet.

I used to find out who the main person in that hamlet was and go and sit in his house. Then I would invite people to his house. Tell them to unite, to attend the workshops, attend the rallies and conferences. Explain to them that if anyone of us goes alone to ask for something, we are thrown out. But if ten of us unite and go, it is difficult to throw us out. And when all of us collectively go and meet an officer, he is scared of us. That is why we have to work hard to build and maintain this unity and organisation. If we have to get land, this is the only way. And so, I used to go around bringing people together, organising them.

At that time there was great enthusiasm. Let me tell you about one incident. We had to organise a *dharna andolan* (a sit-in protest) in Mumbai. Medhatai had to go on some other work. We were unsure and felt we would not be able to reach the dharna. In the end we decided that one way or another we would go to Mumbai. And we did, and everyone was very happy that we made it.

Akrani Tehsil was very backward then, and whether it was Hindi, Marathi or Gujarati, it was very difficult for people to understand these languages. The only language that people spoke was their own—Pawri, or Bhilori. They could understand no other language. They had no interaction with the outside world. Our farms, our homes, our river and our forest—there was nothing else. The Sardar Sarovar Dam had reached us, and it would touch us. But only someone like me who understood Marathi and Hindi could understand what was really happening. In the beginning we were inspired by good-hearted people's support and backing, and so we used to feel that if only we could unite, our success was assured. That is why I put aside all the responsibilities of my home and farm. I managed to convince one of my nephews to look after my house and farm by assuring him that I would get him married, and I joined the Andolan as a full-time activist.

In 1985 I was happy providing food for the parikramavasis who circumambulated the Narmada, a pilgrimage that has been practiced for hundreds of years over many generations. At such a time Medha Patkar came to my house. She helped me to face the reality that if the Sardar Sarovar Dam was built, it would destroy us, so we had to unite against it immediately. And since no one else understood Marathi or Hindi except me, I should translate what was being said into our own languages. And so, with this perspective I went from village to village, from hamlet to hamlet and literally barged into every house to bring awareness to people in the area.

During those times, I must have been the only person to reach every hamlet right up to Bhadal village on one side and Poula on the other. The responsibility of looking after so many villages was entrusted to me. I carried out that responsibility, reached out to lots of villages and managed to complete that work. Our purpose was to see that as many people as possible from different hamlets and villages came together to make our meetings and marches a success. For this we established various committees.

We had been organising the executive committee meetings at Dhadgaon, the tehsil headquarters, to understand the situation and the issues in each village, and then based on that understanding we took our decisions—decisions like whether the next programme should be at the tehsil or the district, the state or the national capital. I have sacrificed my farm and my house for the last fifteen to sixteen years and devoted myself completely to the Andolan, and that is what has given us success and enabled us to reach this far.

Another thing is that after the Narmada Andolan started, Nimgavhan has provided the greatest hospitality. I never asked anything from others. I gave what I had. Okay, take this, grind it, cook it and serve the people who have come, is what I said! After all, most of the meetings that brought the people together from all thirty-three villages took place in Nimgavhan,[57] didn't they?

I never said to anyone, 'Come on, give me a cup of tea!' I never took anything from people! If we sit down and do the accounts, you would see I may have easily spent eight to ten lakh rupees for the Andolan. Not that I want to do the accounts. Suppose I had to go to Mumbai, I never felt comfortable to ask Didi or other people for expenses. A message would be sent, 'Keshavbhai, get so and so person from so and so village.' But that person would not be in a position to spend from his pocket. And so, I would spend for him and see that he reached the destination, and I would never ask for those expenses. If anyone offered them on their own, that was fine. Otherwise, I let it be and moved on. I cannot recount all that history (*Laughs*) because I feel embarrassed. People will say I am boasting, so I do not open my mouth.

Nandini: Why can you not talk about it?

Keshavbhau: Because I have been the giver of food from the start, have I not? Even today I am the same food giver. Right from the beginning whenever there was a visitor in the village, I have been giving. So why do you think I will stop giving now? (*Laughs.*)

In the beginning, according to the decision of the people, a district-level committee was constituted. I was made a member and the work assigned to me was that I would do all the writing for the committee. This committee comprised the member representatives from each village, for example, Batu Patil from Bharad, Khaja Karbhari from Sawarya, Dadala Patil from Bhusha, and then a few from Akkalkuwa Tehsil such as Ukhadbhai, Ambalal Nama Tadvi, as well as Narayan Ranchhod Tadvi. We met every three months. The travel was paid by the government; nevertheless we continued to put forth our own point of view. While the government was presenting their point of view, there was also a lot of discussion on the thirty-five points we had submitted. But the main point was: after being displaced from the banks of the Narmada, where would we be rehabilitated? Where would we be given land?

During that time Deshpande was the collector. He told us that they would have to acquire the extra private land, farmers' land and vacant land in the three tehsils of Taloda, Shahada and Akkalkuwa and distribute it for rehabilitation. He initiated the process of finding such land in every village by instructing the talathis. But the problem was that such land would be in small parcels. Some person's 5 *gunthas*[58] somewhere and someone else's 10 gunthas somewhere else, or some may even have half an acre or 1 acre. Every farmer who had to be rehabilitated was to be given 5 acres of land, so that would be divided into some twenty to twenty-five small parcels. Would it be possible to farm on such land? If we accepted this kind of land, that definitely would be the end of us! And each such piece would be 1 to 2 kilometre from the other. After three or four meetings, it became clear that every time there would be an impasse on this one issue. In the end we refused to accept that land. In this process, we eventually reached Mumbai.

At that time people were not a hundred per cent sure, were they? Some just said, 'Yes, yes. That is true.' Some drunkards would shout and rant and pass unpleasant remarks. Some would side with the government. I was trying to communicate only one thing. There was no gain or loss to me in this. I did not get paid for this work. Nor were we middlemen for the government. The important thing was, if we got organised together and collectively raised our voice that would bring pressure on the government. That was what I tried to explain to the people. Whatever people wanted to say in response to this was put before the executive committee in its meetings.

Nandini: Why would people listen to you?

Keshavbhau: Because of what I was and how I spoke. People thought of me as a straightforward, outspoken person. I was not going to plunder or loot them. I was an adivasi, a tribal, one of them. Even if I duped them, I was from a nearby village fully in their sight. After all I was their own representative.

Earlier, I never stepped out of my home, but now I realised that there was an urgent need to inform people, and an even more urgent need to bring people together and unite them. I also felt that since I could read and write I would be useful to the Andolan. So, I started going from hamlet to hamlet and from house to house.

It made a big difference whether you were educated or not. My explanation helped many people understand the situation. I had begun to feel that if we put forward our points unitedly and collectively to the government, we would certainly gain something.

In the beginning, Dnyaneshwar Patil would be with me. Together we organised meetings in many villages. We gave different names to the meetings of the different groups, such as, hamlet meeting, village meeting or tehsil meeting. Those who looked after and took on the responsibility of all the villages formed the executive committee. And those who looked after the affairs of a hamlet were named hamlet representatives. Among the thirty-three villages of Maharashtra, the twenty-four from Akrani Tehsil were my responsibility. The remaining villages were under Dnyaneshwar Patil. When any meeting was held in a village, tehsil or hamlet, we all would have to rush there to be part of it.

In the old days people used to drink a lot, and factionalism was rampant in every village. But once people developed a clearer understanding of the situation, they came together and even the drunkards and addicts began to join the Andolan.

Nandini: How the organisation was built in the beginning is very important. Can you please tell us about that process?

Keshavbhau: First, Vasudha Dhagamwar came here. After her, Medha Patkar came, and she told us, 'A big dam is going to be constructed in Gujarat. Do you know about it?'

'We don't know too much about it. We don't even know how the water could reach up to here.'

'Look, lakhs of people in Gujarat were displaced due to the Ukai dam. The government had promised to give them land and had also promised to settle a village in exchange for a village. But those people got nothing. They have been rendered homeless and are forced to live on the streets. We must not get into that situation. No one listens to a single person. So, if he has ten other people with him, an official or even a minister may listen. A bundle of wooden sticks cannot be broken, but a single wooden stick can be easily broken into two. We need to organise. One village by itself will have no effect, neither will two villages. So, people from all the submergence villages in Maharashtra must come together and unite. We have to collectively exert our force, and unanimously raise our voice. Only then can we bring about some change. And then whether it is the Government of Maharashtra or Gujarat, we can get what is due to us by law – land in exchange for land, a house in exchange for a house. If we don't organise, we will get nothing, that's for sure.' This is what Medha Patkar put forward before us.

I was convinced by what she was saying. 'This woman is telling the truth, and if we join her, she will not harm us in any way. Otherwise, all the other officers will loot us and destroy us. To unite people, we must give them the full information, take them along with us. Only then will the Andolan be possible.' This is what I thought.

I started working with Dnyaneshwar Patil on some surveys. This was the first time for me.

Dnyaneshwar Patil worked with SETU (Centre for Social Knowledge and Action), an organisation in Gujarat. He was paid some 200-300 rupees per month by SETU. He joined Medha Patkar on the basis of that honorarium. He had the same motivation as her, which was to build the people's organisation, and ensure that our people did not suffer and could exercise the right to demand whatever was justly theirs. Ours was an illiterate area, and we took a lot of inspiration from him. He stayed in Molgi for a few days. Then we managed to rent a room in the name of the NDS in Dhadgaon. He used to stay in that room to maintain contact with the people who used to come to Dhadgaon.

Part of our work was to visit villages. In the beginning Dnyaneshwar Patil himself used to go. After a few days, Virsingh Padvi was sent to look after the nine villages of Akkalkuwa Tehsil. We used to have meetings in two places. One was in Molgi, which was closer for the people from the nine villages. People from Akrani used to meet in Dhadgaon. Dnyaneshwar Patil attended the one in Molgi. We managed the one in Dhadgaon ourselves. We learnt what was happening in each of the villages and understood the problems they faced.

Medhatai could be anywhere. She was always on the move. She never stayed in one place. She would be in Badwani one day, in Vadodara the next day, and on some days, she would be here in Nimgavhan. We had an office in Dhule and also in Mumbai. She kept moving from office to office.

Whenever a programme was taken up, say in Dhule, or in Vadodara, or Indore, or Bhopal or Mumbai, the members of the Narmada Dharangrast Sahayak Samiti would attend those programmes.

In one of the earliest meetings of the executive committee it was decided unanimously that Keshavbhau must be the representative in the committee formed by the government to discuss the issues in all the villages. I would be one to put forward the people's viewpoint.

The meeting was held at the collector's office once every three months. All the officers of the concerned departments participated in that meeting. In the discussions, on each and every point, only soothing promises were made. But there was no action taken on the ground. Meeting after meeting took place and ended. Even after three years had passed, the main issue was unresolved. Every time the officials would tell us, 'There is no land in Maharashtra. That is why you have to go to Gujarat. Since the entire responsibility lies with the Gujarat government, they will be able to provide you good land. There is land in Maharashtra but it is in small parcels—that too not in Taloda, Shahada or Akkalkuwa but only in Gadchiroli or Kolhapur or Thane Districts.'

Our old villages in Maharashtra are border villages, and we had interactions with all three states, namely, Maharashtra, Gujarat and M.P. Our market place was in Gujarat and we had contacts with M.P. which lay just across the Narmada on the other bank. But all the rest of our interactions were in Maharashtra. We had no relatives in Gujarat or M.P. and we felt that as citizens of the state of Maharashtra, if our future was to be secure, we had to be given land in Maharashtra.

Dhadgaon Tehsil or Akrani is adjacent to the three tehsils of Akkalkuwa, Taloda and Shahada. In these tehsils there are thousands of hectares of forest and fallow land that belong to the state or central government. We were willing to take that land. We had given it in writing too. But we were told that since we belonged to forest villages, we would not receive priority in the rehabilitation. According to the survey carried out by the government in the thirty-three villages, altogether only 1,300 families were eligible to get land. And the government had clearly stated that no one else would get land.

At that time, we surveyed every village to find out the total number of people in those villages.[59] We filed a form for each and every family. While conducting this family survey in 2006 we realised that there were more than 5,000 families living in the submergence zone of the dam (in Maharashtra).[60]

And all of them had to be given land. You could not leave anyone out. Since the government had committed in writing that each family would get 2 hectares of land, the 5,000 families would require 10,000 hectares of land. We carried out surveys from time to time and gave them the numbers. Initially, the government did not accept our numbers. The survey that gave the number of families as 1,300 was completely wrong. In each case, the entire village along with its hamlets had not been surveyed. The survey was an estimate based on talathi and gramsevak records. Only those people who had been paying taxes and had land records going back to the British government's time were in their records. They had at best ten landholders in some villages and fifteen in other villages in their records. All the rest were unrecorded.

I had been moving around the villages since 1985, and because the people liked me I was actively involved in the survey work. I went to the district committee meeting to present the number of families we had found against the government's figures. The government answered my points one by one.

Even though we refused their offer, from time to time the collector would tell us, 'Look here, the Sardar Sarovar Dam belongs to Gujarat. The total benefit goes to Gujarat. We may get some share of electricity, but as far as the command area is concerned, the benefits belong to Gujarat. And that is why you should accept rehabilitation in Gujarat.'

Now there was the numbers issue that we brought up, and we said, 'First of all the numbers put out by the government are wrong, and if land is provided only to these few people, what are the others to do?'

The collector said they would give the remaining families some income-generating employment.

We said, 'All this time you have not been able to give us any income-generating employment. How then do you expect to provide it in future and that too, to so many people?'

They began showing us land for rehabilitation from 1985 onwards.

Every month or two a meeting was held in the presence of the collector. Sometimes Medha Patkar used to attend this meeting. Dnyaneshwar Patil was there too, and many times we used to go with him.

I had left my home and started working for the Andolan. My family faced a lot of problems. On the one hand we continued providing meals to the parikramavasis. And now due to my increased interactions, the number of visitors from outside the village also increased. To look after them and their needs was now an added responsibility for my family members. They often took me to task. My wife warned me and said, 'If you continue to move around like this, remember, I have my brother, my mother, I have them all, so I will simply leave you and go away.' My parents were very old. They would tell me, 'Give up this business. You also have a family and a house. If you continue to roam about, what will your wife do?'

But I was not willing to give it up. There was no profit in what I was doing. But I had read the biographies of great mahatmas; that gave me strength. I started work with a clean mind and a clarity that what I was doing was good work. Whatever we could get from farming was our only source of income; we had no other source of livelihood. We had goats as well as milch cattle and a pair of bullocks. My nephew stayed with us for a number of years and looked after everything on my behalf. While I was working, there were a lot of problems. No one was ready to give us loans. Finally, there were some Gujarati moneylenders who gave us a loan, and we could overcome our problems.

I did not get an honorarium for a year. From the second year, the Andolan took the decision to pay me 300 rupees per month. I got the amount through a committee that comprised our Shriram Lagoo from Pune and others.[61] At that time, we considered 300 rupees a big amount. We used it to get around our difficulties.

During that time many shibirs were organised at varied locations, in Thane or Pune, in Gujarat, M.P. and Bhopal. In these shibirs many well-known people from various organisations would present their perspectives. We would present our own.

Based on these discussions we drew conclusions and worked out our strategy.

Today I cannot give you a date-wise or year-wise account of our activities. But I can tell you for sure that to get work experience we had to learn a lot. In Delhi there is some organisation. I forget its name. I went there for a fifteen-day training. I learnt a lot there. There were many activists from all over India. We were taught about different laws. What is the law of the Supreme Court, the law relating to the tehsildar, the BDO and the collector? Or what are the duties of a CM? How are those duties and responsibilities carried out? Our main concern was if we were excluded from a plan or scheme, what kind of action did we need to take? We got the opportunity to learn a lot about these things.

Working as an activist, I was energised. After we formed the NDS in 1985, whether it was a discussion with the CM or the PM or the president, whether it was a secretary or the rehabilitation minister or any other minister, Medha Patkar used to take me along as the main representative.

It goes without saying that the meeting used to start with my presentation. First, I had to present whatever problems and difficulties we faced in the region. Then the discussion would start between the minister and Medha Patkar. Then the follow-up action would be discussed and so on. That is the experience till today. If Medha Patkar had herself presented the situation, the government might not have agreed. But since I was an adivasi myself, and a representative of the people from the submergence area and an activist, the government was forced to answer our questions.

It is only recently that roads have been built connecting many villages. Motor vehicles and boats are now plying. At that time there was dense forest and I was scared to travel alone. But after I became an activist, all those fears vanished. I went from one village to another and this way our work continued.

But one thing was clear—we were not getting land even in Gujarat.

Around that time a serious incident took place. In 1987 in Bamani[62] village, more than 100 children died of malnourishment (gastroenteritis). No medical services were being provided in that region. They existed only on paper. When this news was published in the newspapers it became a serious issue at the national level, as also at the state level. The CM was shocked. He flew in a helicopter to Bamani. He saw the situation himself. Many people were suspended on his orders. A new dispensary was established. And we began to take the stand that we must be provided with all the amenities and services.

The government took on the responsibility of providing the nine villages in the Akkalkuwa Tehsil with dal, rice and other amenities in a big way.

Once the distribution of food took place it also had some effect on the Andolan. We began to take the stand that we too must be provided with all amenities and services. We said, 'We too are villages on the banks of the Narmada. Our movement is called the Narmada Dharangrast Samiti. Our children are also malnourished. In our villages also many children have died. They have been provided with rice and grain, but we have not.' So, when this issue came up for discussion in the executive committee meeting, our friend Dnyaneshwar Patil and I took a decision, 'Okay, we will write an application.'

The tehsildar refused to entertain the application and said, 'There is no space in my office to store this application.' We fought with him, but still he refused to accept the application.

At that time, Borvankar was the collector of Dhule District. We met him personally and gave him the application. We explained to him, 'Sahib, this is a serious situation, as serious as what happened in Bamani. So, we should also get assistance. Whatever assistance you provide for each family we will accept with folded hands.'

The collector was a good person, and he sanctioned the application within a few days. 'In Akrani Tehsil in my jurisdiction within Dhule District, I have a lot of wheat. Will it do if we provide you with wheat?'

I said, 'Whatever food you provide us is acceptable. You may give us rice or wheat or jowar or maize. Anything is acceptable to us.'

We started the family survey. I had collected detailed information on every family. The number of families came to 3,500. The tehsildar and others opposed it. They initiated a fresh survey by sending ten to fifteen talathis and officers to the villages. People were smart! They split one family into five! The survey I had carried out was authentic. Since they could not accept it, they carried out a new survey, and the number of the families doubled! (*Laughs.*)

Again, the collector called us and asked us, 'How has this figure proved to be incorrect?'

To that I replied, 'Sir, I told the tehsildar a number of times that my survey is authentic and asked him to take it as the basis for distribution, but he opposed it. Now if government officials themselves have carried out a survey, let us accept those numbers, else it would lead to fights.' And so, they distributed grains based on the government survey. We were united and the strength of the Andolan was behind us. That is why we managed to get the work done.

That was our first major victory. That year there was a bad drought. No one had harvested more than eight to ten *payalis*.[63] But because of the government distribution of food grains, each household got 2–3 quintals of grain. And that saw us through the year. That was in 1987.

From that day onward people became very enthused. They felt that if we came together and fought unitedly, we could make things happen. Dhadgaon is such a big tehsil. Others did not get grain. Why did only we get it? Because we were united.

Since there was a drought, we asked for employment according to the law through the Employment Guarantee Scheme (EGS).[64] We were supposed to get our EGS card within eight days, so we all applied for it and got the card. We had to put in a lot of work to get the cards. We had to write an application for every able-bodied person in every village and every household. In the application we demanded that we must get employment within fifteen days.

Once you get card no. 4, then no. 5 and no. 6, it is expected that you will get employment. If card no. 7 is in hand and you had not got employment under the scheme, then it is necessary to inform the regional officer and he has to provide employment. And if card no. 8 is not given, then an unemployment allowance has to be declared for that person. We piled up heaps of all the applications with the government. We had shown in which of the villages in Akrani Tehsil, from Poula at one end to Bhadal at the other, it was necessary to provide employment under the scheme. There was no work available in the vicinity. But there were *nala* bunds and roads being constructed in Kundal, on the road to Molgi in Dhadgaon Tehsil, which needed to be completed. So, all the people from Poula, Atthi, Keli, Thuvani, Selakda and Bharad were brought to Kundal. Small huts had to be erected for all of them. The government had to provide them with the necessary tools and equipment. They had to ensure that the people got the prescribed supply of grains through ration shops.

Around 5,000 to 6,000 people in the area got employment. The others just got paper assurances. Many did not get even that.

Our demand that the people who did not get employment should be paid unemployment allowance remained unfulfilled. The case was going on in the courts but remained unresolved. We would have got lakhs and crores of rupees. Because the law was in place for a long time, and it was not being implemented, we should have said that we would not rest until we got the unemployment allowance. We should have remained firm on this demand. The matter of that demand continued in the court for some time. Later on, the case was closed. Our lawyer was Advocate Suryavanshi.[65]

I will share an episode when I faced a difficult situation. There was a fifteen-day shibir in Delhi. My youngest son was critically ill. It was touch and go. Dnyaneshwar Patil came to my home. He stayed there all day saying I had to leave for Delhi next morning.

I told him, 'My son is struggling. His condition is critical. He may not survive. That is why I cannot go.' In response to that Dnyaneshwar Patil told me, 'Listen. In life, that is the one thing we have to leave to God. None of us can say whether he will survive or die. So have faith in God and carry on with your duties.'

I was crying. My wife and children were weeping too. Right there I took the decision that I would leave. My wife began to cry loudly. I just closed my eyes and walked away. I crossed the Narmada at Kadipani. I took the night bus to Vadodara. And from Vadodara I took a train for Delhi. My son was on my mind for some time after I reached Delhi. After a while, I forgot. After fifteen days I remembered him again when I was returning. There is a village named Kavant[66] just after Kadipani. When I reached that village, I remembered him. I wondered what condition he would be in. Would he be there at all or not? There was no way I could find out. It was the rainy season, so I could not cross the Narmada just wherever I wanted to. It was all very difficult.

On the same day there had been a confrontation between the people of Kadipani and Hapeshwar.[67] Murders had taken place. There were crowds of people everywhere on the roads. They were roaming around with thick sticks in their hands. I was thinking, if I go from Kadipani via Kavant to Badwani, it would take me two days or more. If I go via Akkalkuwa, then also it would take two days at least. What to do? Also, I did not have much money in hand. I have been a *bhagat*[68] since childhood, so I smeared my forehead with ash and decided that if I died, I died...what more could happen? And I continued on the same route. I was able to take a vehicle to Kadipani, but from there onward I had to walk.

I met many groups of fifty to sixty people. None of them asked me where I was going! They were busy fighting among themselves. I reached Hapeshwar and followed the river bank until I got to Jalsindhi. I reached around three or four in the afternoon and saw some children grazing cattle. I called out to them and asked them if anyone could arrange a crossing. Sometime later, five or six good swimmers tied together a *tafa*[69] and came towards me. I crossed the Narmada on that tafa.

You know, even then I did not have the courage to ask them, 'How is my son?' I was afraid one of them would turn around and say, 'You left him there and he died.'

I was praying to God all the time: in such a difficult situation I have left everything to you. And believe me, that son of mine recovered and is fine now. I got him married last year. So, such difficulties I have experienced all the time. My wife also used to fall ill frequently then. So many times I have had to leave her and go. I used to get abused a lot. I never bothered about or paid attention to all that.

Till 1988, time and again, whenever we asked where is the land for rehabilitation, the government had nothing to offer. So we also took up the issue that the 33 villages in Maharashtra were not the only ones to be submerged. Nineteen villages in Gujarat were going to be submerged and more than 250 villages (*it is actually 193 villages*) in M.P. We 33 villages could not fight on our own.[70] Nor could the 19 villages from Gujarat. People in all three states had to come together and fight.

In the course of finding a way out of this situation the first meeting was organised at Rajghat[71] in Badwani District in M.P. I too went there. The organisation representing the adivasi region from M.P. was named Khedut Mazdoor Chetna Sangath (KMCS),[72] and it was represented by the activists Rahul[73] and Amit Bharati.[74]

Arch Vahini[75] was active in nineteen villages of Gujarat. Many people had already accepted land in Gujarat but there were also many who had not. According to the executive committee's decision, I was to attend this first meeting. Medha Patkar and I reached the Badwani office. The name of their committee was Narmada Ghati Navnirman Samiti (NGNS).[76] To bring NGNS together we planned a public programme in Rajghat. It was in this programme that Ambaramji[77] participated for the first time. All the representatives from different states spoke at length at that meeting.

You know, earlier there was this Nimad Bachao Andolan in M.P. They had many activists before it petered out. It was revived under a new name: the Narmada Ghati Navnirman Samiti. In Maharashtra there was the NDS. In Gujarat there was the Asargrast Sangharsh Samiti (ASS; Affected People's Struggle Committee). And we all as well as Kashiram Kaka,[78] Shobharam Baba,[79] Sitaram Kaka,[80] Jagannath Kaka[81] and Devrambhai[82] were present in the meeting.

We wanted to build an organisation of all these three states, didn't we? That is why we went there and the decision was taken. In 1985 we established the NDS, which continues to exist. We managed to unite people through this samiti. I had submitted before the meeting at Rajghat that: 'There was no medical facility in our region; many children died of malnourishment. But we managed to remain united and got food grains for every family from the government. But land for land after our villages are submerged is nowhere in sight. We have been staying in this forest for generations. The British government left and then our own government came to power. First the dam was to be built in Jalsindhi but that was cancelled. Now it is planned to be built in Gujarat and there is going to be submergence because of this dam too. But there should be a proper system to take care of the rehabilitation. It is now becoming clear to us that this is not going to happen. That is why we do not want this dam. When the dam is built it will destroy you and it will destroy us too. We will lose our means of life. So, all the representatives from the three states should form a single organisation and oppose this dam under one banner.'[83] That is why this decision to form a joint committee was announced at the Rajghat meeting in Badwani District of M.P.

Representatives of the ASS had come from Gujarat. Bawabhai[84] and others from the KMCS in Alirajpur Tehsil in M.P. had also come. The number of people was very large. I was the only representative from Akrani Tehsil. Noorji and the others were not there. Medhatai and I had discussions with the people there. Then there were speeches. After that we went and stayed with Ambaramji.

At the Rajghat meeting we came to the decision that each village would submit an application to the respective tehsildars, saying, 'All of us are giving you in writing that the Sardar Sarovar has been shown as and promised to be a very large development project, but in real terms the poor people have not received any benefits from it. What we can see everywhere is that this project has only heaped losses upon losses. Based on our experience of the last three years we declare that we will not allow this dam to be completed. Our village is good as it is, where it is, and we want that it be developed.' This was in 1988.

After we submitted the applications from each village, the officials started running around. Everywhere they wanted to show us land for rehabilitation. Here on Dhadgaon Road, at Fatehpura, an official insisted that I should sit in his jeep, and said, 'Just have a look at the land; nowhere will you get such good land!'

'On the one hand, you say that you will give us land, on the other you say there is no land. What kind of a story is this? How can we accept fragmented land?'

'Okay, let us go and see,' I said and climbed into the jeep. A rehabilitation officer along with two or three other officers was also in the jeep. They stopped the jeep suddenly and said, 'Look here, Keshavbhau, all this land is for you.'

'No, but Sir, on what basis do you tell us that this land is for us?'

'The government will buy this land for you.'

'No, but look, there is a standing crop of sugarcane here in the field and a banana crop there. Let us ask these people.'

'No, no, don't ask them. Just tell me whether the land is good or bad. I just want an answer to that question.'

'If the land is good, we would have to say it is good, isn't it? But this land you are showing us is not my father's property nor is it your father's property.' I used those very words. 'Because you are showing us the land from the roadside.'

At Fatehpur Amada there were efforts to give us land for the new habitation, but they failed. Everywhere they would show us the land from a distance. 'Look, this land is for you. That land is also for you.' Just like their posters, along with the contractors and the leaders they say, 'Before the dam is built, you will get this and you will get that.' But once the dam is built, they kick us and say, you will get this (a kick)![85]

We managed to form a people's consensus. We had not gone begging them for anything. In village after village, there is a zilla parishad (district council) school but there is no teacher in the school. We need doctors to come and visit the villages. There is no development work reaching our villages. That is the fault of the government. Our country has become independent but the benefits of this are being plundered by the government. There is nothing for us. Nor do we want anything from them. We have our mother Narmada. We have our land. We have our forest. That is the source of our life. Why should we not try to sustain it? Why should anyone object? This was the decision taken by each and every one of us. That is how the foundation was laid for opposing the dam.

Meanwhile, some people in the village who used to masquerade as leaders raised the issue that if the government was willing to go so far as to give us land, then why would they go back on their word now?

We told them, if you believe them, follow them. Even if *you* do not have faith in it, we prefer our organisation. If we do not challenge this government, they are not going to give us anything. If we have to get anything at all, we have to oppose this dam, and we have to stop this dam right now.

Now I remember, Dnyaneshwar Patil was with me at Rajghat. He stood by me and gave me strength. The support we gave each other brought unity in the work. Whatever difficulties we faced while working, we used to take them to Medhatai and get them solved.

In this way at a gathering of the people of all the three states in Rajghat, we took a decision that because the government would keep making promises but would never fulfil them, it was important that we hold on to our ancestral lands that our forefathers had tilled for generations. We could survive only if we did this.

We decided to conduct the next shibir at Dhadgaon.

This shibir brought together activists from Badwani, from Nimad, from the Bhoomi Sena,[86] and from Kevadia[87] and representatives from Alirajpur, Akrani and Akkalkuwa tehsils. People had come from all over the valley. There was a series of discussions about what our position was today and what it was going to be in the future. Only after a concrete final decision was reached did the people unite for action. A meeting of the village affairs committee was organised in each village, but it was we who drafted a letter for every village. This was because there was nobody else who could write. From each village, we gave one letter each to the police patil, the karbhari and the concerned tehsildar.

'The government is giving you good land. Why are you doing this?' the tehsildar kept asking us.

The government took up the very big responsibility of showing us the land. 'Come, come! Show them the land as soon as possible.'

In Gujarat there was Arch Vahini and also the organisation run by Harivallabh Parikh.[88] Some members of the organisation were trying to get their foot in the door in this process.

'We are not going to Gujarat, so how does the question arise?' we said.

They kept on saying, 'No, it is okay. If not in Gujarat, take land in Maharashtra. But where in Maharashtra do you want it?'

We said, 'Not even an inch of land from Maharashtra will be spared. That is the clear stand the Government of Maharashtra (GoM) has taken, so the question doesn't arise, does it? On the one hand you are showing us private land. On the other, you take the position that not even a pinhead of forestland will be spared. What can we gain from this? We would rather keep tilling the land we have. That is fine with us.' And we kept up our opposition. And then after three years, we simply withdrew from the district committee meetings. We told them plainly, 'From today onward we are not attending your meetings.'

After we stopped attending those meetings, we took out morchas in various places like Mumbai, Bhopal, Indore and Delhi. Whenever there was a morcha we were told, so many people should come from Akrani and Akkalkuwa, so many from Gujarat, so many from M.P., and so on. If Maharashtra was supposed to bring say 1,000 people, I would bring 2,000. It did not take much time. People were very enthusiastic at that time.[89]

Earlier I said that Medhatai had forced the officials to reopen the earlier records which had been deemed to be final and were filed away. She made the officers visit each and every village. In that process it emerged that thousands of landholders had been left out and they had to be added. That proved to be one of the greatest benefits from the organisation.

The other thing was, earlier there were deaths due to hunger, but now people had food. Earlier, people had no work, but now with the help of the law and with a lot of effort from us, people had employment opportunities. The third thing that happened was that extortion and loot disappeared. A new picture emerged in our area. Now the gramsevaks were afraid of us. Nevertheless, the work of the NDA continued—surveying the land in the villages, and so on.

Gradually, by 1988 we had new slogans. 'We Are All One!', 'Who Does The Forestland Belong To? It Belongs To Us, Belongs To Us, Belongs To Us!' The land belonged to us because we were living there for so many generations. But we never got our village converted to a revenue village.[90]

Earlier people used to think that the forest within the village boundary belonged to the government and so also the river and their house—all belonged to the government. But because of the Andolan, every one of us started feeling that the forest, the river and the stones, and everything within the village boundary belonged to the people of the village. It belonged to us. People started saying this because we convinced them. People became firm and steadfast, and that is why we later coined the slogan, 'Our Village, Our Rule!' This slogan was raised only after Ferkuva.[91]

'What Will Sardar Sarovar Do? It Will Destroy Everyone!' This was also one of the slogans created at that time. Another slogan coined was, 'Save Narmada! Save Humanity!' We also had songs. The first song was written in Marathi by Medhatai right in front of me. The song was, '*Dharan alo re, dharan alo*... (The dam is coming, the dam is coming...)' Later on, I translated the song into the Pawri language.

A big meeting took place in our village around 1988. Our Indian commissioner B. D. Sharma[92] had come for the meeting. People simply had one point in mind: 'If he is the Commissioner of India, then why do we need to fight? He should be fulfilling our demands right away, shouldn't he?'

But finally, I was able to explain the situation to the people and convince them. I said, 'Let us start from the beginning. We have the police patil in the village. Above him, his immediate superior is the sarpanch, head of the village panchayat. He is one of the main persons in the village. If we go further, there are higher-level officials, there are different departments, different talathis, there are forest department people, and above them is the circle officer. Then there are other officers superior to them, maybe a police inspector. On the other side are the building department officials. Above them is the zilla parishad (the district council) and above them is the district collector. And then there are district-level political leaders, there are the MLAs and MPs whom we elect, as are the zilla parishad members. They are all elected by us. Then there is the CM of the state. The commissioner is also part of this whole machinery. He takes orders from the president. If he is with us that increases our strength to continue our fight.'

In Nimgavhan, the commissioner took a clear stand. 'I am with you. If you stand up and fight, I will back you.' That is how he gave us strength.

From then onwards we opposed every administrative meeting called by the government. We said, 'From today onwards we will not listen to you because if in spite of discussing it with you a number of times there are no results, there is no use talking to you.'

A few activists from Dhule District had joined the support committee; they also expressed their opposition to the collector and wrote to him very clearly that, 'We are members of the Narmada Dharangrast Sahayak Samiti. We are writing to you on the following points: A submergence area has been shown on the northern boundary of our district. You showed pretty pictures of rehabilitation to the people living on the banks of the Narmada. But it is completely illegal and it will never succeed. And we are bringing to your notice that we will henceforth not participate in the meetings organised to discuss the Sardar Sarovar. From here onward, the Sardar Sarovar will not be built.'

We had never looked at the political aspects before, and we did not know much about it. The political leaders from Dhadgaon Tehsil used to look down on us. They used to think we were uncouth idiots and losers. These very same leaders who thought we were good for nothing were later eager to join us. (*Laughs.*) They started supporting us and arguing on our behalf. Such was the situation in Akrani Tehsil.

In Akrani Tehsil, Dnyaneshwar Patil and myself, we were a very good pair. We also had a person called Ramesh to support us. He got a job as a teacher in the zilla parishad school and left. Ajit Pawra from Bilgaon worked with me and supported me for a number of years. He did a lot of the survey work and the writing work. After all that he has now become a member of the panchayat samiti. (*Laughs.*) He is also sarpanch of his village. We had to handle a very large area, and we fell short of strength. From Sawaria there was Jahangir Bolga.[93] He could not read and write. He was also not able to speak Marathi. But he started working with us.

During that time, I tried hard to push Kevalsingh[94] to go to school until I was tired out. He had to sit for the SSC exam and who knows, perhaps he was afraid he would fail, so he threw big tantrums. Finally, we decided that Jahangir Bolga and Kevalsingh would both join us in our work. The work they did was very important. At that time, it was very difficult for someone to travel from one village to another alone. People even got murdered. For a few days, we used to travel together in pairs. After some time, they too gained the courage to travel alone.

We asked Kevalsingh to take on the responsibility of Akkalkuwa for two years. 'You look after Akkalkuwa, and I will look after Akrani,' I told him. The two of us from one family, we really had a lot to do. For the outside world, it was Medhatai who was visible. But here it was we who had to convince the people and keep them convinced and with us.

Even though from time to time Medhatai did conduct meetings in villages, it was necessary for us to constantly explain things and to make them understand the situation. And we managed to do it. Jahangir Bolga was a hard-core person, and he never could tolerate people who used bad words and cursed. He played a big role in accelerating the work of the Andolan, which was very much required. He worked with us for a long time.

In 1988-89 there was a collector named Gill.[95] He was appointed specially for the rehabilitation work of the Sardar Sarovar. He was very clever. He had the ability to sweet-talk people and break their unity, but the people did not get divided.[96] So, Collector Gill visited the villages for the first time and came to us. His purpose was just this, that the survey work had to be done properly since they did not know the exact number of families affected. As soon as he reached our cluster of villages, he got in touch with me. After that we left for Surung. On our way, we had sent messages to the people that the collector was coming for a visit and we should all gather together. And they did.

At the gathering, I started with my first point, 'Sahib, the rest is fine. But the zilla parishad school in our village exists only on paper. We do not even know who the teacher is. We are running a private school, but you will not accept it and recognise it. There is an ashramshala at Roshmal. But you do not admit students from our village there. We watch the children from urban areas go to school and learn. Our children also want to go to school and study. But there is no school here. And that is a great loss to us. I request you to get these twenty-two children from our village admitted to school. If you do so, it will be a big achievement.' The collector then managed to get all the twenty-two students enrolled in the Roshmal ashramshala. Those students have now been able to complete the first one or two years of college but are sitting at home. Still, they did get educated.

When Collector Gill came to Nimgavhan he was accompanied by fifteen to twenty officers. They came to carry out survey work. The survey did not take place because we were opposed to it. Gill had noted that the children needed education and took care of the issue. But all other issues remained unaddressed. His task was that of displacing us from the banks of the Narmada. Displacement was the government's agenda. So, he was bound to carry out that task.

From time to time, the government invited us to participate in meetings to talk about the Sardar Sarovar, but we refused. And the reason was, if there had been no rehabilitation for the past three years, why would it happen now? We kept on saying, 'Let whatever we have in the village remain with us.'

When the officials came on their visits, they would insist that we go and look at the land for rehabilitation. But we could see very clearly that it was all insincere and false. Whatever the government was giving us was mere promises. They brazenly lied to us. We had no faith, and so from that day on, we decided to completely stop the exercise of looking at land. Arch Vahini tried to show us land in Gujarat. But we were not interested in going to Gujarat, so we opposed that exercise too.

We were not just sitting on our haunches, though. We organised protest marches at Mumbai and Delhi. In the days after we had formed the organisation, we took out a huge rally at the Sardar Sarovar site in Gujarat. There was massive police presence and many of our activists had to face a lathicharge. Under the pretext of arresting us we were taken to Rajpipla. They tried to put pressure on us in many ways. But we were there to give a warning to the Gujarat government, and that we managed to do. We wanted to tell them that it was not a question of one or two villages. This was an issue of a huge number of people and villages, and so they should rethink constructing the dam.

After some days, a rest house that could accommodate high-ranking officers was built near the dam site. Officers from Gujarat, Maharashtra as well as M.P. would assemble and there would be a lot of discussion. All those discussions were inconclusive. But our struggle acquired strength, and we continued to advance step by step.

We now come to the 1989 story. The NBA was now spread over the entire Narmada Valley. In support of the NBA and to seek support from the world, we decided to hold a big rally and conference at Harsud on 28 September 1989.[97] In the Narmada Valley, there was a plan to construct thirty big projects, 3,000 small and 135 medium-size dam projects—a total of 3,165 dam projects. Who can say how many villages would be displaced and destroyed? But we are telling the story of one of these projects, the Sardar Sarovar Dam. So, we had come to Harsud to stop the construction of this dam and with the slogan, '*Vishva Ki Takat Hamare Saath, Bandh Rokna Hamare Haath*' (The World Is With Us, We Can Stop The Dam)!' About 5,000-6,000 of us reached Harsud by train. More than 250 organisations had joined in with the slogan 'In This World, Whose Development? Whose Destruction?' There were spirited discussions. Many leaders addressed the gathering. We too spoke and put forward our views.

Baba Amte[98] and others also participated in the two-day Harsud gathering. The 250 organisations that had come together took a unanimous decision that wherever destruction was taking place in the name of development, we would oppose it with our lives if necessary.

I too spoke.[99] I said that this Sardar Sarovar Project which was bringing destruction in the name of development was going to submerge many villages. But we would not allow these villages to be submerged. We popularised the slogan 'Whose Development? Whose Destruction?' all over the world. Many leaders were saying that big dams have their benefits. If we did not allow big dams to be built, how can we achieve development? But we could see, one Sardar Sarovar would kill one to two lakh people, and in lieu of that, how many people would get food and an opportunity to live? Why did two lakhs need to die? We would die, but for whom should we die? For the benefit of urban residents? The position we took was simple: we would not die. From that day onward, if any person tried to take away anything from within our village boundaries by force, we would oppose it. We put forward this viewpoint of ours and returned from Harsud.

After we returned, we entered politics! We began to think: we do not know what kind of animal this politics is. We had the same sarpanch for thirty years—Lotan Sangana Pawra. We took a decision—myself and Dnyaneshwar Patil—that this time why not try and have a sarpanch of our choice. We asked Murlidhar to contest elections, and out of a total of eleven seats, eight who got elected were from our panel.

But those opposing us attacked us physically by hiring 1,000 people. This happened in 1991. This was a big fight that went on for a long time. That day we were not allowed even to reach the panchayat office. They kept attacking us with stones. A lot of us were injured. The presiding officer too was a fraudster. He lied and declared that the sarpanch and the deputy sarpanch had been elected. False thumb impressions were taken. They managed to falsify three thumb impressions and declared, 'Our sarpanch has won'. No activist was present at that time. I was not well and had developed high fever. I kept thinking what should I do? What should I do? All the people had returned to Nimgavhan. Everybody was served meals. Altogether there were 2,000 people on our side.

Kevalsingh, Ulya from Mal, one other activist from Nashik and Jahangir were surrounded and were openly threatened with their lives. We waited and waited for them until we were tired out. We got word that Kevalsingh and others had been trapped in some valley and had been killed.[100] So, all 2,000 of us decided to go to Dhadgaon in the morning. And it was decided that all of us would carry weapons.

We sent messages to the remaining villages that those opposing us had declared that they had killed five of our people. And so, we had to go to the police sub-inspector's (PSI) office at Dhadgaon. Present there were our MLA and other national leaders.

We were now more than 5,000 people. All of Dhadgaon was full of people. As soon as I reached, the PSI said to me, 'Keshavbhau, come here. We have declared Section 144, and so you move about only in twos and threes, not more.'

'Why was it not declared earlier and why now?' I asked.

The tehsildar said, 'The election of the sarpanch and his deputy has already been declared and so nothing can be done about it now.' And he declared the same old Lotan Sangana Pawra as sarpanch once again.

The gramsevak was there. We asked him to explain to us what had happened. He was scared of us. He kept on saying, 'I cannot say anything.' Jahangir Bolga had then raised his axe at him. I stopped Jahangir and asked him to let it go.

The PSI was also scared. All the officers were scared. They were running about all over Dhadgaon town. We were 5,000 people after all, weren't we? And we all had weapons, didn't we? After all the hullabaloo, all that the PSI told us was that the law would be strictly followed. So, from there, I sent everyone back and left for Dhule. At Dhule, with the help of Shyam Patil[101] and Dashrath Tatya I called a press conference and told them everything about the illegal process of election and our demand for re-election. I went to the collector as well, who came and allowed himself to be photographed with us.

Then the collector announced that a re-election would take place! It was a long and fierce struggle. In that process Murlidhar Vasave became sarpanch for the first time. And Kushna Balaji Padvi became deputy sarpanch. From that time, the political leaders were afraid of us because they saw that we had very strong support.

After we took the panchayat into our hands, a question came up. We now had our own sarpanch in the village, but no development work could be undertaken in the submergence villages.[102] The issue was created by the government itself. So, we did not allow them to work in the villages outside the submergence zone either, no matter if the funds lapsed. Of the twenty villages in the panchayat, fifteen were in the submergence zone!

They falsely implicated Murlidhar Vasave in a case of murder. Murlidhar had to be in jail for forty-five days, and the case continued for fourteen years, after which time the final judgement was passed, and he was freed. Such is the politics of the government.

In the Murlidhar case, Medha Patkar, Dnyaneshwar Patil and Advocate Suryavanshi from Dhule helped us a lot. And because of that Murlidhar was released. Otherwise it would have been a very difficult situation. After that we managed to get Geeta[103] elected sarpanch. Kevalsingh contested the zilla parishad election. Andolan representatives contested sarpanch and panchayat samiti elections. Those who opposed us offered 500 rupees to every voter for their vote. They distributed lakhs of rupees. We never distributed any money. We managed to get elected based on our spoken word. This brings the story up to 1990.

Now we come to Ferkuva. After the Harsud rally, the GoM entered into a contract with the World Bank.[104] One issue kept coming up. Since private land was not available, forestland should be considered for rehabilitation and resettlement (R&R). There was pressure on the World Bank for this.[105] Finally, the World Bank proposed this to the state government. At that time Gill was the collector. Gill told the government that the adivasis had been eyeing the forestland all along. So if we offered them forestland, they would come forward and accept it without resistance. And we would not have any problem with R&R. So, the government sanctioned the release of 4,200 hectares of forestland for this purpose.[106]

But the state government gave the Centre a false reason—that the people have a single demand, and that is, they are ready to accept R&R only if they are given forestland in the three tehsils of Taloda, Shahada and Akkalkuwa.[107] So, if we have to build the dam, then the central government must release forestland for this purpose. Only then would this issue be resolved. Based on the World Bank's report, the GoM demanded that the Centre release 2,769 hectares out of a total of about 18,000 hectares of forestland in the three tehsils. We would then accommodate all the displaced families, they said. Sharad Pawar followed up this demand and managed to get a sanction for the release of 2,769 hectares of forestland. There were supposed to be 529 trees standing on that land, and the GoM had agreed to compensate the Centre for the cost of those trees. Accordingly, the compensation was paid and the forestland was released for settlement.

The second point that emerged as soon as the land was sanctioned was whether it would be sufficient to resettle all the displaced people because the government had said they would give 2 hectares per family. Their maths was something like this: there were 1,300 families. Two times 13 is 26; so 2,600 hectares. And another 100 hectares or so for the housing plots. With this thinking, 2,769 hectares were sanctioned. After getting the sanction, I had a detailed talk with Gill Sahib.

He said, 'Look, we have managed to get sanction for the release of forestland just as you have demanded. You should be very happy.'

But I did not say I was happy. I said, 'Is so much land meant for building houses, Sahib? Where is the land for cultivation?'

He said, 'No, no. This will be sufficient for cultivation.'

'Oh, I see. I thought it was for housing. But will it be sufficient?'

'No, no, we have prepared another proposal for Akkalkuwa for an additional 1,500 hectares.'

Within a few days the 1,500 hectares was also sanctioned. So, a total of 4,200 hectares of forestland was sanctioned.

That was the time of the Ferkuva struggle. That happened in 1990. In the Ferkuva struggle, around 5,000 of us from the adivasi areas joined together. Each of us packed our own provisions. And off we went on foot to Alirajpur Tehsil. We walked in the day and camped in the night. Men, women and children—all of us were there. I returned only after thirty-six days when the struggle was concluded. All the others, they kept coming and going.

Ferkuva was planned as a programme in which we travelled on foot from village to village, camping every day in one of them, until we reached the dam site. Many different organisations from all over the country participated in it. There were journalists. And media people shooting their videos. Baba Amte was with us. As we walked towards the dam site, we were stopped at the border of M.P. and Gujarat. There were 10,000 police on one side and 10,000 of the public on the other side. It was as if it was a battlefield with both sides face to face and ready to charge.

On the Gujarat side, we could see people being brought every day. We came to know later that they were handsomely paid to be there.[108] They thought if we people reached the dam site and began a sit-in, they would not be able to construct the dam. So, they were determined, come what may, that they would not allow us to enter Gujarat. That was their plan.

We asked them, why were they not allowing us to enter Gujarat? Wasn't it a constituent state of our own republic? This is the dam that was submerging us. That is why we wanted to stop the construction of the dam. We had some discussions with the secretary of the Government of Gujarat (GoG) and some Gujarat leaders, but no concrete solution emerged. So, we proceeded to sit-in right there.

Sometime later, the Gujarat government and M.P. government colluded and were preparing to pick us up and disperse us. But we showed our strength and managed to make them leave. Our hunger strike continued. But we saw that even after thirty-six days no solution was forthcoming. None of the issues was getting resolved. The government was not willing to take any decision. We realised that continuing the sit-in was not of much use. We decided that we would retain the strength we had shown and watch and see what the government would do. So, with the slogan 'Our Village, Our Rule', we ended our satyagraha and returned to our homes.

Then there are the later events of 1991. A meeting was organised that included the CMs of the four states, namely, Maharashtra, M.P., Gujarat and Rajasthan, the central government minister Ramvilas Paswan, Manubhai Kothadia and our own B. D. Sharma. I still have that leaflet with all the names. The question was, should we attend this meeting? We decided that if it was convenient for all, then we could attend it. We took the decision, and I left for Mumbai to attend the meeting. At that meeting they had brought three or four persons who opposed me all the time. One was Ambalal Nama Tadvi, second was the sarpanch of Gadher Village in Gujarat, and there was also Biharilal from Bhavati Village in M.P.

The district rehabilitation officer took me there. But I went there with everyone's consent. 'Remain a campaign activist; do not become a government person,' they advised. The collector, Mr Gill, showed me all of Mumbai from his car—'This bungalow belongs to Minister so and so, that bungalow belongs to Minister so and so....' He showed me all the important places.

After showing me around, he asked me, 'Look Keshavbhau, would you like to have a Jeep? Take a new Jeep. I will buy it for you; why are you afraid?'

'No, I will not take it, Sahib. There is no road for it in the village.' (*Laughs.*)

'Okay, tell me, can you survive on that land there?'

'Yes, Sahib, if it produces 5–6 quintals of grain, it is sufficient for us for twelve months, and we are quite happy with it.'

'Okay, will you look after the rehabilitation work in your tehsil? I will enrol you for 1,100 rupees honorarium.'[109]

'No, Sahib, that won't be possible for me.'

'Just sit there at least. I will write you up for 1,100 rupees a month. And secondly, how many acres of land do you want?'

'Hmm. If I am allotted the land then I would get 5 acres, wouldn't I, Sahib?' I said.

He asked me, 'But will 5 acres be sufficient for you?'

And I said, 'Sufficient or not, I will only get whatever is due to me, wouldn't I, Sahib?'

'Oh, come on, why do you hesitate? I will give you more land; just accept rehabilitation.'

'No Sahib, I cannot survive alone, can I? It is everybody's problem. Everyone should get land. How many people will you fit in 4,200 hectares of land, Sahib?'

He said, 'There will be sufficient land for all.'

'Do the calculation. How many hectares are you giving per family?'

'Two hectares.'

'If each person gets 2 hectares, then with 100 hectares how many people would get land?'

'Fifty.'

'And with 1,000 hectares, how many people?'

'Five hundred.'

'Suppose there are 4,000 hectares, how many people?'

'Two thousand families.'

'Then where would the remaining families go and die? That is why, Sahib, 4,000 hectares will solve nothing. You need 10,000 hectares to solve this problem.'

And Collector Gill said, 'No, Keshavbhau, why do you think like this? Everyone should look out for themselves. Look, now, there is going to be a big meeting over here. There are four chief ministers attending this meeting. The rehabilitation minister will also be there. Put forward some good points before them.'

I said, 'Okay, I will put forward whatever best I can.'

After I was shown the whole city of Mumbai, I went into the meeting hall. Our names were written beforehand on the nameplates. Here would sit Keshav Vasave, here Ambalal Nama Tadvi, etc. I sat behind my nameplate. The meeting was scheduled for two and a half hours. Remember, this was a very important meeting. We had very hot exchanges in this meeting. At the beginning of the meeting, the Chief Minister of Maharashtra Sharad Pawar introduced us all. Here is the Honourable Chief Minister of Gujarat Chimanbhai Patel, and there was loud applause. Here is the Honourable Chief Minister of Rajasthan—what was his name? He who went on to become president or maybe vice president? Oh, yes, Bhairon Singh Shekhavat. So, here is the Honourable Chief Minister of Rajasthan; here is Sunderlal Patwa, Honourable Chief Minister of M.P. There was applause from every corner. Then it was the central government ministers—Ramvilas Paswan of the Rehabilitation Ministry, and Manubhai Kothadia of the Water Ministry, etc. After this the rest of us were asked to introduce ourselves. The others were not cleverer than me; they were assholes. The others were introduced by K. C. Padvi.[110] Then it was my turn. I stood up and said, 'I am Keshav Vasave. I am an activist of the Narmada Andolan.' I told them my address. Ambalal did the same and so did the Gadher sarpanch.

The Chief Minister of Gujarat, Chimanbhai started the ball rolling. 'Brothers, the representatives from the Narmada Valley, Central Ministers Ramvilas Paswan-ji and Manubhai-ji, keep in mind brothers, the Sardar Sarovar is held to be the largest such project in the world. It is going to irrigate a lot of land. It is going to produce a lot of electricity. For those people who are deprived of drinking water, it is this project that is going to quench their thirst. There are a number of adivasis in the Narmada Valley. There are no doctors or medical facilities in their villages, no educational facilities, none of the other facilities, and for many years to come there cannot be any development work in these areas. Such remote areas, and such monstrous lives they live! Because of Sardar Sarovar, we will be able to bring these adivasi people and settle them near urban areas. We will make them human and give them education. We will make them advanced. We consider it our responsibility, and that is why we are building the Sardar Sarovar Project. We have to build this project as fast as possible. That is why we have invited you as representatives. That is why we have to vacate the villages as soon as possible. This project is a large-scale inter-state project. All we are saying is that with this project our entire country is going to prosper. That is why this project is called "Narmada Development Authority". It is our fervent hope that we will go ahead with this project.'

After he had spoken, people started saying, 'Come, let us start, let us go ahead.' But no one was getting up. I got up. I had come there to speak, hadn't I? I said, 'My name is Keshav Vasave, Village Nimgavhan, Tehsil Dhadgaon, District Dhule, Maharashtra. I am representing the 220 villages on the banks of the Narmada.' I had only said this much, and there was a furore. I was fiercely opposed. Which 220 villages? Tell us their names. What kind of representative is he? Who has invited him here?

'Look here, I got this invitation letter to attend this meeting, and that is why I have come. I have come here to put forward our position.'

Sharad Pawar asked everyone to keep quiet. 'Silence please, silence please.'

'What kind of representative is this, and who called him?'

'I have come here as the representative of all 220 villages on the Narmada banks, and I have also come to put forward our viewpoint,' I said again.

Then I began to speak, 'What the Gujarat Chief Minister has just said is a big thing—there is going to be a lot of irrigation, a lot of water and a lot of electricity which is necessary for the development of our country. But on behalf of our movement, there are many people who do these calculations, and they have also done these calculations. We are talking about water reaching Rajasthan, but water from this project will not reach Rajasthan. You say people who have been living in the dark for the last fifty years will get electricity. When are we going to get it? You talk a lot about development, but I do not accept it. There is no talk here about how so many people will be rehabilitated. So, you may keep calling this project Narmada "Development", but until my last breath, I will call it Narmada Destruction Project!' That is the language I used.

There was great opposition, so fierce you would not believe it. 'What kind of representative is this? How can he talk like this?'

But Sharad Pawar kept on asking me, 'Do you have anything more to say, Keshavrao?'

'Yes, Sahib, I still have something to say,' I said, 'So, the Minister Sahib told us a lot of things about the Narmada Valley. For all these years, it is only adivasi people who have been living in the entire Narmada Valley. Now you are going to take them near the cities, teach them, school them, make them literate, knowledgeable. Fifty years have passed, why didn't you teach them, educate them all these years? Those areas could also have been developed, no? Then why has that development not taken place until now? Only now they are talking about Sardar Sarovar. Second thing about the project, a lot of electricity is going to be produced. Who is going to get that electricity? It is for the big cities. Poor people like us will continue to stay in the dark. Who will get water? Big people? Industry? This Sardar Sarovar Project is being planned for these people. So, our objective is that if we are not getting its benefits on a priority basis, then we will not allow the dam to proceed further.' I said this and sat down.

'Okay, next one please.'

Ambalalbhai started to speak, 'Sahib, we have chosen the land near the minister's village. Our Chimalkhedi village should be rehabilitated there as early as possible. That is all we want.'

A lot of applause all around, 'Very good, very good!'

After listening to this, I raised my hand. Sharad Pawar again asked me, 'So, Keshavrao, do you want to say something about this?'

I said, 'I am an activist working in the thirty-three villages of Akrani and Akkalkuwa tehsils. This Ambalalbhai was also our friend. But a few days back, he left us. In Chimalkhedi there are ten families of the Tadvi tribe. When we had organised a meeting there, we ourselves suggested to them, explained to them, that if they wanted to go to Gujarat, we would help them move. We offered to transport their houses to the dam site at the earliest. We said we would put all their stuff on a raft and launch it on the Narmada. But he refused. But Chimalkhedi is a large village. There are 150 families of Vasavas. Till today the Vasavas are saying that we will drown and die but we will not move from here. Look, this Ambalal is connected to the government and government officials. We do not accept him at all.'

Poor fellow, he sat down without saying anything! Then the Sarpanch of Gadher got up and said, 'There are nineteen villages in Gujarat which will be submerged. Most of these people have chosen land in the villages they like. Still a few families have been left behind, but they are also willing to move in large numbers. That is why our demand is: rehabilitate us as soon as possible. And vacate the banks of the Narmada as soon as possible.'

After listening to him, I raised my hand again. I said, 'Gadher is a very big village, Sahib. I know the story of that village. Though he is Sarpanch of Gadher, only a few people have accepted land. The rest of them are still staying in the village. Some of the people from the lower hamlets are in touch with us, and they say the quality of land being offered is so poor that they will not be able to make a living.'

He too fell silent.

After him, Biharilal stood up. He started on a long story. 'The people from M.P. are willing to move right now, my adivasi brothers. But we should be provided the land.'

I raised my hand and said, 'Dear Biharibhai, you are not from the Narmada submergence area, are you? You are from some other village, aren't you? Why would you need rehabilitation? It should be provided to the people whose land is going to get submerged, isn't it so? You are not even an activist! You are trying to suppress the important question of the survival of so many people.'

So, he too sat down. No one gave any answer. After this K. C. Padvi put forward his views. Then he asked me, 'Why are you opposing everyone?'

I said, 'I have to oppose them. It is necessary that these things be said.' Upon this the Gujarat CM said, 'People are willing to settle in Gujarat, but only a handful of bad people from the Narmada Andolan are opposing it.'

B. D. Sharma tried to intervene and say something, but there was strong opposition to him. Yet he was not intimidated. He raised his voice and said, 'The President of India has given me the responsibility of this powerful post as commissioner. It becomes my duty to see if poor people are dying, and if they are, I must prevent that. And so, if there is a person who is saying that he represents 220 villages and says that they would prefer to die rather than move out and leave their place, but ten families want to leave and settle in Gujarat, why don't you move just the ten? Move them immediately, and allow the rest to lead their lives in peace.'

The meeting went on for two and a half hours, but one and a half hours were taken up by the arguments between me and the minister, and there was only one hour left for the other people. The meeting was not successful. They were asking me to stay for lunch, but I left without lunch. I just came back. What a meeting, and what kind of talk!

In that meeting I also said, 'I am using this language today, but I promise you, after ten years also I will be using the same language. I will keep saying that the Sardar Sarovar Project is a destructive project. It is these same words that you will hear from me even after ten years.'

We refused to be intimidated by the ministers. That day, protesters—the support group in Mumbai—had taken out a protest march, and they were to march to the venue of the meeting. They had been arrested even before I reached there.

K. C. Padvi, who was sitting with me, did not have the courage to speak out. So, I was forced to lay it all out. I fulfilled my duty and continued to do whatever was needed to be done. We were apprehensive about getting forestland, but we managed to win on that point. It was not clear whether all of us would get rehabilitated or not. Nevertheless, at least most of us in Maharashtra, we remained united, and we could fight and move ahead. Later on, the government was even forced to buy private land and give it to us.

The strength is not that of one person. It is a united strength. We the people of the banks of Narmada, we held fast to our courage and our resolve. Only after we got support from each other could we build our strength and move ahead. It is because of this strength that Medha Patkar was to receive a renowned award in 1991. Medha Patkar refused to accept that award because there were so many battles we still had to fight.

The issue was discussed in the executive committee meeting. Many people from the banks of the Narmada said that the (award) money received should be distributed among everyone, and that we should accept. Some said, we have a lot of expenses in the Andolan and we should use that money to cover those expenses. Someone said this, someone said that. Finally, it was decided that Medha Patkar should refuse to take it on her own behalf and should say that the award should be in the name of the movement and that an adivasi person from the movement should receive it on its behalf.[111] And after a lot of discussion about who should go and all, it was decided unanimously that Keshavbhau should go.

It was November 1991 and I had to go, but first I needed a passport. One month was spent in the process of getting the passport issued. The Indian government did not want that we should receive the award. It is for this reason that Medha

Patkar was arrested in Shahada. The news spread all over the country which put tremendous pressure on the government. If she was receiving the award for her social work, for good work, then it was not good if the Indian government was arresting her. She should be immediately and unconditionally released. That was what was being said, and soon there was pressure on the CM, and on the president's orders Medhatai was released forthwith. On 30 December we left Mumbai for London and stayed abroad for about fifteen days.

We accepted the Right Livelihood Prize[112] in a foreign country. On that day, every newspaper in the country carried our photograph accepting the prize. That was a precious and important prize.

I myself had signed on the dotted line saying that the money from the award would not be used in the Narmada Valley. So, none of the award money was used in the Narmada Andolan. The interest on the prize amount was to be used to support needy organisations doing good work. That prize money is still intact. Over the last five to six years, I have visited many places as a member of the Jan Sahyog Trust.[113] Even now good work is being supported.

Nandini: You have travelled to many foreign countries. How was that experience?

Keshavbhau: We travelled for fifteen days and visited various countries. I did not get a ticket to Germany. So, after Medhatai went to Germany, I was told, 'Come directly to Stockholm.' In our country, we can go by bus, or railway or taxicab. It is different in those countries. They are all countries in the midst of the sea, aren't they? That is why one can travel from one to the other only by aeroplane.

Once I was selected for the visit to foreign countries, I went to Mumbai for a month to complete all the paperwork. Before that, I visited the local government offices one by one so that they could furnish me with the police patil's certificate, the gram panchayat sarpanch's certificate, the talathi's certificate, the certificate from the Dhadgaon Tehsil police station, the tehsildar's certificate and the deputy superintendent of police's (DSP) certificate. So, we collected all the certificates from all levels, and I left for Mumbai.

In the course of getting the passport one more issue had emerged: 'Suppose, you happen to die in an accident overseas, your dead body would be sent to Mumbai. Where should we send it in Mumbai?' You have to give the Mumbai name and address. After submitting the Mumbai address, they say, 'You belong to Dhule. So, where in Dhule should we send it?'

I gave Dashrath Tatya's address.

'Okay, fine. You are from Dhadgaon Tehsil, so where in Dhadgaon do we send it?'

This became an issue.

'Which is your post office?'

'It is Surwani.'

'Where in Dhadgaon?'

I told them that once they contacted Dhadgaon, the message would reach my village. And at last, the chain stopped there.

I also told them that once my dead body reached Dhadgaon, my panchayat, Roshmal Khurd, was a big panchayat, and the sarpanch was my brother, so my body should be sent in his name.

In Mumbai, YUVA[114] had allowed me to stay in their office in the Mahim area. I used to stay there all by myself. After I reached there, I began imagining all kinds of things. I had left my wife and children behind and had been in Mumbai for almost a month. I was going to visit a foreign country. I started out on this foreign trip thinking I would get the opportunity to travel in an aeroplane. I had to go there and accept an award. And here people were asking me directly where they should send my dead body! Even in my sleep I had nightmares about it. After this, I began to think, what if I decided not to go? What was the harm? My children were so young, and I had left them behind. What if something happened to me on the way? Man! There may be no trace of me left behind!

Instead of going through all this, I felt I should just lie to Medhatai's mother[115] and run away. Why shouldn't I? I picked up the phone and called Medhatai's mother. And lied to her.

'Grandma, I have not come prepared to visit a foreign country. I have left all my clothes and everything behind in my village. I had come to get a passport. But I have to get my clothes and other things, so I am going home to get them.'

She said, 'No, no, Medha will be mad at me! You can't go!'

I said, 'No, I will leave today and will be back tomorrow or the day after.' (*Laughs.*) I was not able to concentrate. I was fed up with my one-month stay in Mumbai. I was living on *vada-pav*.[116]

'Okay, but be sure to come back by the morning the day after tomorrow.'

I said, 'Oh, yes. I will surely come back.'

She said, 'If you don't, Medha will be so mad, she will chew me out.' That is what she said.

'Grandma, please send somebody to help me reach the ST bus stand, because I have never been there,' I told her, and within no time a young boy came and escorted me to the ST bus stand. The bus to Shahada was already waiting at the platform. I boarded the bus at eleven o'clock and reached Shahada between eight and ten o'clock. From Shahada I went to Dhadgaon and from there to Nimgavhan. But I was not able to sleep. I had spent a lot of money so that I could go abroad. I had taken out a passport. I had got all the certificates issued. I had been dreaming of travelling in a plane for such a long time. Now, none of these things would be fulfilled. So, I got up the next morning and reached Dhadgaon, and from there I went back to Mumbai. (*Laughs.*)

The passport was issued the same day. We reached the airport, and at the right time, boarded the plane and sat in our seats. I was not able to figure out when the plane would leave. We had separate seats when we flew out. I got a seat on the lower floor. The plane had two floors. Medhatai had a seat on the upper one. After take-off, flying higher and higher, the plane would raise this wing once, then the other, and every time I thought, 'Oh my God! Look, it's gone... It's gone... gone!' (*Laughs long and hard.*) I had a window seat, so I could see all the lights and everything on the way. Once we took off there was a rush for the toilet. And one had to stand in that queue to relieve oneself. In this way we reached London after twelve hours.

A person from Ahmedabad, Gautam Appa,[117] had a job there. I stayed with him for four days. There you cannot survive in our clothes. You need to take a lot of warm clothes with you. One has to be fully prepared to face the cold. In the four days we spent in London we addressed many meetings. The subject of these meetings was—Big Dams: Beneficial or Destructive? I spoke, and someone translated. 'The World Bank is a big moneylender. Poor countries like India take big loans from these wealthy moneylenders to build dams like the Sardar Sarovar, and in that process we poor people have our lives destroyed. We are not getting anything out of it. That is why we are making a strong appeal to you—do not lend money to such projects. These big projects are taking our lives.'

The next programme was to be held in Stockholm the following day. Medhatai had to leave without me because I did not get a ticket on her flight. When she was leaving, Medhatai said, 'Keshavbhau, Gautam Appa will take you to the airport. From there onward you have to manage to get into the plane and come to Stockholm by yourself.' That's when it hit me that I would not be able to return to India from this foreign country. I was finished!

The first thing was, I was not sure I would be able to bear the cold. Then, I was not sure I would be able to find my way back to Gautam Appa's place. How would I manage what to eat? Nor could I understand their language. Anyway, the next day, Gautam Appa took me to the airport. London is a big international airport. There were thousands of planes on the ground. I was confused. Which plane was I to board for Stockholm? I could not make out. Then I went around from line to line with my passport and managed to board a plane. My boarding pass had the number 15 written on it, so I went and sat down on seat number 15. If someone was to come and ask me to vacate the seat, then I was in the wrong plane! But no one asked me to get up. After some time, the plane took off. On the way we were served meals and tea, after which, I finally reached Stockholm!

At Stockholm, I sat inside the airport for half an hour. Outside, there were many important people eagerly waiting for me. They kept calling up Medhatai. She had told them the whole story, that I was an adivasi, and that I have a tattoo on my forehead, and all that. After half an hour I ventured outside. A woman came running, calling out, 'India? India?' Within seconds a crowd had gathered around me. The welcome began right there. They took me to the hotel in a procession accompanied by music played on different instruments. It was a big hotel named Gumla. We were given two separate rooms. One was in the name of Keshav Vasave and the other was for Medha Patkar. When I saw Medha Patkar's name written there, I felt reassured that she would definitely come. I was very happy. Up to that point, I was scared whether I would ever be able to get back to India.

So, we spent eight days there. We accepted the award on Monday. Ten to fifteen similar awards were given. I gave a small speech. I also sang a Pawri song, *Dharan Awyo, Dharan Awyo* (The dam is coming, the dam is coming). (*Laughs.*) Everybody liked the song.

We were to stay longer, but from 1990 the Manibeli satyagraha was going on. In 1991 they were going to relocate the Shoolpaneshwar Mandir away from Manibeli using bulldozers.[118] After we received the award, we called the Vadodara office and came to know that a large police force comprising 700 policemen from Gujarat and 500 policemen from Maharashtra had assembled at Manibeli. They were supposed to be moving the Mandir brick by brick, or so we were told.

We decided to shorten our stay. We visited different countries—England, Germany, France, Sweden, Norway, and New York in America—but curtailed the time we spent there. We were supposed to do it in a month, but we finished the trip and returned within fifteen days.

We visited many places in our free time. There was a big office which displayed adivasi culture. There one woman was shown grinding grain. Another was shown carrying a head-load of two *ghagar*s (round metal pitchers) one on top of the other. Another woman was spreading cow dung in the fields from a container on her head. A big meeting was organised there. At every place I visited, I talked against the World Bank.

In the beginning I used to feel there was no city like Mumbai anywhere in the world. But after I visited other countries, I saw broad roads, plenty of electricity, tall buildings, and so on. In comparison to the world out there, Mumbai is a small town.

Today, whatever can be done in this age of science with the power of money has been done and the world has gone far ahead. Even though I stay in a small corner of a river valley, I have had the opportunity to see it all. We were surviving on a little bit of greens and coarse jowar bread. But the government was trying to snatch away even that from us. Those little bit of greens and coarse grain bread are the most important things for us—they are our life. If we are to save them, our struggle must become strong. So, I did my duty towards this end by going on this trip abroad.

Regarding this award, the biggest allegation in Gujarat was that we were 'building the Andolan with foreign funds.' Our response was that the award has been given to us, and we will accept it, but we will not spend a single paisa of it for the Andolan. We would deposit this money and use the interest earned on that amount to support all those different organisations that have no funds but are setting good examples for everyone.

When we returned to Mumbai after receiving the award, a very large number of people had gathered at the airport to receive us. We felt that it was the kind of reception a visiting CM receives. That crowd was there for an adivasi and Medha Patkar who had received one of the highest awards one could get, the world-famous Right Livelihood Prize. We were escorted to Mumbai by this crowd singing and playing various instruments. A big meeting was held in Mumbai. We were both felicitated. The event was written about and reported in all the newspapers. And after two days we returned to our villages.

After I returned, there were all these people who had opposed us who were saying, 'He has just been to Mumbai and back! Do you think he could really go to a foreign country?

Who would allow him?' But it was the government officers who would tell them, 'Come on. You don't know a thing! We have read in the newspapers. He has got a big award in a foreign country.' And so on.

The real issue cropped up after I reached the village. Adivasis do not think too far ahead. They began telling me, 'Do not eat all this award money by yourself. Share it with everyone.'

I told them, 'The award is not for sharing like that. (*Laughs.*) The Gujarat government is always criticising the Andolan for taking foreign funds. That is why we announced that we would not use a single paisa of it for the Narmada Andolan. The Gujarat government is saying that it will provide Sardar Sarovar water to Saurashtra and Kachchh but they will not be able to do this. So, we are going to spend that money on some experiments to support people and set good examples for others.' After that they stopped. But they still kept grumbling, 'You are very cunning! Why did you give it away? They have a lot of money. That money should have been shared amongst us.' And so on.

The MLA from Akrani, K. C. Padvi, heard about the award, and he too felicitated me. He spoke well of me, and said that even he, who was an MLA, never had the opportunity to visit a foreign country. But one of us, an intelligent adivasi brother, getting that opportunity and winning one of the highest awards in the world, was no small thing. It is a matter of great fortune. He said, 'You received it in Stockholm. We congratulate you,' and so on, and welcomed me with flowers and a coconut.

Now let us move ahead with the story. We were demanding and insisting from the beginning that the dam had to be rethought. In 1993 the Manibeli satyagraha was in full swing. Since there was no change in thinking, we were forced to take the next step and announce our intention of *Jalsamarpan*[119] (sacrificing one's life by drowning). This had been discussed and decided in the villages, and many people had come forward to join the Jalsamarpan. The government was avoiding the issue of a review. Finally, 6 August was decided as the day for the Jalsamarpan. There was a huge public meeting on 1 August and thousands of policemen had been called up. Since the eyes of the entire world were set on whether Jalsamarpan would take place or not, at the 1 August rally, I publicly warned the government, 'If you are not going to rethink the dam, we will commit mass suicide by drowning.'

In Maṇibeli, Kesubhai Tadvi had a house,[120] and that site was submerged. We had a number of sit-in protests at the Mantralaya in Mumbai about it and also had discussions with Sharad Pawar. Kesubhai's house had been shifted to the village Parveta in Gujarat. We opposed it and said, 'Why has the house been shifted to Parveta without our permission? How did you shift his house to Parveta when he does not have land there? You must shift it back and rebuild it here.'[121] We held a large protest with slogans on 1 August. 2 August went by, 3rd went by, 4th went by, and on 5 August, this central—who was that person, son?' (*Turns to Kevalsingh for response.*)

'Yes, the Water Resource Minister at the Centre announced, 'Okay, we accept your demand.[122] We have begun the process of rethinking. Please do not perform Jalsamarpan. So Medha Patkar came out of hiding.[123] In these five or six days, the entire world was shaken. The whole of the Narmada Valley was full of policemen. Anywhere you looked, you would find policemen. All over the world the radio carried no other news. Every news report would end with Medha Patkar. On the 6th, Medha Patkar appeared publicly in the midst of the people. After that as a matter of formality, she was shown to be arrested and released by the Vadodara collector. Our people had been jailed. They were told not to stay in Manibeli. They were loaded onto vehicles, transported to Molgi and then released. But our people would manage to turn up in Manibeli again!

In that same year, with the idea of accelerating the dam work, 30,000 college students were brought to Kevadia Colony from all over India. They were called to dig pits and plant trees in the area surrounding the dam. To explain our standpoint to them we had opened a small booth at Kevadia Colony. The arrangements and expenses for the comfortable stay of these students came to thirty crore rupees. They had special tents, and sturdy pits and vehicles at their beck and call.[124]

We had put up our information booth at Navagam.[125] Wherever there were a large number of students present, we would go there and call out to them from the road, 'Oh, brother! Come here and watch. This dam named Sardar Sarovar that is being built is going to submerge all these adivasi villages. This government is planning to kill all these adivasis. Thousands of hectares of forestland will be submerged. Standing forests will be destroyed. They are asking you to plant these trees as a replacement for this destruction. The number of adivasis affected is very large. The government is giving them nothing in lieu of their land which they will submerge. You have been invited here in the name of development. Do not be fooled by their talk. Do not be carried away by their propaganda.'

Many students were convinced and returned to their homes. We continued to run the booth. I was there. Medha Patkar was there. Old woman Dedlibai was there and also Ranya Dahya and Noorji. Kevadia Colony resident Prabhubhai[126] and Baliben[127] were there. Then suddenly in a monster-like vehicle a big policewoman arrived on the scene. She easily picked us up in twos and threes, and the police put us in the van and took us to Rajpipla and left us there.

By then a lot of publicity had taken place. The news had reached almost half the students. First those students were physically taken away from our booths and sent back to their places. But many of the students kept coming back to listen to us. So, finally the police had to remove us from there. We wrote articles in the newspapers describing what was happening. That this was a violent attack on the adivasis. At that time the construction of the dam had just begun.

In 1994 the height of the dam began to increase rapidly. It reached something like 69 metres, I think. But we were not silent. We organised various programmes—protests in Delhi, Mumbai, Dhule, Indore and Bhopal.

This is something that happened in 1993. Eight talathis and gramsevaks came to my house and stayed over. They had probably been asked to visit on the instructions of Kunte, the collector of Dhule and P. P. Sharma, the superintendent of police. Gill Sahib had been transferred, and he later joined the World Bank in 1992 or 1993. Later, he may have felt sorry for what he had done, or maybe not, who knows? We had punished him in many ways. He was a good officer. But he did not have sufficient determination and courage to think, 'I will do whatever is needed and see it through.' Nor was it in his hands to do so. Their main objective was to divide and destroy the main people of the struggle.

So, back to 1993 after Kunte became collector. The officers began to realise that if we adivasis of the NBA continued our ban on government officials entering our villages, it would make things very difficult for them. So, they decided, 'Okay, we'll go ahead and crush this movement.' That is why they had sent the eight gramsevaks and talathis to our village as an advance warning.

They tried to tell us, 'Look here. This is a development programme. This project will give electricity and irrigation water. Everyone will benefit. And you people will get land in exchange for land. The government is much stronger than you. Why are you opposing them? One SRP (State Reserve Police Force) policewoman will be more than a match for ten of your men. So, what is the point in resisting the government?'

I told the people that the officers were saying one SRP woman would be a match for ten of our men, so let her come and we would see. Finally, we sent them a message saying that until they gave us a final decision on our demand, we would not be able to negotiate. Till then it would be, 'Our village, our rule!'

Since we would not allow the police to enter our village, they set up camp at Roshmal Khurd. Imagine how much money must have been spent on the thousands of police who were called there! From 15 November 1993 the police force from all over Maharashtra had been called in. By eight in the morning on 19 November, people from all over had gathered at our village limits. After sometime, the police started coming in batches. 'They are coming, they are coming,' we announced; we had a loudspeaker with us.

'SRP police, pay attention, we are warning you! Do not take a single step forward! This is a question of life and death for us. What business do the police have here? It was the officials who were to come. Then why have the police come? You are coming to crush our spirit and destroy us!'

One batch of our people went to the Bharad side. The Nimgavhan people were on the opposite side in large numbers. The police were sandwiched between the two. They panicked and started firing. In that firing Rehmal Vasave was killed.[128]

The news of the firing and death of Rehmal reached Vadodara, and soon after that it reached the Badwani office, Dhadgaon office, Dhule office and Mumbai office. Activists of the Andolan rushed to the spot immediately. Each and every activist including Medha Patkar from Badwani reached the place where Rehmal was shot. They stayed over and joined the collective vigil.

We did not allow the survey to take place. We told them very firmly, 'If you want to carry out the survey then you will have to bomb us. Only then will you be able to conduct the survey. Or, alternatively, if you want to survey our village, you will have to put us all in jail, and then carry out your survey. Otherwise, with you and us face to face, it is impossible.'

After Rehmal Vasave's post-mortem and his last rites, we held a protest march in Dhule to express our grief and to hold the collector responsible for his murder. The march was fiercely lathicharged. With that lathicharge, we were arrested and put in jail for eight days to make a big show that we were the murderers, we were the criminals. And in those few days the police used the opportunity to enter the village in the name of the survey. All this happened in 1993.

We had erected a stone in Rehmal's memory, but we have not brought it here to the rehabilitation village. It was submerged. His memorial stone was treated like a god, wasn't it?

We have not brought our gods and goddesses over here either. But every year some offering is made in their name. Rehmal sacrificed his life for all of us. No one could say that he died for his personal interests. People here in Vadchhil,[129] and the rest of the world, will always treat him as a martyr. Despite Rehmal's sacrifice, his brother is still not included in the official list of the dam-affected persons. But at least Rehmal should be included, that is what we said. Finally, last year (2006–07) Kailas Punya Vasave received land as Rehmal's heir.

Nandini: Keshavbhau, before we go on to what took place after 1991, can you please tell us about the Morse Committee and the Jayant Patil Committee reports?[130]

Keshavbhau: There was lot of pressure on the World Bank, so they established the Morse Committee and sent the committee members here for a review. Morse was the head of the committee. When we came to know that he was to come to Manibeli to have a discussion with the Andolan, we gathered on the banks of the Narmada. The satyagraha at Manibeli was still going on. We decided we would not allow Morse to enter the village unless he heard us out. He was to travel by boat. We had a discussion right there on the Narmada bank. One person who knew him introduced him to us. 'This is Morsebhai and he is something, something, etc.' After that we raised slogans, and I opened the talks. I told him clearly that if he was really interested in listening to us, he should know that we would not allow any helicopter to enter our village. If he came in a helicopter then along with him thousands of police would come, officials would come. We did not allow anyone to enter our villages.

'But, brother, I cannot walk. Then how do I reach your village?' he asked.

'Do not worry. We will manage all that. But we will not allow a helicopter to enter our village. First, you have to accept that condition. Second, you will have to listen to our side of the story in full. And record it in full. You listen to the government. So you must listen to the stand of Andolan too. If you accept all these conditions, we will allow you to enter our village.' Morse agreed. We took the responsibility of taking him on a *khaat* (a bed made of rope) from Manibeli, where the satyagraha was taking place, to other villages. We would put Morse on the khaat and four people would carry him.

We were not sure we could believe him, or that he would listen to us adivasis. But in the end, we managed to put forward our viewpoint in full. The government put forward its position. Poor thing! He visited one village after another. He ate adivasi food. We were not expecting the report to be favourable to us. But the Morse Committee report completely accepted the Andolan's objections. And this brought great pressure to bear on the government. The World Bank had to withdraw from the Sardar Sarovar Project finally. This was a big victory for the Andolan.

People's representatives from all the affected villages of the three states were present. The first thing I told Morse on behalf of everyone was that all our villages were going to be submerged. The Gujarat government was illegally submerging our land, and we were protesting that by sitting in satyagraha. Huge funds had been borrowed from the World Bank. That had made it possible for the dam project to gather strength, and the government was going ahead with its construction and drowning our adivasi brothers. If the World Bank withdrew from the picture, the Gujarat government would be responsible for the completion of Sardar Sarovar. That is why we had decided to work towards the withdrawal of the World Bank from the project, to which it agreed.

A huge victory rally was planned at Kasrawad in Badwani District. People from all the villages in three states came together to celebrate the World Bank's withdrawal and to raise their voices against the dam.[131] Many issues cropped up at the rally. Even if the World Bank had withdrawn support, what if the Gujarat government decided to provide its own funds and build the dam? But we were sure that would not happen.

Then, in 1994, there were heavy rains and floods such that no earlier generation had seen. The slight increase in the height of the dam meant that many houses from Bharad up to Pipalchop in Akkalkuwa Tehsil were washed away. None of them received any compensation.

That massive deluge completely washed away all the houses in the lower parts of the villages. People got wood from the nearby forest and constructed their houses once again. All their belongings were gone. They got no help from the government. But the Andolan managed to give them some grains, clothes and utensils. People in Manibeli village had to be given a lot of support from outside.

There was a huge satyagraha at Bhopal against raising the height of the dam without any kind of rehabilitation of the displaced people. We were on hunger strike for twenty-nine days. It was then that Kevalsingh went on hunger strike. Meanwhile, we also registered a case in the Supreme Court. In the end the court stayed the construction of Sardar Sarovar. That hunger strike made it possible! After the court stayed the construction of the dam, the next seven or eight years were peaceful. People were also at peace. Houses did get submerged but depending on the rains, the waters would rise and then subside. It was still possible for the water to flow away. So, while the Gujarat government kept on with its attempts to raise the dam height and the Andolan kept up its opposition, various committees were formed to complete the process of rehabilitation.

In Maharashtra, the Dawood Committee was formed that brought many benefits to the people of the state. The committee pointed out the flaws and shortcomings of the rehabilitation process in Maharashtra. Because of this, the responsibility of the Maharashtra government increased manifold.

Since 1994 some people started accepting land. Forestland had been sanctioned in the four villages of Rozava, Dekati, Amoni and Amalibari.[132] Rehabilitation also began to take place in Somaval village. Some people decided to accept land there. New resettlement sites came up in these five resettlement villages. There was resistance from the local people.[133] There were fights and confrontations, there were murders and there was destruction. Now it is somewhat peaceful. But this was not rehabilitation with people's participation. These resettlement villages were set up by force by the government. There was only lip service to due process. Due process was neither followed nor implemented fully. For example, there are a lot of electricity poles but there is no electricity. There is a school but no teachers. There is a dispensary but no doctors.

Nandini: So, in 1994–95 some people accepted rehabilitation although the work on the dam had been suspended?

Keshavbhau: Yes, in 1994–95 work on the dam was stopped. Some officials were very clever. They used to call people and tell them, 'Look, good land is being distributed now. Hurry up and claim it. Those who come first will get good quality land. If you come later, you will get rocky, bad land or land in the nalas.' In this way the officials would lure people. Only the greedy people came forward. After the establishment of R&R sites in these five villages, they announced that rehabilitation of all villages had been completed.

Nandini: Whom do you mean by greedy people?

Keshavbhau: They were our own people, weren't they? The government gives a person 500 rupees and that person is ready to become an agent, isn't he? And if he is not, then offer him 1,000 rupees and he will be ready in no time, right? That Gill Sahib, when he saw that people would not budge, he started showing them money. That money corrupted people. Jahangir and Dadala Patil of Bhusha crossed over. Rotya of Poula and a few representatives from Akkalkuwa also did the same. We did not. Our demand was that everyone should get land. The Forest Department was offering lakhs of rupees to take up tree plantation work. We told them we did not want their lakhs of rupees. We would not allow plantation on our lands. We told them, 'Remember, if you plant trees over here, there will be murder.'

We even gave it in writing. 'There is so much thick forest all around. Why the hell do you want to plant more trees here?' The objective was simply this, that 15,000 hectares of forest was going to be destroyed and they wanted plantations to replace it. That is why we opposed the plantation. On the one hand there was the Andolan and the satyagraha at Bhopal, and on the other there was the case in the Supreme Court. Because of this there was a stay on the Sardar Sarovar. The construction of the main part of the dam was stopped. The work outside that part continued to take place but construction in the middle, gated portion was stopped completely.[134]

At that time the height of the dam was 80 metres. And we were saying, what is the need for a 455-foot high dam? If you build the dam up to a lower height—which would allow free flow of water through the canals to Gujarat[135] and prevent the displacement of all the other villages—it would be a big thing.[136] We tried to explain to the government that lowering the height of the dam would greatly reduce the responsibility and cost of rehabilitation, but the Gujarat government was adamant and continued to argue that only a high dam would ensure electricity and water supply.

The news that the dam construction was stopped reached our adivasi brothers in the submergence zone. They were a little shocked by the news, because they felt they might not get land. On the other hand, there were attempts to get people off their land. Since R&R sites had been established in five villages, representatives of some of the villages went there and acquired land. For the other people in the submergence zone a rosy picture was being painted that people in the R&R sites were getting a lot of benefits.

In the Narmada Valley, there are streams and nalas on the way from one village to another. Once the waters rose, it entered these streams and flooded them, and it became difficult to travel from one village to another. We would have been happy if the construction of the dam was stopped altogether. But after a stay that lasted many years, construction was being reconsidered. In spite of there being thousands of people yet to be resettled, the government began to show on paper that everyone had been resettled and began to seek permission to increase the height of the Sardar Sarovar dam. In the courts the Andolan continued to put forward its position and the government its own.

Succumbing to the Gujarat government's pressure, the Supreme Court permitted the government to gradually increase the height of the dam, in steps of 5 metres at a time, on the condition that 'rehabilitation would precede construction'.[137]

Hundreds of people who were entitled to land had been left out of the lists, and they had not been officially identified. To hear complaints and to keep the government informed of the progress of R&R, every state issued a government regulation (GR) and established a Grievance Redressal Authority (GRA) under the leadership of the central government.[138]

Since under the GR the Maharashtra state was to hear complaints and officially decide about those who had been excluded, it appointed the Kurdukar Committee[139] to carry out that work. Kurdukar was a retired judge. The Kurdukar Committee did hear complaints under the GRA. In those hearings we put before the judge the many difficulties people were facing. Kurdukar was unaware of the problems faced by adivasis in these remote areas, the lives they led and the basis of their lives. What if he was a judge? We tried to explain these things to him many times. He heard hundreds and hundreds of complaints. But not in a single instance did he officially accommodate even one excluded person.

So, after the 1994 Bhopal satyagraha we set up different committees under the Loknivada (roughly, people's decision)[140] to bring into the open what was the truth and what was the untruth. The government was trying to show that all displaced people had been resettled; but the world got to see that on the Narmada banks, thousands of families were still staying on. While fighting for their rights, people were lathi-charged, arrested and jailed simply because they opposed rehabilitation. For all those years we had been applying for work under the Employment Guarantee Schemes, we were asking for roads, but we never got anything. But here in the name of rehabilitation, roads were built between the villages within a month with the help of bulldozers!

We had been consistently demanding that adivasis staying in one village needed to be resettled as a single village. That had not happened. They just accommodated as many people as possible in the five villages, whichever village they may have belonged to. For those who remained, they had no land; that land was only on paper. And even that land had been given ex parte.[141] Some were given land in Gujarat. One piece of land had been given ex parte to four or five people. But through the Loknivada as well as the Task Force Committee report[142] it was brought into the open that there were thousands of people who were not given land. The Gopalpur village R&R site was set up without the participation of the people. A few people were allowed to resettle, and without a proper purchase of the land, people were shown any piece of land and were fooled. So, the Andolan took up the cases of many of these people, brought it to the notice of the government and helped the adivasis get their land.

The government felt that this one village might not accommodate all the remaining oustees, so one more site was opened in Tarawat without the knowledge of the villagers. The collector said, 'This is good land here. Take it. Tell us in the next five minutes whether you are taking it or not, otherwise you will not get any land.'

We had been trying to tell the collector time and time again, 'Sahib, it is a matter of life and death for us. We cannot give you an answer within five minutes. We need five days.' At this, Collector Sahib would get very angry and ask for the idiots to be sent away. Later this same collector who used vile language was asked to explain his behaviour to the CM.

In the case of the site in Vadijavada village, we publicly declared our position. 'This cannot be an R&R site. There are too many problems with it. The land at this site is infertile. So please cancel this site.' In the end, many adivasis were brought there with false promises and were given these lands. Today, the whole world can see that this site gets regularly submerged during the rains. They cannot grow any crop. The land is saline. And today, those very same people are clamouring about the injustice done to them.

Nandini: Why did people accept rehabilitation? The construction of the dam had been stopped. Government officials were not allowed to enter the villages. Then how did they make contact and make the people leave and accept rehabilitation?

Keshavbhau: From 1991 to 1993, for three years, we did not allow the officials to enter the villages. 'Our Village, Our Rule', that was the condition. At the time Rehmal Vasave was murdered, the police were straining all their muscles to destroy the joint strength of the adivasis. The police used to force their way into the villages. After 1993, villages began to be submerged. And again, in 1994. In 1994, in each and every village from Manibeli onward, a police station or camp was established. Manibeli, Domkhedi, Nimgavhan, Surung—all the villages had police camps. We tried to oppose those camps at the time they were being established. We held demonstrations before the police and at their camps. We had sit-ins, campaigns, and marches to warn them. But in 1994, when the submergence was very high, and many houses were washed away, people were willing to leave. All our village wanted was that all of us should be resettled as a single village. But our village was split into four.

There were other reasons too. The main reason was that the village heads became greedy and decided to leave. When that happened some people felt, 'Oh, my God! Once he leaves who knows what will happen to us?' and they too decided to leave. Another reason was that people felt, 'Oh dear! If they are going to drown us one way or the other, maybe it is better to leave.' Some people thought, 'Our houses have been washed away right in front of our eyes. If this is going to continue, who knows if the government will compensate us later or not? At least the government is offering us something right now. Why refuse it?'

There was fear and uncertainty on the one hand, and greed on the other. Some people on the banks of the Narmada had land which was not very productive. Some had land inside streams and ditches. Because many were forest villages, people did not have land in their own names; the land was in the name of their ancestors. Many of these people therefore willingly accepted rehabilitation. After the submergence, acceptance increased. A large number of people left after 1994.

Nandini: I would like to ask you some questions about yourself. From 1990 to 1994 the Andolan was at its peak. What were your special responsibilities in this period?

Keshavbhau: What I say, Tai, is that right from the beginning when I became the people's representative, I was considered the main person, whether it was in Akrani Tehsil or Alirajpur or Nimad. People thought of me as second only to Medhatai. People had trust in me. They felt I was a person who would take them down the right path. I was not a person who would ditch them and take advantage of them. 'He abides by the truth. We will accept whatever Keshavbhai tells us.' Since I had people's respect and the leadership role, wherever Medhatai went, whether to meet a CM, the president, the PM or a secretary—now things have changed (but earlier)—Medhatai never went to a meeting by herself. She always took me along. When we met the minister, she would not allow me to sit on the back benches. I was seated right in the front. After the introductions were over, the discussion always started with me. 'Speak, Keshavbhau, start the discussion. What do you have to say?'

Today things are different, and so I am sharing that Medhatai never started a discussion, whether it was with a collector or any other important person, without calling on me. So how did she go alone today? This is the issue. Even in Ferkuva I was in the forefront of the discussion. In Ferkuva, when that secretary had come after thirty-six days of struggle, I was there. Medhatai was there. The arguments were intense and hot. Everyone was speaking in English. I kept objecting from time to time saying, 'No, no. Speak in Hindi too. We must also understand.' The discussion with the secretary was going nowhere so we sent him packing. Secondly, there was Haribhai (Harivallabh Parikh) who used to come and explain the government's position to us. Chunibhai[143] also used to come. I would say, 'Chunibhai, you are showing us the development in your state, but you don't seem to be aware of what is happening in our area. So, until all the affected people's issues are addressed, no one touches the dam.'

Nandini: So you would always begin the discussion with the authorities. Do you remember all the prime ministers and others in front of whom you put forward your viewpoint?

Keshavbhau: First was the meeting with V. P. Singh in Delhi. At that time, Medhatai, Noorji and I were there. Then we presented our case in front of Chief Minister Sharad Pawar many times. Then there was Vilasrao Deshmukh, and later on we presented our case in front of R. R. Patil and Patangrao Kadam. With our M.P. Swarup Singh Naik, we got into a big fight—Dadala Karbhari, Pinjaribai of Mal village and me. And I was the one to put our case to the ministers of different departments as well as commissioners.

In Delhi we put it to Manubhai Kothadia, and Kamalnathji. And to our Chief Minister, Digvijay Singh, in Bhopal. We used to sit together like brothers, didn't we! He used to say to me, 'Oh! Come here brother; let the representatives of Maharashtra sit near me. Why are you sitting so far away?' This way he used to make me sit right next to him. In his first five-year term he talked so nicely, but in his next five-year term he showed us his real colours. What a person he turned out to be, this Digvijay Singh!

At the various press conferences that were held we presented our case so many times. At public meetings, I was always the first speaker. This is what the history of the Andolan and the history of our people will say.

We also sought people's support from all those places where there were active organisations. Right from the beginning, Bhoomi Sena, the organisation from Thane, supported us. That is why I went to Thane. Whenever we organised a protest against the dam or a protest march in Mumbai or a massive struggle in the Narmada Valley, we needed full cooperation from everyone. Wherever in India there were organisations, we used to send them food grain as invitation, the way we send a letter. 'We are inviting you to come and support us.' We used to send wise and old people like Ranya Dahya, Pankya Karbhari, Batu Patil, to make these invitations, even to people in faraway places. Jahangir and Batu Patil visited Bastar district. And Dadala Karbhari visited Kerala.

I have been to Pune side a number of times. In Pune I made many presentations at Baba Adhav's[144] shibirs. I used to request them to be with us in our struggle. I visited Mumbai, Pune, Thane and organisations like Bhoomi Sena more than anywhere else. Then Adivasi Mukti Sanghatana and I got the organisation from Sendhwa to join. And, then there was this place where there had been a firing? Chhattisgarh Mukti Morcha? Yes, Shankar Guha Niyogi. He came over a number of times, and I had been to his place too. There was a big shibir held at Chitrakoot. There were participants from many different places in the region. There we presented all our issues. We also requested them to come to us whenever we invited them. Their support and cooperation were sorely needed.[145]

Most of the meetings were held in Nimgavhan, whether they were conducted by Medha Didi or by other activists. Another thing is that there was a lot of corruption in Akrani. People used to approach us also for their personal matters. Take for example, that my land has been taken away by force. Or say we are so many brothers and the land should have been shared equally between us, but one of them has taken by force much more than his share. Resolving these types of issues was one of the biggest tasks we carried out. I managed to successfully resolve almost a hundred and fifty such matters relating to either the police station, the tehsil revenue office or the forest ranger. Even after I came to Vadchhil, people find that if they go to the village official there is very little response, but if they come here, they get a full response and a full answer.

Other relatives also came to us with various kinds of problems. Some involved fights over witches or over land. But I decided beforehand in which disputes I would intervene and in which I would not. I used to tell them upfront. I would tell the people who came to me not to fight, to show some understanding and accommodation, to try and resolve the issue. And that when we fight, that itself causes loss. I would explain it to them, counsel them and send them back. Sometimes I would have to write out an application for them.

In some cases, it became imperative for me to look into it in person. This is the way we have been working. And that is why all the people have faith and trust in us.

Then there was the satyagraha at Domkhedi. People stood fast in their village and in the rising waters, saying 'We shall drown, but we shall not leave.'[146] During the Domkhedi satyagraha when the floods came, there were two barges full of police. We did not allow them to come anywhere near us. For forty-eight hours people were standing in the rising waters. And then water rose up to our chins. We did not know what to do. We were clear that we would not allow Didi[147] to drown.[148] Even though the shameless government would not listen, it was our duty not to let her die. We took that decision right there, without the knowledge of anyone and took care to keep it a secret.

There was a big police camp. The entire police force had collected on the river banks! There were so many people who had joined the satyagraha in Domkhedi, and now the question was, how to take them all out? They were scared. The collector was scared. At the last moment, I took a decision without telling anyone. I made Ulya Patil my go-between. My wife was standing in the lowest portion of the water. All the other people were in the higher portions. I had so many worries, you can't imagine! All the people were inside the house holding on to each other's hands. Had the water risen a little, just one wave, they would all drown! Not one of them could have escaped. That was the fix we were in. So, I told Ulya Patil, whose farm was near where the police were camping, 'Those police who have just gone away, they will come running to you to make inquiries. Answer them only after they ask you anything, and only say what I have told you. Go right away.' So, I sent him to his field and told him to pretend that he was there to shoo away the birds. 'Keep making that noise to scare away the birds.'

As soon as police heard him shout, they ran to him and asked him, 'Patil, how much has the water risen?'

'It must have reached their mouths by now. I was there till now.'

'Oh no, but what can be done?' they asked him.

Patil told them, 'If Medhabai dies, not one of you will be left alive. They will drown you all.'

After that, there was a spate of wireless messages between Dhule, Dhadgaon and Mumbai. Police asked for additional police force, and two barges full of police immediately joined the one barge that was already in Domkhedi. Then we vanished from there. I took shelter in the bushes. The main people like us were not at the forefront of the fight, and that is why the others were not feeling very confident. But the collective strength of the women was remarkable. The police entered the homes and took the women out by force. They were arrested, dumped into the barge and taken to Dhadgaon. We were all jailed for fifteen days in Dhule. And to the world outside we had to make it a big issue. In those fifteen days we successfully carried out our slogan, 'We Will Drown, But We Will Not Leave'.

In 1994 or 1995 we managed to build a shelter for the satyagraha in Domkhedi. We started the satyagraha after a day's fast. So many people had collected there. So many activists from foreign countries had come—from America, England, Germany, France, Sweden, Norway, Australia and Japan. People from different parts of India were arriving in batches. In the Domkhedi satyagraha we raised some issues relating to Akrani tehsil as well. In Akrani, in the whole of Dhadgaon Tehsil, seventy-three villages had been declared forest villages. It was important that they be classified as revenue villages, so we added on that issue.[149] It also helped increase our strength.

At the same time, we were also arguing that as the dam height was being increased, the low-lying farms[150] were getting submerged. The lands on the upper side were not in the people's own names.[151] From 1995 to 1998 the satyagraha continued. In 1999 the Supreme Court gave its verdict. I stayed in Delhi for fifteen days during that time. The things that went on in the Supreme Court were a joke. I felt terribly ashamed.

I went out of the hearing from time to time and talked with the officials. All these officials were well known to us. I took the rehabilitation officers of the Narmada Development

Authority aside and asked them, 'What is this, Sahib? What will you achieve by such blatant lies? Why are you destroying our lives? Show whatever is the truth! Why not say truthfully that we should compel these people to accept rehabilitation by force. Why do you lie and say that not a single one has been left out, and that everyone has been rehabilitated?' Such are the falsehoods perpetrated in the Supreme Court!

We didn't get a chance to speak in the Supreme Court. Our advocates Shanti Bhushan and Prashant Bhushan[152] argued very strongly on our behalf. They faced a lot of opposition. I was in Delhi for two weeks. There were so many lies being bandied about. After hearing everything, the final verdict was as follows: decide who all come under the next 5-metre submergence zone, rehabilitate them first, and then raise the height by 5 metres.

But they never followed that verdict. (*Laughs.*) They submerged us first. (*Laughs.*) So, even the directive of the Supreme Court was not observed by the Gujarat government. And though the verdict went against us, and though it was in their favour, they did not follow it. The Court had decided that the rehabilitation of the people falling within those 5 metres had to be completed, and only then could the dam height be increased by 5 metres. What the government did was exactly the opposite. They destroyed every one of us. Now again dam construction has been suspended with the dam height at 122 metres.[153] That too because there was such an outcry against it. Maybe the construction has been stopped because they are thinking of putting a gate at that height and perhaps, they may not have enough funds for it.

Medhatai says, the remaining people should continue to stay on the banks of the Narmada. But there is no life there. There will be no development. It is impossible to live there. Our demand is that all the people remaining behind must also be rehabilitated. Because in a few days, in those parts, the situation will be so bad that boatloads of thieves will come, plunder and go away. It is not that bad yet, but it is sure to happen. One or two isolated families cannot survive there. Only if there is a sizable number of families can they survive.

The forest is gone, isn't it? What is there if anyone is to stay on? They would take away even the huts. Bawabhai[154] is already expressing these fears.

A few adivasi villages from Alirajpur Tehsil in M.P. are demanding land for rehabilitation. I feel that demand should have been taken up. We are on this side of the river and they are on the other. We came away here for rehabilitation, but today they have to survive there somehow. They are in a very bad situation. So, we feel there needs to be one common law for all.[155] Madhya Pradesh should have the same law that Maharashtra has. And so should Gujarat.

In the beginning the Maharashtra government was not willing to listen and was insisting that an adult son would get only 1 hectare of land. But after the Supreme Court order we got our demand of 2 hectares. In the same way we should register a fresh case in the Supreme Court on behalf of these people that they too should get land. If we had put in all our efforts that wherever it may be, all the people affected by the project should get land, then perhaps their issues would have been resolved.

Nandini: Till which year did the Domkhedi satyagraha go on?

Keshavbhau: It went on up to 2002, didn't it? From 1990 to 1994 it was in Manibeli, but in 1994, 1995 and 1996 it took place in Domkhedi. In 2002, Asimkumar Gupta was the collector. That year there was a very big flood. At that time the submergence was very large. The collector had also come. He gave us his usual warning to move out, but we disregarded it. After he left, the water level started rising fast. I got the satyagrahis shifted from Bula Dahya's house to Jugi's house. After shifting to Jugi's house we then decided to move them to Baljya Dahya's house and hold the satyagraha there. But I was sure that this year there would be great danger. The officers came, the boat came, the police barge was there, but there was something missing. It was all very casual.[156]

Medha Didi had told me that I too should stand in the water. But I could not stand in it for long. I had decided that I would allow others to stand in for me and I would move aside. I had warned Ulya Patil that this time there was great danger because within five minutes I could make out that the water was rising very fast. This water would submerge everything. All the houses would be submerged and this hillock[157] too would go under water. So, what was to be done? I decided to leave as fast as I could. I would go home. But after that, once the water reached up till here (*points to his chin*) then someone would have to pull Didi out. That was our stand. Otherwise, that year Didi would not have come out, I am telling you! That is the truth. Ulya Patil did exactly what he was told. He pulled Didi out. (*Laughs.*) What else could we do? We had no other option![158]

(*At this point Kevalsingh adds*) 'After the verdict of the Supreme Court the responsibility of the state government was greatly reduced, wasn't it?'[159]

Keshavbhau: Yes, indeed it was greatly reduced! That is why Ulya Patil did exactly what I had told him to do. He implemented my suggestions completely. Didi was pulled out by so many people....She gave Patil such a thrashing, a regular thrashing, I tell you. She realised that he must have followed Keshavbhau's instructions. So there! (*Laughs.*) But to answer,[160] I had to go to Nandurbar. And because I went to Nandurbar, I also had to suffer a loss. That same day they had come to the village to carry out a *panchnama* to evaluate the damage to the land.[161] The village people did not evaluate the damage on my land. So I got nothing. A fat zero!

Nandini: In 1994–95 many people left the Andolan. A lot of effort had to go into seeing that they did not leave. Can you please tell us about it?

Keshavbhau: We had a tremendous responsibility. We used to monitor each and every person. No one should split away, and the village must remain united. So many different kinds of disputes arise in the village. A boy falls ill and some woman is immediately identified as a *dakin* (witch). That man is farming on my land; he hasn't left me anything. We tried to resolve these disputes with love, affection and understanding. In the village if some officers had come and convinced someone, it used to be a big effort to wean him away. Sometimes there were disputes over children and over women. In such cases we needed a lot of patience and understanding.

The police patil of our village had a strong influence. It was his responsibility to ensure that nobody in the village splits and leaves the Andolan. But Dadala Patil and Ulya Patil themselves had a big fight over the post of police patil. Ulya Patil insisted he should get the post. Eventually he did become the police patil. The old police patil held me responsible. He said if I had not sided with Ulya Patil, the latter would have never become police patil. Ulya Patil and the old patil Jahagya are on good terms with each other now, but the old patil has not been talking to me for the last fifteen to twenty years—even today he does not talk to me!

So, he said, 'Because you sided with Ulya Patil, I was forced to leave the village.' That is why he accepted the rehabilitation offer in 1994–95. He now stays in Rozava. Many families left with him, about ten or fifteen.

Later, the gram panchayat elections took place. We managed to get five seats and lost three. So Ugranya Gumana Vasave was made deputy sarpanch. We wished to see him become sarpanch. But who knows what they[162] decided? Straightaway Shivaji Jodha Pawra became sarpanch. Ugranya remained deputy sarpanch. They took that decision. Later he blamed us for losing the position of sarpanch and accepted rehabilitation at Amali.

I had done nothing wrong in that case. But Ugranya made up a mistake he could point to. He had to make a show in front of the people saying that on my own I would never have accepted rehabilitation, but because these people didn't support me, I am accepting rehabilitation. This is the way people left the Andolan to take resettlement.

The other thing was to keep a watch on the people from other villages, to see in what way they behaved. Not everyone could manage to meet the officials. Because of that a lot of our unity survived. Later on, after people had become clever and got an opportunity to speak, it would have been difficult to maintain unity. But in those times, unity was maintained by words. At times, it became necessary to visit a person and talk to him two or three times in a day.

For this it became imperative for us to complete a tour of the villages every month. When we felt that some people were drifting away, we had to contact them several times. For example, the entire Sikka village was about to leave, and we tried very hard to stop Thabdya Karbhari and the others from leaving. But in the end, they all accepted rehabilitation and left. We also tried very hard to stop the Bharad people from leaving. They did stay on. Sikka split away a little earlier. The Sikka people had some contacts in Gujarat as well as in Maharashtra. And so, people accepted rehabilitation in both the states. A few left for Gujarat and a few for Maharashtra.

We began to notice another thing. It is true that people listened to us. Later on, outsiders kept on trying to wean them away. They would tell people, 'Tomorrow these same people will become sarpanch. They will keep you down by force.' This was what our people were being taught. That is why they were splitting away. On the other hand, they were also afraid that if they left, who would help them with their problems? They feared that too. That is why people were not accepting rehabilitation very easily.

But it is important that all the people stayed on right up to 1994. Which means that people started accepting rehabilitation only after ten years had passed. In the beginning, we were told there is no land in Maharashtra; go settle in Gadchiroli, go to Solapur, go to Thane; or someone would say go to Navapur. At that time, the government was not even ready to show us the lands. Even then, people fought, they struggled, took great efforts and maintained their unity for so many years; even when they could not fight the actual submergence of their lands, they stayed on. But after the forestland was released for rehabilitation, things changed. The officials said, 'Why don't you take that forestland? You were the ones who demanded those lands. You asked for it. Why then are you opposing it now?' It was after they were faced with this argument that people started accepting rehabilitation.

'If you delay things now, all the good land will be taken. If you leave right now, you will get good land.' That was the point. On this issue, people split away on their own and accepted rehabilitation. The people were not wrong in this, at least that is what I feel. Because on the one hand, the village is getting submerged, and on the other hand, land is actually being offered. Then to keep on saying, no, I will not take it, I will see about it later—gets a man to think, doesn't it? People were scared that once all the land the government was offering was distributed, and if the government did not give any more land, they would be left without land.

We ourselves had asked for forestland and insisted on it, and now that it was being offered to us, why should we not accept it? Later on, once the dam was constructed and the backwaters rose, there would be no land to be had in the higher reaches. It would also be very difficult to survive on the forest that would remain. So, if they had to leave anyway, then either everyone should leave together right then, or else each one would leave on their own. That is how many people left. We tried hard to convince them, but they were not ready to be convinced. They had not thought ahead about the difficulties they would face later on, about who would help them out in that situation.

On the one hand, the backwaters of the dam began to submerge the village and on the other, people started to accept rehabilitation. That process began with the Somaval village. The second was Amoni resettlement site where the leaders of Bhusha accepted rehabilitation. After that other villages rapidly followed suit and accepted rehabilitation. They did not do the maths. How many people can be settled in 4,200 hectares? We can do the maths easily. If every family was to be given 2 hectares, then a little more than 2,000 families would get land. Where would the remaining families go?

I could stand up and ask the CM, 'Sahib, you say you have sanctioned 4,200 hectares of forestland. Is it to build homes or play games?' I could ask such questions, but the others could not.

About 60–70 hectares and up to 100 hectares is needed for the village settlement itself. The land surrounding that village settlement then needs to be allocated for farming. So, for five villages let us say, 500 hectares of land is given for the village settlement. Subtract 500 out of the 4,200 total and 3,700 hectares land remains. Out of that only 2,700 hectares can be distributed as 1,000 hectares is barren land, fallow land, land under streams, stony land, etc. What we then found is that by giving someone 1 hectare and someone 2 hectares, they had rehabilitated 2,000 families in those 4,200 hectares. The problem of all those who were left out then became a big issue.

Those 2,000 families were named, and in the report to the central government it was declared that everyone had been rehabilitated. So, in the award process, in the different committees, in the CM's committee, we raised the issue that these 2,000 families were not the only ones involved. In the beginning they started out saying there were 1,300 families. After a few years the government itself revised that figure to 3,000 families. We now know that there are many more than 3,000 families, for sure. There were many people who had been left out. And after those declared so by Kurdukar, the total number of families who had to be given land would come to between 10,000 to 15,000 families.

By that time the government began to accept this number somewhat. Which meant that in discussions with us they would say, 'Yes, there are people who have been left out. We have to give them land too.' In front of us, the collector would always say, 'Eleven hundred families have not yet been rehabilitated. We are in search of land for these 1,100 families.' But the reports given to the central government always said that they had completed the rehabilitation of all the displaced people and that no one was left out!

Nandini: When did your village get submerged? What happened then?

Keshavbhau: When the dam wall reached a height of 80 metres there was a big flood and the low-lying land in our village began to be submerged. Then the dam height was raised to 85 metres, and then 90 metres, and the water began to find its way into our village. More and more land came under submergence. So we submitted an application to the tehsildar claiming compensation for the submerged land and managed to get the compensation for that. When the dam wall rose to more than 95 metres, even more land was submerged. Much of the farmland was lost in that submergence. That year there was also a big flood.

Evidence of the loss was recorded in a panchnama. But the government was trying to avoid giving us due compensation. So, just before the dam height reached 95 metres, we organised a very big satyagraha in Mumbai. Close to 2,000 people converged on Mumbai and forced the government to sanction due compensation. The compensation was widely distributed.

After this, the next year the dam wall reached 100 metres. Most of the lands were submerged. So, we forced the government to carry out a fresh survey. From A to Z, we submitted the full information to them. But the government tried to avoid paying compensation saying that they would not pay for the fresh damage. So, 2,000 people from Akrani Tehsil went to Nasik and we organised a sit-in in front of the commissioner's office. The sit-in continued for fifteen to twenty days, and finally we managed to get the compensation.

So, in this way, we managed to get compensation for the submerged land for three consecutive years. That year the total amount of compensation decided for Akkalkuwa Tehsil based on the panchnamas was sixty lakh rupees. That compensation has not been paid till today. But the compensation for Akrani Tehsil was paid.

At a wall height of 110 metres, nothing in the village remained. People in our village almost went mad. The village was submerged, the land was under water, everything was washed away. Then there was the rehabilitation issue. We visited the sites, but no land was available. The Vadchhil site we had already selected, but it was not being made available to us. All that land had been distributed ex parte.

What could we do?[163] It would have been better if we had taken land in the first 4,200 hectares. That land had already been distributed. Where could we find land now? We travelled all over looking for land for the village settlement. In the end, in 2004, the Alivihir satyagraha took place. We occupied forestland, saying if the government did not give us land, we would occupy forestland. Then they set up a conflict[164] with the local people over the forestland.[165] Thousands of police were stationed there, and they managed to get a stay order. And then they said no land would be sanctioned. This entire conspiracy came to a head there.

At this time, I managed to get Ulya Patil and Irmya Karbhari to Alivihir at my own cost. I felt if I left them by themselves, they would just wander about, and might even hang themselves, so depressed were the people at that time. So, I just caught hold of them and got them there. Because it is very difficult to bear it all alone, by oneself, isn't it? So, all of us who had been left out, we had to stay together and accept land in the same place.

On that day (the day of the satyagraha at Alivihir), the heavy rains truly thrashed us. There was a small hut in which we sat and somehow saw the night through. Next day, as it dawned, everyone wanted to go back home. That day I must have made twenty trips meeting people (at the place of the satyagraha) and persuading them not to leave and to stay on. After a while the rain stopped. There was some relief. Then I met Medhatai. 'What needs to be done now, Tai?'

'I got a phone call from the commissioner. He is visiting the day after tomorrow. Don't go anywhere. When he comes you better be there to meet him. The secretary will be accompanied by the commissioner, the collector and officers from all the departments. That is why you must not leave. We have to put our position collectively in front of these people,' said Medhatai. Then she left.

The commissioner did not come, but the secretary did. Much of my attention was given to the meeting, but I was paying even more attention to these two (Ulya Patil and Irmya Karbhari). They wanted to run away from there.

I asked them to stop and stay overnight and convinced them that it would give us an opportunity to listen to what the commissioner, collector or the secretary had to say. There were about 2,000 people present and at least 1,000 policemen. Then Medhatai came back to Alivihir where the satyagraha was going on. She introduced me and the others. She said Keshavbhau will begin, and so I spoke addressing the secretary.

'Sahib, my name is Keshav Vasave. I have been the main activist of the Andolan right from when it began. I am also a member of its planning group, the secretariat committee, the government's planning committee and the Task Force. I am a member of the district-level committee under the collector's presidentship. While working in all these committees, I have been presenting our demands to the government for a long time now. I have raised the issue several times before Gupta Sahib that we should get the land as soon as possible. They keep harping on this…ex parte. Our old village has been submerged three times before the wall of the dam reached 100 metres. Now at a dam height of 110 metres, there is no land left to be submerged. If we stay on there, on the banks of the Narmada, we will die. We cannot survive. We will die anyway. Then what is the big deal if we die on the plains in sight of the whole world? I am telling you, what is the future of all those on the Narmada banks. And if the police say, "Why are you harming our Sahib?" and if they shoot us, that is fine with me. I will not resist or oppose it. So far, they have maddened us with their chant of "ex parte, ex parte", and that there is no land. When they tell us it is *ex parte,* most likely they have distributed it to someone else. The lands which we ourselves have selected and that have been approved are just lying vacant for the last twelve–thirteen months. I am tired of asking for that land. So, today, all I have to say is this: I will not leave unless I tie Vats Sahib to this tree with this rope. The rope will not be untied till we get our land. The day we get our land, we will release him. Vats Sahib, please tell us what you have to say to this.'

Everybody was surprised to hear me say this. Vats Sahib started scolding the Collector Sahib. Then it was the Commissioner Sahib's turn. He told them, 'These people will not let us leave. So, we must distribute the land today itself.'

Finally, they pleaded with Medhatai, 'It is not possible to go to the settlement site today. Instead, we will begin land distribution from tomorrow.' Only after they accepted this were they allowed to go. It never came to tying them up to a tree, but it was only when we used such words that we got sanction for the Vadchhil settlement site. The land was then distributed in the presence of Vats Sahib himself.

Within five days, we took over the settlement site. Some people shifted to it the same year (2004), and most had shifted by the year 2005. Our house, which was in my wife's name, was shifted from the banks of the Narmada to the site on 13 July 2004. We reached there at midnight. After it had been shifted, on 14 June,[166] twenty vehicles from the Ministry with flashing red lights and all came there, along with a large staff. They had come expressly to welcome me. 'The Narmada Andolan has ended. There are no more problems. Everyone has accepted rehabilitation. It is a moment of celebration and joy. We felicitate you for this.' That is what they said.

That day Medhatai had also followed them to the site. She said, 'What felicitation? Even while accepting this Vadchhil rehabilitation there are so many unresolved issues.' If we had to say something in the same vein to Medhatai today, we would say that just because we accepted rehabilitation it does not mean that we have left the Andolan. This Andolan needs to continue over here, over many generations too. Because not all issues have been resolved. Issues will always remain. When we went to see the land, we had told them that the farmlands are far away from the houses in the settlement area. We were told that an approach road would be built from the settlement to the farmland. That road is yet to be built. That road can be completed only after lakhs of rupees are spent on it.

Another thing is that we selected lands that are served by canals. So, we cannot say the land is bad. But some get water and some do not.[167] That affects the crop. For this to be sorted out, due process must be followed. And that can happen only if we keep continuous contact with each other.

In this settlement site there are many of our adult children who have not been declared as project-affected persons (PAPs).[168] This issue was closed by Kurdukar, but we had filed suits for the court to reconsider the issue. The matter is still pending. We need to leverage the pressure of the Andolan and demand answers to our questions. When we go individually and try to ask for answers, some of the Andolan activists ask us, 'Have you broken away from the Andolan?' That is why we do not go to them.

To make the village a living place we demanded that 8,000 trees be planted in two years. We planted a large number of trees. To maintain live sources of water in the area, we got the Agriculture Department as well as the zilla parishad to build bunds at various places. The bunds stored water which infiltrated into the soil and improved the groundwater levels.

Then there was the issue of drinking water. After a lot of protests and agitation we got a 600–700-foot-deep borewell dug for drinking water. That borewell is working right up to this day. But in this area the motor frequently burns out and then it takes up to fifteen days to get the motor repaired. Until then we have to wander around here and there looking for water. So, we have demanded that the five hand pumps in the settlement be repaired. Till this day they have not been repaired. We keep raising our voice and protest from time to time.

We have named our new village site Shobhanagar.[169] We are demanding that it be officially recognised, and that this new village should not be made part of the older village within which it was situated. We should have a separate, new gram panchayat for this village. We should have a separate dispensary with a separate staff. Another thing is that at the time of planning the settlement site, some things escaped the concerned officer. Some of the drainage pipes on the culverts are placed too high, and the water does not easily drain away. The roads are higher than the surroundings, so the water does not flow away. Instead, it comes back and enters the houses and everything becomes muddy and marshy. In the planning group, the government had agreed to and sanctioned the construction of raised foundations for the houses. But till now this has not been done. Until all the work in the village is completed, we will have to pursue these things.

We lived happily on our small farms in our old village, so here also we can live happily if we work hard. But life here has become very expensive. There in the forest, at times, we ate vegetables without oil. We could gather vegetables from the forest and eat them. The fish eaters could eat fish and carry on most of the days. Over here if we have to cook a single vegetable it costs us fifty rupees. This is what life here has come to.

In the past we did not need money. There was no going and coming and giving and taking. We simply got up and went to the forest and gathered vegetables. If we went to the Narmada, the fish eaters caught their fish. We wanted for nothing. We grew food grains on our own farms. We did not have to give or take. Once a year we needed money to buy salt and clothes. The implements, axes and sickles we got made from Kavant. We ate from earthen pots. We cooked in earthen pots. These pots were homemade. That was what the old women of the community did. They made the earthen pots. We made our *bhakari*, rolled the flat bread dough in earthen pots and roasted it on earthen pans. It used to be so very tasty. Today the bread roasted on these iron pans does not taste as good. But is there an alternative? That kind of roasting needs more wood. There the forest had plenty of wood. We never fell short.

We run these *Jeevan Shalas*,[170] but how long will we keep running them this way? We have to see that they get government approval. The Andolan needs to pay much more attention to this. The ones who have been rehabilitated on dry land go on digging wells, but it doesn't look like the wells will have water and their problems will end. There is a need to give more attention to finding a permanent and long-lasting solution for them. It is the responsibility of all of us to help those who have been left out and help them get land by filing new applications and putting in new efforts.

Since the day we accepted rehabilitation, the Narmada Andolan activists have not come to our village even though we have invited them many times. That is the one thing that makes us sad.

Nandini: Don't they come here anymore?

Keshavbhau: No, they really don't! No meeting has been held. Even Medhatai has not come for the last one or two years. She did come once, stayed the night and left in the morning. She did not even ask us about our issues.

The others may have come two or three times. But they should be here for all the programmes. Once they were there for a sit-in agitation, and there was a big uproar. Oh my, my! What an uproar there was! It was about rooting out corruption. The second time, it was for a meeting on 15 August, Independence Day. Only for these two programmes did they come. Then last year they came for Holi, but they missed the festivities. So it was no fun.

We don't expect that Didi herself should come. Didi has activists over here. She has clearly told us, 'Look here, the world is so large; your village cannot be my only objective. I will come, maybe once a year, or once in six months, or may be in four months. I will come when we have a big programme dealing with all-embracing issues. I will speak about them and leave. But to resolve these issues, there is Yogini,[171] there is Chetan.[172] Talk with them. If an issue is not resolved, then get in touch with me. We will get in touch with officials and follow it up.' But no one asks us anything! I keep on saying that we must have a proper meeting once, find out what the issues are, think about them and discuss them. Till now, that has not happened.

Nandini: Does a meeting of all the main activists of the thirty-three villages in Maharashtra from all the sites take place?

Keshavbhau: No, it doesn't take place. Suppose, I go to the collector's office. The next day I get questioned, 'What work did you have there?' They (activists) get scared thinking, 'Why did he go there?'

Another thing, suppose a meeting has been organised in Indore. People are to leave for it the next morning, and I get a call the previous night. 'How many people are coming?' We have not even been intimated of the meeting, and we are asked, 'How many people are coming?' That is the way it is! Then we have to ask, 'When is the meeting?'

'I will have to ask people; I have to call a meeting,' I tell them. How is it possible to just get up and go?

These issues can be resolved only by the Andolan. They cannot be solved by individuals. We say this very clearly. The Andolan must get united again and raise their voice. Since the Andolan's voice grew feeble, the officials also have turned cold. If an issue is not getting resolved, we have to come out in large numbers and raise our voice.

The activists have become weak. In my view, the activists are unhappy because the dam could not be stopped. They expected the dam to be stopped halfway. It did not happen. But people did get rehabilitation, didn't they? We say this is a victory. But the activists in their heart of hearts feel the dam should have stopped halfway. Because of this mindset other things have got ignored.

Nandini: Can the Andolan regain its former strength?

Keshavbhau: Yes it can, by all means. Because so many issues remain unresolved. People can come together in large numbers to ensure that they get the benefits of whichever schemes the government takes up for implementation. The schemes are many, but to benefit from them, you need each and every document. This Shahada Tehsil is truly a big, big dacoit. Everything is costly. Understand this. These sellers make big money on every single pipe they sell. If the Andolan gains momentum once again, I tell you, in Shahada Tehsil all these people will be saying, 'Beware! These are Andolan people!' But today what do they say? 'These people, they have got everything; now they are just lazing about, having fun. They got the land, they got the money, what more do they want?' That is the language people use, I tell you!

The Andolan needs to continue for at least eight to ten years. Though, ideally it should be there permanently. Now just look at this. In this region there is this big canal area.[173] If the canals are lined with concrete, all the people would benefit. It they are unlined, the water seeps away into the soil. If we take up issues like these one by one, the Andolan will continue for a long time. The local people will also join.

Now, we have accepted rehabilitation here on our own. It is my lookout all the time, to get land occupation receipts and the Form 7/12[174] land records showing the ownership of land. When people like me and others raised our voices, we were able to get Form 7/12 records for forty-eight landholdings. Now we are again trying to organise to get the Form 7/12 at the earliest for those who have been left out. If these same issues had been raised by the Andolan activists with, say, the collector or the tehsildar or the Electricity Board or their officers, things would have proceeded more smoothly. Since none of the Andolan activists visit us here, all these questions have remained unresolved.

For example, the borewells sunk by some farmers earlier—their electricity charges have been billed at one lakh rupees for one person, two lakhs for someone else, and three lakhs for another. Who can pay these sorts of amounts? These issues cannot be resolved without Medhatai's presence.

It is true that the farmers who were rehabilitated earlier might have got ready-to-till farms, but they still have a lot of difficulties. Some land is dry land, at some places there is no approach road, some lands are not levelled. Some farms get submerged in the monsoons and whatever is planted dies. There are so many different problems. They have not disappeared.

The government has taken the responsibility of building the foundations for the houses. But after a few days all the material of the road itself will be washed away. It is not within the means of the farmers to repair the roads. The government had said, 'We will build a pakka connecting road.' The road construction should have started by now. I keep raising my voice from time to time. But the answer is, 'Okay, it's all right. It is being sanctioned. It is being sanctioned.'

The farmland that has been allotted should have been within 8 kilometres of the settlement site. But land is given outside of the law—settlement in one place and farmland somewhere else. The gram panchayat would not be able to deal with such a big issue. If the Andolan raised its voice every two months, then these problems could be resolved much more easily.

Another important issue needs to be taken up. In other settlement sites so many people who were eligible but had not been declared as affected people have now been declared to be affected. But in this settlement site Medhatai needs to talk with the Collector and Commissioner, Brahme Sahib to take a decision. In no time they will be declared as affected. In this village many more boys have not been included. Leave aside those too young, we have to select at least those from the report of the Task Force.

Nandini: I would like to ask you about the work done by the Andolan activists and how they are remunerated. At one time, you used to receive an honorarium. Do you still receive it?

Keshavbhau: I would have been receiving it even now, but I had declined because even when we were working day and night, the situation was such that we would receive the honorarium for December in the next December. By then my loans would pile up. I had to go and ask for the money.

Then I would have to listen to a lot of things. 'Okay, give me a daily, monthly account of the work you have done. Where had you gone on the first of the month?'

'I had gone to Dhadgaon.'

'Why did you go there?'

'I stayed at the Andolan office.'

'Okay. What work did you do on the 2nd?'"

'On the 2nd, I reached home.'

'What work did you do at home?'

'It took me the whole day to reach home. Then I stayed at home.'

'Okay. Where were you on the 3rd?'

'On the 3rd I had gone to Surung to conduct a meeting.'

'What was the outcome of the meeting?'

'It was a village meeting, and I had joined it.'

'Where were you on the 4th?'

This was the kind of questioning, so I declined the honorarium. This was in 1994–95.

Nandini: The honorarium you received was only 300 rupees, wasn't it? Your expenses must have been more than that.

Keshavbhau: They must have been five times more than that! (*Laughs.*) Okay, so we used to work because we got an honorarium. But these questions, what you did on the 1st, and on the 2nd? She (an Andolan activist) would fix a meeting, make arrangements and then wouldn't turn up for the meeting. People used to wait the whole day and would abuse her and go home angry and frustrated.

I thought to myself, oh, look, these are all people from the same submergence area, what difference would it make if I do not take an honorarium? From that day onward I decided I would not take the honorarium, and so I declined it. I even received a letter from the *Kritadnyata Nidhi* [literally Gratitude Fund which sponsored the honorarium], but I did not reply to them. The letter asked me: Did I want special support from the Fund? Did I need it in connection with the Andolan? But these people would level charges, so why accept anything at all?

Nandini: I know it is perhaps wrong to ask you this. Still, could you estimate roughly how much you may have spent?

Keshavbhau: It is not possible to work out how much I spent. My own estimate is that I must have spent four to five lakh rupees over all these years. In my house we kept goats; we had oxen of a very good breed. In the end, I sold them and managed to repay my loans. I also had to spend a lot on the parikramavasis who were on their Narmada pilgrimage.

All these expenses I am telling you about—the four or five lakhs—are related to travel. To travel from here to attend a meeting scheduled in Delhi you had to have 2,000 rupees with you. By the time we came back, that money would vanish. Some was spent on bidis and matchboxes, some on tea and snacks, and some went to whosoever was short of money and asked for it. I travelled to Delhi and Mumbai hundreds of times. And also to other places. I took Ulya to Mumbai hundreds of times, but I had to bear all the costs. Then there was the matter of the well that Rama had dug. He told me he would repay me as soon as he got the money (from the government) for digging the well. I took him to Dhule hundreds of times. But nobody is able to pay. There were so many such things, I tell you! (*Laughs.*) I have never disclosed the details of what I had to spend to anyone.

Another thing, I will tell you honestly and clearly. Now suppose I had to go to Badwani to attend a Jan Sahyog Trust meeting. I go from Nimgavhan to Hapeshwar, Hapeshwar to Kavant, Kavant to Chhote Udaipur, Chhote Udaipur to Alirajpur, Alirajpur to Badwani and from Badwani to Kasrawad. That was the route I had taken and charged to cost of travel. But I had to answer so many questions. So why should I ask for travel costs? That is why I decided not to attend the Jan Sahyog Trust meetings. Spend so much on going there, spend again on coming back—and all I had put in was a single night's stay over at Chhote Udaipur. Because I had to stay over, didn't I? Why should anyone spend from his own pocket to travel to a meeting? I almost had to get into a fight over that money, and they finally did pay. But that day I decided not to travel to their meetings anymore. It is now three years since then. If the situation hadn't been like this, I would never have remained absent for a meeting of the Jan Sahyog Trust. Didi said, 'If you are not going to attend meetings, then you'd better resign.' At that very moment I wrote out my resignation letter and handed it to her![175]

Nandini: Till what year were the executive committee's meetings held?

Keshavbhau: They went on for eight to ten years and then they stopped. The committee met from 1985 to 1995 and after that the people did not feel the need for it, did they? People were going their different ways. (*Laughs.*) Some of them split away from the executive committee.

Nandini: All these big programmes that you organised, how did you decide on them? How did you decide on the strategy?

Keshavbhau: We were the ones who took the decision. The main activists would meet separately. Suppose a satyagraha or a fast was to be organised—throughout the day there would be discussions. What shall we do tomorrow? What is needed to bring pressure? Representatives from all three states would be there. That committee used to be called the executive committee.[176] If we did not want large numbers, then Noorji and I would represent Maharashtra. There were two representatives from Nimad, one from Gujarat and another one or two activists; all of us together would take the decisions. Suppose we were to organise a big programme in Delhi. Delhi is for all of us, isn't it? Even when we discussed Maharashtra issues, we would invite someone from Madhya Pradesh as a representative.[177]

Today, there are no decisions, do you get me? Three years have passed. After 2004, there are absolutely no decisions being taken.

Nandiniben, I am telling you honestly and very clearly. I have not said anything so far. In Nimgavhan, as I told you yesterday, there were two sets of families or clans, the Vasavas and the Tadvis. In my family there were three brothers, Nimba, Sika and Supa. There were five shares, all in the name of our eldest brother, and the remaining five were in the names of the sons-in-law. For a number of years, we used to manage our earnings jointly. But later on, the way the land got divided, I got half an acre of land as my share.

That was the situation there. Since our life then was based on the forest, we could keep our lives going. Now I have got 5 acres over here in lieu of that half an acre. There was plenty of forest in Nimgavhan, but then it wasn't our ancestral property, was it? They could have taken away that forestland anytime they wanted, couldn't they? It was not in our name, was it?[178]

Nandini: Wasn't that an old encroachment?[179]

Keshavbhau: No doubt, it was. It was a 1972 encroachment, and it should have been registered in my name. But the government never wanted that.

Nandini: Lawfully, they should have registered it in your name, isn't that so?

Keshavbhau: Certainly, they should have done it. Even today, Didi has left this issue of encroachment incomplete. That is also very wrong. In the seventy-three villages of Akrani, the issue of encroached land had come very near to getting resolved, but then it was completely forgotten, completely ignored! So, whatever was earlier on record remained on record. Take this electricity project that came up in Bilgaon just a few days ago;[180] at that time it was declared in a meeting that within eight days we would get our Form 7/12 records. We haven't got them yet. (*Laughs.*) This is the story of seventy-three villages of Akrani.

This issue has remained unresolved forever. K. C. Padvi has forgotten about it. Medha Patkar also has forgotten about it. We should have continued our fight until we had those 7/12 forms in our hands.

Nandini: What do you consider as the biggest achievement of the Narmada Andolan?

Keshavbhau: The world is so big—it has 142 countries. What is it called...the World Bank? The bank of 142 countries! Our first big victory was at the World Bank.[181] We were many times stronger than even the government. That the World Bank report favoured us, I consider our big victory.

The second thing was the Review Committee report which also favoured us. That too was a big victory for us. The third thing was the Dawood Committee report which presented the situation to the government very truthfully. That is similar to a victory. If we had not fought, we would not have got any land. That we did get land because of our struggle is also a big victory. It is true that not everyone got land. The people of M.P. have been left out. But in Maharashtra we got land. In Gujarat too, some people got land, and they got it because of the Andolan.

We fought a battle with the government for twenty years. That is why we got whatever was rightfully ours. That is why, you can see, I am able to say all this with pride and self-respect. Lokmanya Tilak had said *swarajya* is our birthright. In the same way we too have a right to live our lives in this country. We fought until we won that right and didn't leave the battle halfway. This is a very big victory. If we had not fought that battle, we wouldn't have got this settlement site. I visited many different places like Bargi and Koyna. Everywhere I found that the government paid the people a little money and chased them out of their homes. Nowhere did they get land in lieu of land. But this Andolan, with help from organisations all over the world, put such pressure on the government that in the end they had to give us land.

Nandini: What have you achieved in your personal life, as an individual?

Keshavbhau: In a way I would say I got nothing. I had spent twenty years in religious work and the next twenty years I gave to the Andolan. All I want now is a happy life. What more can I ask? I worked, I laboured and most of what I got, I gave to charity, and whatever I have left now has been given to me by the government which is for my children, for the generations to come. But I have nothing left for myself. (*Laughs.*) Whatever I got I gave away.

The hard work that I have put in no one can put in, and no one will. I say only what is right. Fetching water from one and half kilometres away and serving it to each parikramavasi pilgrim, cutting and carrying home ten or fifteen head-loads of firewood and then have them burned away in a single fire by the pilgrims – no one would do these things.

I used to think, this is our own struggle, our own Andolan, and I would spend whatever was in my pocket. In 2002 there was a Task Force meeting in Mumbai. I had carried 3,000 rupees with me. I wanted to buy a radio-cum-tape recorder. But the meeting kept on being extended day after day. I thought I would spend 2,000 rupees on the radio, and the rest would cover my expenses. But I will tell you the kind of expenses I had to incur. To visit the toilet every time it cost three or four rupees. To take a bath, another three or four rupees. Whenever I had a cup of tea there would be ten or fifteen people along with me, so I ended up paying for everyone. What else could I do? I had to spend all the money in this way. Someone would come to me and say, 'I do not have money for soap, Keshavdada,' so I would give him ten rupees and tell him to go get some soap. Someone would say, 'I have a severe stomach ache, but I do not have money. Where do I go for a shit?' So, I would say, 'Okay, take these ten rupees and go. Go fast. Run!' All our people used stones[182] in the toilet, and they would choke up the toilets. The fellow in charge would be furious and would keep scolding me. (*Laughs.*) So, I paid money to help people go to the toilet. What else could one do in the city of Bombay?

(*Laughs.*) Once it so happened that I had a stomach upset and urgently needed to use the toilet. I had gone to Churchgate Station and stood in the toilet line thinking, today I will be shamed for sure. I thought if I waited in this two-rupees line, I was sure to get my trousers soiled. What to do? I took an instant decision and decided to offer 100 rupees to jump the line and save myself from shame and embarrassment. I told the person looking after the toilet, 'Bhaisahib, take these 100 rupees, but allow me to jump the line.' He took the money and put me into the first booth available. But then he also returned ninety-eight rupees. I couldn't even have gone to the sea shore. I had a severe stomach ache and it felt as if it would come out anytime![183] (*Laughs.*)

Nandini: Keshavbhau, the Andolan went on for so many years. A lot of good things have happened. But there were also some things that hurt you, made you think that this should not have happened...

Keshavbhau: When I was in Dhadgaon I used to get an honorarium from the Kritadnyata Nidhi, and I had also taken up a job. Not a big job. I used to get twenty-five rupees per month, and I used to think that it was a very big job! (*Laughs.*) I did that work for almost twenty years. I had to draw blood from ten or fifteen people and send it to be checked. I distributed chloroquine tablets. After four or five years, I became what was called a Community Health Volunteer, and I used to get fifty rupees more. As a requirement of that post, I had to complete a course. I had to stay in Dhadgaon for eight days, and I was given a big tin of medicines. My work was to distribute those medicines and submit a report every month. So, the original twenty-five rupees and the fifty rupees I later got meant that I used to get seventy-five rupees a month.

After three or four years, I was told to go around the hamlets every month and report whoever had fallen ill to the doctor in Dhadgaon for which I used to get ten rupees. I used to get eighty-five rupees in all. I got a lot of experience. I knew which specific tablet and injection were to be given for which particular illness. I used to give injections too. I could manage to put people on saline as well. I was not a trained doctor and I used to be afraid. If someone suffered an adverse reaction, what would I do? If someone died, I would be jailed for sure.

And then in 1987, the Bamani episode happened. In that episode 103 children died. In Domkhedi an entire family died. The monsoon had started and the rest of the people were busy with their own farms. I could see that no one would spare time, but I said I would report this. So, I put my farming aside and rushed to Dhadgaon. I wrote a report and informed the officers immediately. I managed to get fifteen officers to come immediately to the village. By the time we reached, the few who died did die, of course, but we were able to save all the rest who were ill. Then the district health officer and the collector ordered the officers to find out, 'Who is this man?' I gave a copy of the report to the doctor, a copy to my police station, a copy to the tehsildar and one to the panchayat samiti.

After a few days I was made a multi-purpose worker (MPW). The order was issued right from the top under the signature of the collector and the DSP. But I declined. Today an MPW gets 14,000–15,000 rupees, but if I had agreed to become an MPW, the Andolan would have remained incomplete. That is why I decided not to take up the job. (*Laughs.*)

Nandini: Is there anything else that you wish to share with us in the end?

Keshavbhau: For the last twenty years I have spent my life on the basis of sacrifice by giving away food and following the path of devotion, *bhakti*. I have given very little time to my family. I have forced hardships on my children and have been constantly abused by my wife. I never answered back. 'You went away with them. But I too have an emotional bond with you. You keep wandering all over the place. Who will look after the house? Is your father going to come and do it?' she would shout at me. But right up to this day, I have never told her, 'You used to abuse me.' She was doing it for the right reasons. She had to cope with everything all by herself. But it was because of my guru's advice that I was able to lead a life of sacrifice and devotion. Because of it I became and remained an activist of the Narmada Andolan from 1985. And that's how I could develop activists like Kevalsingh from my own family. More like him should have been developed. Others helped me do this but for a short while. I would lie awake in the night thinking about how to sustain the person. About how to bind him to the movement. How to ensure he did not go astray.

Since 1992 I knew that the main responsibility of continuing the Jeevan Shala schools would have to be mine, and that is why they are still running. The hostel was receiving no food grains from the Andolan. I asked everyone in the village for food grains, but no one was willing to give. Finally, I would wait for my wife to go to the river bank and then secretly steal some grain from home and provide it to the hostel. There were so many such days; it is not possible to describe them all.

Nevertheless, this Andolan exists because of the inspiration it has taken from Medhatai. I bow to my guru and tell you this, that Medha Patkar contacted me because of whatever little my guru had taught me. She contacted me because I spoke a little bit of Marathi and Hindi. And so, I got an opportunity to put forward a few words in front of the world. Otherwise, who would have known someone like me from such a remote area? Today we are being felicitated in the presence of hundreds of people.

Kevalsingh is the youngest in my family, but he has done a lot of work for the Andolan. It is his support that helped the movement to gather such momentum and progress so far. We were able to get activists of the calibre of Noorjibhai and Vesta[184] from Sikka. Luharya and Manglya from here and Rama from Keli have remained activists even today. I must say Manglya is a real hero among them all. Udadya's Ranglya was a man with such a strong voice, but today the poor man is so much under the influence of his in-laws that we can hardly hear his voice.

Activists like you supported us. Doctors like Baranth,[185] the support committee from Dhule and activists like Nagesh Hatkar[186] and the activists from Delhi, all of them supported us fully. That is why we could fight such a big battle, and we had the good fortune to get land.

Earlier we were unaware of the law. But while in the Andolan we came to know about various things in the shibirs; we acquired a full knowledge about the law and the legal structure. That turned out to be very important. We can identify and resolve a dispute in less time than it would take for a lawyer to consult his law books. I even taught Kurdukar a lesson. Because of that Kurdukar announced the number of PAPs as 4,000. If I had not confronted him, he would not have taken steps to resolve such a major issue. I told him, 'You might feel you are a great person because you worked for seventeen years as a judge, but I do not give it any consideration. You might be getting a daily allowance of 25,000 rupees, but I do not give that any consideration either. Because I am an adivasi from the Narmada Valley. And I am trying to explain to you the conditions in which we have lived here for generations, and if you do not listen to what we have to say, you are of no use to us.'

There are seven or eight cases against me.[187] The forest officers used to go to the villages to plant trees. We stopped them, so they have gone and registered a case.[188] Before the Domkhedi satyagrahas there was a *Rasta Roko andolan* (Block the Roads agitation). There is one case related to that time. They made me run almost three quarters of a kilometre to avoid arrest. Had the police caught me then, they would have beaten me up pretty badly, I tell you. Then once we managed to close down the office at Dhadgaon. There is a case related to that. I may receive a warrant anytime. There are two cases registered at Dhule. One is related to the Rehmal lathicharge. The second is a fifteen-day jail sentence for the Domkhedi satyagraha. We had gheraoed a World Bank official in Mumbai. That is one more case. In this way, there are seven or eight cases.

I have not gone to court until now. I am absconding. If I go, they will surely arrest me and will not release me for a long time. There will be so many expenses. Who is going to bear them? Kevalsingh has many cases against him. The police tell me, 'Explain to him, Keshavbhau, and bring Kevalsingh to court. We promise he will not have to spend anything; we will take care of it.' But I know this is not at all possible. They will arrest him and put him in jail, and they will not release him for two to three months. He will not be released till all the persons concerned are present. Even the PSI could not argue further on this point.

'Sahib, if I get Kevalsingh here, would your word be honoured by the judge? And suppose the court puts him behind bars. What will you do then?'

'No, no. We will get him out on bail.'

'Will you? And if bail is denied? What will you do?' After this they used to fall silent.

The following is Keshavbhau's second interview, on 2 February 2012, four years after the previous one in 2007.

Nandini: Keshavbhau, we are meeting after four years. In 2007, there were a number of issues related to rehabilitation. Has the situation improved?

Keshavbhau: In a way, the situation has not changed much since 2007. That is what we are thinking about these days. The young ones who are now educated are staying home without jobs or occupations. The future is bleak. Sending applications is not going to be sufficient. The government might be under the impression that the Andolan is over, but it is not. And then the new generations have to find their own paths. That is why we have to be alert. We are going to conduct a shibir for the youth in the coming eight or ten days. We can see that many of them have the potential to be activists themselves. We will get well-known people and supporters to participate in these shibirs, raise our voices and put these issues before the government. Wherever possible we will resolve the issues at the tehsil level;

otherwise we'll raise our voices further and take the issues to the district level.

The Narmada Bachao Andolan has been active since 1985, and we will surely build a new andolan along those lines. Without such an andolan, issues will not be resolved. So, we will give it a new name and call on the new generation to take up the challenge. All the officials, from the gramsevaks to the collector, are transferred every one or two years. And then they evade the issue. 'We are new here. How can we answer you unless we get full information about these issues?' That is a big problem for us. And by the time the new officials become familiar with the issues and get to know the Andolan, it is time for their transfer.

First, give jobs to those who are educated. If not, give them land. These should be our demands and that is how we have to intensify the Andolan. Only then can we survive. If a person has 5 acres of land and has four or five children, how will they survive? We will have to ask the officials, you tell us what we should do—let our children survive or let them die? We will do whatever it takes. If we have to go to Indore or Mumbai, we will go just like in the old days; we may have to organise dharnas, agitations and protest marches. The reason is that the right to livelihood is the right of every citizen in this country.

If the Narmada Valley had not been submerged, there were many resources the forest would have provided. Even if your land was poor, you could get tubers and roots and gum and such things from the forest and survive. People never went hungry. But here if you have dry land, if your crop is not good or if the rains fail, then you will have to go hungry for sure. It is going to be a very hard life. There's another thing. In our old village we had pure breed grains, and we never used chemical fertilisers. But here without chemical fertilisers, we will not get any crop. The lands have acquired the habit of being supplied with chemical fertilisers, so without them nothing will grow. We used organic fertiliser or compost because on the Narmada banks we kept cattle, fowl and goats. But here there is no fodder to feed the cattle. The government has not provided us any grazing land.[189] Here goats get diseases and they don't survive. None of the animals we brought with us from our old villages survived. There is only one pair of bullocks now. A few people may have one or two buffaloes. There are no other means for survival!

So, we have to build a new youth organisation, organise programmes around the country and appeal to the world's people to once again come to our help and support. We have to put pressure on the government. So long as I live, even if I am lame in one leg (one of Keshavbhau's legs had to be amputated), I will certainly go to nearby places to support their activity. It may not be possible for me to attend all the programmes, but I will surely attend those from where I can return the same day. The NBA was nothing but a group of all of us. But if we have accepted land, accepted a settlement site, we have not committed a crime. We say very clearly and emphatically that we have accepted this because our village and our land have been completely submerged. But the way the Andolan has left things halfway and ignored our problems—we consider it a very bad thing to have happened.

Nandini: You are the oldest activist from Maharashtra, right from the days the first executive committee was formed. We had adopted one primary strategy, 'We will drown, but we will not leave'. What are your views on this?

Keshavbhau: In all the big programmes we organised, for example, the battle of Ferkuva, or the gathering at Harsud or the Manibeli and Domkhedi satyagrahas, the many hunger strikes and sit-in protests in Mumbai—in each of them it is the people who had to suffer the hardships. Okay, we took a firm stand—as long as our demand is not met, we will not leave or stop the hunger strike. But for that we needed the backing of a huge number of people. We had to be unwavering and firm. Because the people had never left their villages or been in the city, after four or five days, they would get fed up. Where do we bathe, where do we relieve ourselves—all these issues came to the surface. So, we had to work very hard to keep them in the city and retain their participation. We even had to provide them tea, soap, etc. Adivasis habitually smoke bidis, so we had to buy stocks and provide them with bidis. You know how uncomfortable one feels if one does not have a bath for a couple of days. So everywhere, at every event, after two days, the people would get tired and irritated. But we managed; people stayed on till the end of the programme and that put pressure on the government for sure.

In 2003, we had a 21-day-long agitation at Nashik. There, with the combined efforts of the NBA and Punarvasan Sangharsh Samiti (Committee for Struggle for Rehabilitation)[190] compensation was finally sanctioned. In the end, people felt there was no use staying on, so they began to leave their villages in batches and accept rehabilitation. The height of the dam reached 100 metres at that time. Now that the government had obtained permission to raise it by another 10 metres, it was going to be very difficult. Everything would be ruined. People in the villages also began to speak very differently. So, in the end, we had to take the stand of accepting rehabilitation.

This was at the time of the 2003 submergence. Since I was one of the main activists, people started abusing me. 'He is the one stopping us. Everything is getting destroyed. This compensation we have been offered, how many days is it going to last? How do we live our lives in the future?' Some said they would go to Gujarat, others said they would go and stay at their in-laws. Then after consulting the people, we started the Alivihir satyagraha in May, 2004. We took control of the forest. We do not know what conflict developed between the NBA and the Punarvasan Sangharsh Samiti then. Neither of them talks face to face. There must have been some disagreement. But we could not really understand what it was all about.

The Rehabilitation Secretary of Maharashtra was scheduled to come and visit. I was the one who was asked to initiate the discussion and present the issues. I said, 'We have been pleading with the collector and the commissioner for so long, and still they are not giving us the land, so we are left with no other option. If we go back to the Narmada banks, we will certainly not survive. If we stay here, we will have to engage in robbery, and we will one day be killed by someone. So, until we get land, we are going to tie you to the trunk of this neem tree. Tell us what you feel about it.'

In the end the sahib was very angry and started scolding the collector and the commissioner. 'Why have you not given them the land they have been demanding? Today, tomorrow, right away you had better hand over the land to them, else action will be taken against you.'

From that day onward although Vadchhil is talked about sweetly outwardly, the main person of the movement has anger towards it (Vadchhil) inside.[191] And that is why I am of the firm opinion that we did not get support till date. (*Laughs.*) But I took a firm decision when I found that the people were scattered and dispersed. That is why they were forced to give us land at one go. They made all sorts of plans to break me. But I did not break. Because if I had, I would have become rich all by myself and others would have been left in the lurch. And I avoided getting into the clutches of the government. That is why my situation is no different from anyone else in the village, neither more nor less. Those who broke away from the Andolan built pakka houses. But we had our houses submerged every year and were moving in and out of them. We had no money to spare. We could not build pakka houses.

We organised the Domkhedi as well as the Manibeli satyagrahas. We organised huge programmes in Nimgavhan, Badwani and Kasrawad. They must also be counted as successes. The government was refusing to establish a sixth settlement site. But because we put pressure on them they were forced to establish the sixth site. Then they had to go on to establishing numbers 7, 8, 9 and 10. The government will surely have to build two or three more.

The main activists of the Andolan must have been of the opinion that we could sustain our struggle only if we stop construction of the dam. But the dam did not stop at any point. The height kept increasing step by step. Everyone wants to live, no one wants to die. So, we had to decide.[192] We had to put pressure on the government. And we did win our rights.

The dam did not stop. Everyone was taking the Narmada water in their hands and swearing, 'We Will Drown, But We Will Not Leave.' But I refused to take that water in my hand—the water of Mother Narmada. During the battle of Ferkuva some people had written the slogan in blood. I said, 'I will not do that.' I refused to take the Narmada water in my hand.[193] Many people were watching me. Medhatai was also watching me. 'Why are you doing this?' she said. But I remained firm.

However, when I realised what people wanted, we lost no time in putting pressure on the government and we got us the land. If we are being opposed now because we accepted the land, it is meaningless. Have we committed a crime in accepting land? No, we have not.

We also got fooled in the process. By the Andolan activists. We had taken 2,000 people to Bombay, for a ten-fifteen-day hunger strike and that too in the rains. We sacrificed a lot. At last, the Chief Minister of Maharashtra took the decision that a Task Force Committee would be set up to decide on what was right and what was wrong through a survey. They did a survey of each and every village in which information was taken about the landholders and the landless. How were the landless left out?

In the end Medhatai called us and said, 'It is my firm stand that whosoever had their names in the Task Committee survey report will all be given land in stages. But if you break away from me and go to government redressal machinery or somewhere else, that is not acceptable to me.' People here already had faith in her and Medhatai broke that trust. We came to know of this only on 14 August 2011. We are greatly saddened by this.

Even when Medhatai was travelling all over the world, we used to feel that she was with us. But then why did the people get left behind from time to time? In Indore we gathered in large numbers, thinking that the issue of the sons not being declared as affected persons would be taken up. That issue was not even mentioned. We used to go to Mumbai to solve the issue of undeclared sons' rights, and no one took up the issue. The people are mobilised for important issues, and then no one utters a word about the issue. That is why the organisation came apart.

In Maharashtra, twenty-four villages in Akrani have been considered forest villages from British times. There were no papers indicating their status. There were no receipts of fines paid from the British times. Those villages were not considered as revenue villages. That is why in the beginning when we got organised as the NDS, we had coined the slogan, 'To Whom Does the Forestland Belong? It Belongs To Us, To Us!' Then came the slogan, 'What Will the Sardar Sarovar Do? It Will Destroy You!' The issue is still unresolved (the issue of converting the villages into revenue villages).

So, this is the story of the forestland. From 1980 to 1985 the government must have faced problems because this is a forest village from very old times, but they would not know what kind of land it was unless it was surveyed. Akrani has seventy-three such villages of which twenty-four are on the Narmada banks. How much is the land in each of these villages? Who are the land owners? Nothing was clear. So, they undertook a survey. At the time of that survey, no organisation existed, but there were corrupt officials. Whoever could feed them chicken, pay them money or get them liquor, his farm would be measured and recorded. That was how it was. So, a very large number of people had no land in their names. And those who had the land had it from ancestral times. Then there was the Forest Department. Their practice was that the land would be in the name of the eldest brother. So, it turned out that in the villages on the Narmada banks there were only 1,300 landowners. Only after we raised our voice saying, 'We are not only 1,300, we could be 13,000', took a huge protest march to Mumbai and raised the issue in the year 2000 could we get the Task Force appointed.

Some were declared affected by the collector, some by the Bagul Committee,[194] some by the commissioners. Some were declared by the redressal machinery. We reposed total faith in Medhatai because she had told us that we will get everyone declared as affected according to the Task Force Committee's decisions. We trusted her, and were left out in the process.

In Dhadgaon Tehsil, seventy-three villages on the Narmada banks were surveyed. There is some evidence of that survey. But no decision has been taken till now. If that decision had come in time, there would have been no need to go begging to the government. But the Andolan did not push for those demands. In 2005, a case had been registered in the Supreme Court that the Form 7/12 record should be made out in the name of the actual tiller. The Andolan did not pursue it further, and the matter met a natural death. Pratibhatai[195] has now taken up the issue of encroachments in Ambabari and other places. That has helped many people. But the Andolan had not taken up that issue. That is why this issue of forestland and encroachment has been sidelined. If encroached land had been registered in the name of the actual tiller, not one of us would have been left out.

The files pertaining to forestland – they remained wherever they had been put away. Perhaps they are at the tehsildar's office. Who knows where they are? Forms were filled out, but there was no implementation. The Andolan was only interested in whether the 'people are with us'. After people started accepting rehabilitation, that (the forestland issue) was kept aside.

The other thing was that, people kept thinking that adult sons of landholders would also be declared as project-affected families (PAFs) and would receive land. They remained bereft of hope! Their issue should have been resolved. We will have to take the stand that we will not rest until all outstanding issues are resolved. And we won't rest until we build a new Andolan.

NOTES

[1]Nimgavhan, in Akrani Tehsil of the then Dhule District (now Nandurbar District) is one of the 33 adivasi villages of Maharashtra falling in the submergence zone of SSP. Nimgavhan is now submerged in the Sardar Sarovar dam waters.

[2]Acharya Vinoba Bhave was a social reformer and a mentor for *Sarvodaya*, the constructive wing of Gandhism.

[3]Dashrath Tatya Patil was a founding member of the NBA, Dhule, Maharashtra. A renowned Gandhian, Tatya's entire family is active in the NBA, and his house is an extension of the NBA's office in Dhule.

[4]The march might refer to the historic one led by Vinoba Bhave on 3 March 1959.

[5]Vinoba Bhave led the famous Bhoodan movement in the 1950s, appealing to landlords across India to donate part of their lands to a common pool for disbursal to the landless poor, as a step towards voluntary land reforms.

[6]*Ashramshalas* are residential schools in Adivasi areas broadly modelled on the idea of an ashram.

[7]The *Varkari* sect is part of the Bhakti movement centred around devotion to the deity Vitthala, an annual pilgrimage to Pandharpur, the seat of the deity and regular bhajan-kirtan.

[8]Devachi Alandi is an important seat of the Varkari sect and also the place where its oldest saint Dnyaneshwar attained samadhi.

[9]*Madhukari* is an accepted practice of going around houses asking for cooked food or meals.

[10]*Bhajans* are devotional songs; *kirtan* is a traditional form of religious storytelling through songs, music and performance practiced in Maharashtra and in other parts of India.

[11]*Haripath* is the recitation of God's name.

[12]Although adivasis had been inhabiting these villages and cultivating these lands for generations, the government had not conducted the process of land settlement in these villages as they fell in the interior and inaccessible forest areas, and therefore classified them as 'forest villages'. The lands were not transferred in the names of the tillers, who were considered encroachers of forestlands with no land records in their names.

[13]A string of tulsi beads worn around the neck and considered holy, and among the Varkari, wearing the *maal* (becoming a *maalkari*) is a mark of the firm resolve to lead a pure life.

[14]*Khashi* is the fertile land of a river bank.

[15]The Narmada is a revered river among the Hindus. A unique religious practice associated with the Narmada is the *parikrama*, a circumambulation of the 1,312-km long river, to be undertaken carrying nothing but the bare essentials. It can take about three years to complete. Thousands of *parikramavasis* undertake this exercise every year and are fed and hosted by the villages on the banks of the Narmada. The many dams built on the river have disrupted this Hindu religious tradition.

[16]The *Dindi* is a team of Varkari travelling to Pandharpur with musical instruments, singing bhajans.

[17]It was believed that passing through the dense Shoolpaneshwar forest during the Narmada parikrama was dangerous and so no one stopped while crossing the forest.

[18]Rajghat falls in the Badwani District of M.P.

[19]Keshavbhau discontinued feeding the parikramavasis when his village Nimgavhan was submerged in 2004 due to the Sardar Sarovar Dam, and he shifted to the Vadchhil rehabilitation and resettlement site (R&R site) far from the Narmada.

[20]Donkeys were the only means of transport in these inaccessible adivasi areas with no roads.

[21]The late Dongare Maharaj was a popular religious figure and a preacher. His public readings of the *Bhagwat* drew large crowds, particularly in Gujarat.

[22]Keshavbhau is possibly referring to a trust set up by Dongare Maharaj.

[23]Keshavbhau's brother.

[24]This could be the year 1972.

[25]Keshavbhau means that Alandi was predominantly a brahmin town.

[26]One of Mahatma Gandhi's favourite songs, this is a popular devotional song which promotes communal harmony.

[27]Also known as Didi or Tai, both of which mean elder sister.

[28]After being displaced by the SSP, many project-affected families and persons (PAFs and PAPs) from the 33 affected villages in Maharashtra have been resettled in Shahada and other tehsils of Maharashtra.

[29]Though the people paid fines regularly for the forestlands they were cultivating, they were given no receipts as the forest department personnel pocketed the money. Later, when such lands were regularised and ownership given to the tillers, the adivasis in this area suffered great injustice because the lands were not regularised in their names as they had no proof of the fines they had paid. This had far-reaching consequences for the adivasis in the Narmada Valley when they were displaced. Because their lands were not regularised, many families were considered landless and were discriminated against in the land allocation for resettlement.

[30]A government employee in a village, *gramsevak* literally means one who provides services to a village or assists village people.

[31]Parveta, one of the earliest rehabilitation sites in the Sankheda Tehsil of Gujarat, is where PAPs were shifted as far back as the early eighties.

[32]According to the Narmada Water Disputes Tribunal (NWDT) award passed in 1979, PAPs and PAFs could choose to resettle either in Gujarat where the SSP was being built or in their home state.

Although the oustees in Maharashtra and M.P. were not keen on moving to sites outside their own state, there was immense pressure on them to choose resettlement in Gujarat.

[33]The villages of Sikka and Surung fall in the state of Maharashtra and are neighbouring villages of Nimgavhan, while Jalsindhi is on the opposite bank of the Narmada in M.P. The dam site as well as the height of the dam had undergone many changes before the present site and height of dam were finally chosen for the SSP.

[34]Initially there was a plan to build a dam on the Gujarat and M.P. border called the Haranfal dam which was shelved later.

[35]Here Keshavbhau is referring to the inter-state dispute over the dam height and sharing of Narmada waters between the state of Gujarat and other party states—mainly M.P.

[36]The Narmada Valley Development Plan (NVDP) consists of 30 large dams, 135 medium and 3,000 small dams on the river Narmada and its tributaries. A large number of villages, forests, and agricultural lands has already been or will be submerged by these dams.

[37]Initially the foundation of a much smaller dam of about 161 feet height at Navagam in Gujarat was laid by Pandit Nehru in 1961. However, the state of Gujarat wanted a much higher dam but that would have submerged large tracts of lands in M.P. and an interstate dispute over the height of the dam and dispute over sharing of the Narmada waters arose between the party states. The NWDT under the Interstate Water Disputes Act 1956 was set up in 1969 to resolve the dispute. This was while Indira Gandhi was the PM of India. It is popularly believed in the Narmada Valley that it was only in the late seventies that the NWDT gained momentum when Morarjibhai Desai, who belonged to Gujarat became the PM of India in March 1977 to July 1979 and the NWDT gave its final decision in August 1978 for a higher dam, while he was still the PM. The Narmada Control Authority (NCA), established to implement the directions of the NWDT award, on its website also confirms this as it notes, 'On 16 August 1978, the final order and decision of the Tribunal was published'. The NWDT increased the height of the dam, now called the Sardar Sarovar Project to 455 feet, much higher than what was envisaged earlier when its foundation stone was laid by Pandit Nehru in 1961 at Navagam. For details about the setting up of NWDT, see: http://nca.gov.in/imp_date.htm; and 'History less known: The history of the Narmada Water Disputes Tribunal' (nandinikoza.blogspot.com) [accessed 15 October 2021].

[38]The group gram panchayat of these submergence villages was situated in Roshmal village near Dhadgaon, in the then Dhule District. It was at a distance of some 20 kms from the submergence villages, and people had to walk to Roshmal as there were no roads.

[39]People had decided in 1984 not to accept R&R in Gujarat but to remain in Maharashtra itself. This was before NDS, the people's organisation, came into being. The NWDT award also recognised the right of the people to resettle in the state of their choice.

[40]This charter of demands by the PAPs in 1984 became the foundation on which the demands of the people took concrete shape in the future.

[41]The PAPs had demanded from the government that they be given forestland in Dhule district itself for resettlement of all the villages falling in the submergence area in Maharashtra. This demand was made as people felt that these forestlands offered large enough pieces of land to settle the adivasi people as a community, and that these lands were closer to their original homes and had a similar socio-cultural-economic milieu.

[42]Submergence villages of SSP in Maharashtra located near Nimgavhan.

[43]Dr Vasudha Dhagamwar, a lawyer by profession, was one of the earliest persons from outside the Narmada Valley who visited the valley over the issue of SSP and displacement in the Maharashtra villages. As a lawyer, she had earlier taken up the issue of land rights of adivasis in Akkalkuwa Tehsil of Maharashtra in the seventies and was familiar with the area. Her earlier work in Akkalkuwa helped her win the confidence of the people in this inaccessible area where outsiders were looked upon with suspicion. It was Vasudhaji who later on introduced the activists of SETU, including Medha Patkar, to the submergence villages in Maharashtra. Vasudhaji was the founding member of the organisation MARG and also associated with several other NGOs and social movements. See: http://www.ngo-marg.org/about/history (accessed 23 September 2021).

[44]Medha Patkar, leader of NBA. When Medha visited the Narmada Valley with Vasudha Dhagamwar, she was working with an organisation in Ahmedabad named Centre for Social Knowledge and Action (SETU), founded in 1982 to mobilise marginalised communities against exploitation. Achyut Yagnik, Rajni Kothari, D. L. Seth, etc., are among the founding members of SETU. SETU and its activists like Ashok Shrimali, Dynaneshwar Patil, Medha Patkar, Rohit Jain, etc. played a significant role in the formative years of the Narmada struggle and in building the NDS in the 33 submergence villages of Maharashtra.

[45]Dynaneshwar Patil of the NGO SETU played a key role in building the NDS in the initial years.

[46]Talathi is a government employee who maintains the land records of villages.

[47]Manibeli, in the Akkalkuwa Tehsil of the then Dhule District was the first village in Maharashtra in the submergence zone of the SSP. Situated on the banks of the Narmada and its tributary, the beautiful Dev, surrounded by forest on two sides, and with the magnificent Shoolpaneshwar temple at its doorstep, Manibeli seemed a divine village. Manibeli was so close to the dam that the bright lights on the dam could be seen from the village. However, Manibeli itself never had electricity. The battle of Manibeli has been as extraordinary as the village itself. Even today people defy the state and continue to live in the partially submerged village braving great odds. Manibeli was once the nerve centre of the NBA, drawing worldwide attention to the NBA.The Manibeli struggle was so powerful that when a large number of organisations the world over called for a moratorium on the World Bank funding of mega dams, it was called the Manibeli declaration. See: https://www.culturalsurvival.org/publications/cultural-survival-quarterly/2000-ngos-support-manibeli-declaration (accessed 23 September 2021).

[48]Bhadal is the last among the 33 villages in Maharashtra to be submerged by the Sardar Sarovar Dam.

[49]The NDS was the organisation of the people of the dam-affected 33 submergence villages in Maharashtra. Prior to the formation of the NBA as an umbrella organisation, there were different organisations of people affected by the SSP in the three states. In M.P. there was the NGNS. In M.P. itself, in the late 1970s the Nimad Bachao Andolan had taken place demanding the reduction in the height of the SSP. Then the Khedut Mazdoor Chetna Sangath (KMCS) that existed since the early eighties in Alirajpur, M.P. was formed to work for the rights of the adivasis. In Gujarat, the people of six adivasi villages who had lost their lands in 1961 to the construction of the Kevadia Colony struggled for their rights since then. Later they were associated with the Rajpipla Social Service Society (RSSS), and then with the help of Muljibhai Tadvi and NDS, the RSSS and the Lok Adhikar Sangh from Ahmedabad working on civil and human rights together formed the (Narmada) Asargrast Sangharsh Samiti (ASS). All these groups together came to be known as the NBA. While NGNS, NDS and ASS more or less merged and took up the single identity of NBA, the KMCS, RSSS and the Lok Adhikar Sangh and some others continued to maintain their independent identity and work. Arch Vahini, an NGO in Gujarat, had started work on the issue of rehabilitation of the Gujarat oustees in the early eighties prior to the establishment of NDS in Maharashtra.

[50]Places like Dhule—the district headquarters—Molgi, etc., were crucial administrative centres for the villages falling in the

submergence zone of the SSP, and it was important to establish a base and support group in these places.

[51]Noorji Padvi of village Danel in Akkalkuwa Tehsil of Maharashtra is one of the senior adivasi leaders of NBA.

[52]Dr Chaudhari, Dashrath Tatya Patil and many other eminent people had formed a strong NBA support group in Dhule. There were support groups all over the country but those in Malegaon, Pune, Mumbai, Vadodara, Ahmedabad, Indore, Hoshangabad, Bhopal, Jabalpur, Delhi, etc., were the strongest and it would be appropriate to call them extensions of NBA itself, particularly those closer to the valley like the groups in Dhule, Indore and Vadodara. NBA support groups carried out a series of activities like fundraising, campaigning, awareness generation, lobbying, liaisoning with media, legal work, and participating in the struggle. Many of these groups are still active.

[53]Charter of demands.

[54]Already 13,000 hectares of forest was being submerged by the SSP. Use of other forestland for R&R would have meant additional loss of forest. Besides, central government permission is required for the diversion of forestland for R&R.

[55]The adivasis did not follow the English or Gregorian calendar and had their own unique way of remembering dates.

[56]Adivasi villages had many hamlets, each called a *pada* or a *falia*.

[57]The village of Nimgavhan was very active in the NBA and was strategically located near the borders of Maharashtra, M.P. and Gujarat. Being an important centre of the NBA, crucial meetings with representatives from submergence villages across all the three states often took place in Nimgavhan. This is not only because Nimgavhan was centrally located and its people were powerful *andolankaris* (people who constitute the movement) and were very hospitable, but also because senior adivasi leaders like Keshavbhau belonged to Nimgavhan.

[58]A *guntha* is a fortieth of an acre or roughly a hundredth part of a hectare and measures approximately 100 square metres.

[59]The NBA continued its surveys in the Narmada Valley almost every year for different purposes, including for placing the data before the Supreme Court.

[60]The estimates for the number of families that would be affected due to submergence in each state kept on increasing as more and better surveys were conducted due to the pressure exerted by the struggle. Only because of the people's struggle did the government declare that the total number of PAFs was around 4,500 in the 19 villages of Gujarat, 4,200 in Maharashtra and 33,000 in M.P. The NBA maintained that the actual figure of PAPs would be much higher as

there was underestimation of project impacts and losses, as is the case in every such project.

[61]Progressive and well-known cinema and theatre personalities of Maharashtra like Dr Shriram Lagoo and Nilu Phule performed on stage to raise funds to set up the 'Samajik Kritadnyata Nidhi' to support activists of people's movements and social workers in Maharashtra. This assistance to the activists was an important support to the NBA.

[62]Bamani is one of the 33 villages falling in the submergence zone of SSP in Akkalkuwa taluka of Maharashtra.

[63]A *payali* is a measure roughly equal to 4 kg.

[64]Maharashtra state already had an Employment Guarantee Act many years before the current National Rural Employment Guarantee Act (NREGA) came into being.

[65]Nirmalkumar Suryavanshi, a well-known lawyer based in Dhule, represented NBA in many cases in Maharashtra. It is because of the support of lawyers like him and an excellent network of lawyers that NBA could fight the many false cases clamped on its activists and the many legal battles from the district to the Supreme Court.

[66]Kadipani and Kavant, in the predominantly adivasi Chhota Udaipur District in Gujarat, are the only market places for the villages on the Narmada banks that have bus connectivity. The popular weekly bazaar at Kavant draws adivasis from all the three states of M.P., Maharashtra and Gujarat, and is a place for social interaction. Kavant is so colourful and eventful that the Gujarat State Tourism Department promotes it as a tourist destination. See: https://www.gujarattourism.com/fair-and-festival/kavant-fair.html (accessed 9 March 2022).

[67]Hapeshwar, an adivasi village in the SSP submergence zone in the Chhota Udaipur District of Gujarat, had a heritage Shiv temple which was submerged by the Sardar Sarovar Reservoir. Many such temples were submerged by the several dams built on the Narmada.

[68]Here, *bhagat* means a devotee who has renounced intoxicating substances and one who has pledged to live a disciplined and austere life. Bhagats can be identified by their attire and appearance.

[69]A raft.

[70]The NDS felt that though rehabilitation did not seem feasible, it would not be possible to take a 'No Dam' stand and fight for the rights of the oustees without the coming together of the people's organisations that were already active in other states, including the KMCS and NGNS in M.P.

[71]The samadhis of Mahatma Gandhi, Kasturba Gandhi and Mahadevbhai Desai are located at Rajghat on the banks of the

Narmada near Kukra village in M.P. The meetings of the NGNS used to take place at Rajghat.

[72]KMCS founded in the early eighties is an organisation of the adivasis in Jhabua district, now Alirajpur district, of M.P. and was already active before the formation of NDS in Maharashtra. KMCS is registered as a trade union and has done extensive work for adivasi rights. See: http://anar-kali.blogspot.in/p/khedut-mazdoor-chetna-sangath.html (accessed 23 October 2021).

[73]Rahul Banerjee, a graduate engineer from IIT Kharagpur, joined KMCS in its formative years. Through KMCS and Dhas Gramin Vikas Kendra he has played an exemplary role both as an activist and a thinker. For over three decades now he has been involved in the struggles for adivasi rights and promotes the indigenous knowledge, livelihoods and culture of the Bhil community. His writings have been published as articles and books. See: https://anar-kali.blogspot.com/ (accessed 20 October 2021).

[74]This should be Amit Bhatnagar. Amit left his studies as an architect to work with the people of rural and tribal India. He joined KMCS during its formative years and played a key role in strengthening it. His stirring songs continue to inspire several people's movements even today. Amit and his wife Jayshree Bhalerao, who was also an activist with KMCS as well as NBA, currently run a school for the children of members of the Adivasi Mukti Sangathan in Sendhwa, M.P. See: http://adharshilalearningcentre.blogspot.in/ (accessed 20 October 2021).

[75]A pro-dam NGO based in Gujarat, Arch Vahini was officially appointed by the GoG along with several other NGOs to carry out R&R work in the 19 submergence villages of Gujarat. It was also a member of the land purchasing committee appointed by GoG to buy lands for oustees in Gujarat. In the initial years, Arch Vahini was instrumental in lobbying for some progressive provisions in R&R policy for the oustees in Gujarat. However, later on, Arch Vahini joined the GoG and the World Bank in pushing for the dam even though R&R was far from complete.

[76]The NGNS was established by several veteran Gandhians and well-known freedom fighters like Kashinathji Trivedi (former minister in the M.P. Government), Prabhakarji Mandlik, along with local leaders like Parasmalji Karnavat, Phulchandbhai Patel, Shobharambhai Jat, Ambaramji Mukati and Surajmalji Lunkad, among others. NGNS was active prior to NBA on the issue of dams on the Narmada in M.P. and consisted of affected people from the plains of Nimad in M.P. NGNS undertook programmes like yatras, awareness campaigns and exhibitions around the issue of Narmada

dams. This helped in generating awareness among the people in M.P. regarding the adverse impacts of large dams on the Narmada, including the SSP. The work carried out by NGNS subsequently helped in building the NBA in M.P.

[77]Ambarambhai Mukati, a well-respected senior farmer leader of Nimad, belonged to village Borlai. He was also one of the founding members of NGNS and played an important role in the formative years of NBA.

[78]Kashirambhai Yadav of Badwani, M.P., popularly known as Kaka, is a senior leader of NBA. He was also a firebrand leader of the Nimad Bachao Andolan in M.P. in the late seventies and fought for the height reduction of the dam.

[79]Shobharambhai Jat belonged to the submergence village Bagud in M.P. He was a senior leader of NBA as well as the founding member of NGNS.

[80]Sitarambhai Patidar of the submergence village Kadmal, M.P., has been one of the committed leaders of NBA. A great orator and mobiliser, Sitarambhai has donned several responsibilities in the NBA and has undertaken many fasts, one of them being 26 days long in Bhopal. He was a part of the NBA's *Samarpit Dal* (the contingent ready to lay down their lives).

[81]Jagannathbhai Patidar of the submergence village Kundia in M.P., popularly known as Kaka, is one of the pillars of the NBA. His home can be considered an extension of the NBA office in M.P. Kaka was also an active member of the Nimad Bachao Andolan.

[82]Devrambhai Kanera of submergence village Khaparkheda, M.P., is one of the senior full-time activists/leaders of NBA, and part of its Samarpit Dal. Devrambhai's entire family including his wife, Shakuntala Bhabhi, and two daughters Sangeeta and Swapna have been active in the NBA.

[83]It was when the people of the Narmada Valley realised that the government not only had no land for resettlement, but did not even have the mandatory rehabilitation master plan in place as required, that complete opposition to the SSP was declared in 1988. By now they were also aware that the government had not resettled those displaced by earlier dams like the Tawa, Bargi and the Ukai, and that the condition of those displaced was abysmal.

[84]Bawa Mahariya of submergence village Jalsindhi, M.P., is one of the senior adivasi leaders of KMCS as well as NBA. A highly committed leader, Bawa continues to reside in his partially submerged village braving all odds and refuses to move out.

[85]Keshavbhau is referring to the popular cartoons created by cartoonist K. P. Sasi concerning the maltreatment meted out to the oustees by dam builders. One particular cartoon shows how a

politician promises the sky to the PAPs before the dam is built, and then kicks them after it is built.

[86]Bhoomi Sena (literally, land army) is an adivasi movement for land to the tiller, which began in the early 1970s in Maharashtra.

[87]The lands of six adivasi villages—Kevadia, Waghadia, Limdi, Navagam, Gora and Kothi falling in the Narmada District of Gujarat—were acquired in 1961 for the construction of the project colony named Kevadia Colony near the SSP dam site. The people of these six villages have never been considered PAPs, and were given paltry cash compensation at the time of land acquisition. Most of the nearly 1,000 families displaced by the Kevadia Colony work as casual labour either at the dam site or have ended up as domestic workers in the homes of the project officials or are doing lower-level jobs in government offices. They have been fighting fiercely as part of NBA.

[88]Harivallabhbhai Parikh, a Gandhian, had stalled the construction of the Lalpur dam in Gujarat in which his Anand Niketan Ashram was to get submerged. Initially opposed to large dams including those on the Narmada, he later became one of the strong proponents of SSP and joined hands with the GoG to proactively oppose the NBA. Anand Niketan was also one of the many NGOs officially appointed by the GoG for the resettlement work of the oustees along with Arch Vahini.

[89]The programmes undertaken by the NBA like the campaigns, demonstrations, fasts, road blockades, were not limited to the concerned three states but were undertaken before the Prime Minister's Office in Delhi, at different ministries and administrative offices, and at the World Bank office. Public programmes were also undertaken at Jantar Mantar, Rajghat and the Boat Club in Delhi.

[90]Revenue village is an administrative unit where agricultural lands as well as other land uses of a village and land ownership are well defined, with proper land records. The agricultural lands in a revenue village are well demarcated from the forestlands, grazing lands, waste lands, residential lands, etc. In revenue villages mostly individual as well as family land ownership records are maintained and available. Often in remote areas, particularly adivasi areas, the land records are not updated and maintained so the lands belonging to the people are often not registered in their names in government records.

[91]In 1990, the NBA organised a peaceful long march (Sangharsh Yatra) from Rajghat in M.P. to the dam site in Gujarat, in which thousands of people participated. However, the Long March was not allowed to enter Gujarat and was stopped at the Gujarat border at Ferkuva by the GoG by deploying thousands of police. This

became popularly known as the Ferkuva programme. For details see Kevalsingh's interview.

[92]Dr B. D. Sharma was then Commissioner for Scheduled Castes and Scheduled Tribes, GoI. A founding member of Bharat Jan Andolan, an alliance of adivasi movements in India, he played an important part in the NBA.

[93]Jahangir Bolga, a senior adivasi activist, played an important role in the organisation in Maharashtra during the early years of NBA. He took the decision of accepting R&R in the Andolan's initial stages.

[94]Kevalsingh Vasave is Keshavbhau's brother's son.

[95]Maninder Gill, the then Deputy Collector for Resettlement, Dhule District, later joined the World Bank.

[96]After the people took a no-dam stand, the government adopted different tactics to break the people's resolve by dividing them.

[97]In September 1989, thousands of people from all over the country belonging to different movements assembled at Harsud, a town in Khandwa District of M.P. and resolved to oppose destructive development and struggle for sustainable development. This programme can be considered a watershed in the history of struggles against destructive development in the country. Many years later, Harsud was forcibly evicted and submerged due to the construction of the Indira Sagar dam.

[98]Senior Gandhian, Padma Vibhushan and recipient of the Magsaysay award, Baba Amte shifted to the Narmada Valley in 1990 from his *karmbhoomi* in Maharashtra to reside on the banks of the Narmada in the submergence village Kasravad in M.P. He pledged that he would drown but would not move if the dam was raised and waters entered his home. The coming of Baba Amte to the Narmada Valley gave a tremendous boost to the NBA. Baba Amte and his wife Sadhana Tai spent over a decade in Kasravad in spite of their age and failing health. Before coming to the Narmada Valley, Baba Amte had successfully spearheaded the struggle against Bhopalpatnam and Inchampalli dams in Maharashtra in 1982. As an outcome of such protests a meeting of social activists and environmentalists across India was held in Anandvan in July 1988, and the Anandvan Declaration to oppose big dams across India was adopted. For details on Bhopalpatnam and Inchampalli dam struggles, see the 2nd and 5th Citizen's reports by Centre for Science and Environment (CSE).

[99]Thousands of people from across the country had assembled at Harsud to participate in this historic programme; therefore only a few select activists/leaders and eminent people could be invited on stage to speak, and Keshavbhau was one of them.

[100]Fortunately, the activists managed to escape.

[101]Son of Dashrath Tatya Patil, Shyambhau Patil, is a very active member of the Dhule support group of NBA.

[102]All developmental work in the submergence area was stopped right from the time the Narmada Projects were announced. People of the submergence area were deprived long before they were actually displaced as even work on basic amenities and development was not undertaken so that people would be compelled to leave their villages sooner.

[103]Geeta Vasave, Keshavbhau's niece became the first woman sarpanch in the area.

[104]In 1985, the World Bank had given a loan to the Indian government for the SSP, subject to several conditions. Around 1989, the Bank came up with several more conditions for the continuation of the loan. Ultimately due to the people's resistance, the World Bank had to withdraw from SSP, the project it was funding.

[105]Displaced villages and people needed to be rehabilitated as a community as a whole as mandated by the NWDT. For this, large chunks of lands at one place for rehabilitation of thousands of oustees were not available except forestlands in the then Dhule district of Maharashtra. Clearing forestlands for rehabilitation purposes required special clearance from the government including from the central government. What Keshavbhau means here is that the World Bank was facing international pressure to ensure proper rehabilitation of people displaced by SSP as it was funding the project and in turn, it put pressure on the government for release/diversion of forestland for rehabilitation of the Maharashtra oustees.

[106]Apart from a loss of 13,000 hectares of forest due to submergence of the dam, another 4,200 hectares of forestland was released for rehabilitation in Maharashtra.

[107]The demand of the people by then was 'No Dam' and implementation of sustainable and equitable alternatives. This was after due consideration when people realised that it was not possible to rehabilitate 245 villages spread across the three party states as well as those who were to be impacted by the project infrastructure. The demand of the NBA was to stop the project and that the government undertake a time-bound review of the SSP with the people's participation. The demand of the people was not the single demand of release of forestlands for rehabilitation of Maharashtra oustees.

[108]The GoG, under the chief ministership of Chimanbhai Patel, along with powerful and moneyed religious trusts like the Swaminarayan trust, etc., sponsored the opposition to the NBA's long march at Ferkuva. Gujarat State Transport Corporation buses were used to bring people from across Gujarat to Ferkuva without cost to them, and

the many religious trusts and NGOs of Gujarat fed the participants sumptuously. Government schools were ordered to bring school children to Ferkuva to display strength.

[109]The government had appointed many persons as paid *punarvas sathi*s to persuade PAFs to accept R&R.

[110]An MLA.

[111]It was the policy of the NBA that it being a people's movement, no individual within the movement would receive any award. Awards, if conferred, should be conferred on the NBA movement as a whole. The Right Livelihood Award, which is given only to individuals, was therefore denied, till the organisers accepted that it would also go to the NBA, along with Medha Patkar and Baba Amte. It was decided that Medha Patkar and Keshavbhau Vasave would receive it on behalf of the NBA. Later on, the NBA policy changed and individuals within the NBA began accepting individual awards.

[112]Also known as the 'Alternative Nobel Prize'.

[113]The NBA had set up the Jan Sahyog Trust with the Right Livelihood Award prize money. Keshavbhau was one of its trustees.

[114]YUVA, a people's organisation in Mumbai, was an active supporter of NBA. Later, NBA established its own office in Mumbai, and it was run by the well-known feminist Lata P. M., along with many other Mumbai-based activists.

[115]Medha Patkar's mother, Indutai Khanolkar, retired from the Indian Post Office in 1987. She was a senior women's rights activist associated with the organisation 'Swadhar' started by Mrinal Gore. Indutai was also active in the Rashtra Seva Dal and very active in the NBA.

[116]Popular street food where the vada is deep-fried and is eaten with a bun. Adivasi people are not used to such food.

[117]Gautam Appa, a long-time supporter of NBA, teaches at the London School of Economics.

[118]According to government plans, the historically important temples to be submerged by the SSP had to be physically relocated. However, most of the magnificent and very old temples like Shoolpaneshwar and Hapeshwar were never relocated and went under water.

[119]In 1993 the NBA announced Jalsamarpan, demanding that the Government of India (GoI) should appoint a committee by 6 August 1993 to review the SSP, otherwise a small group of activists would sacrifice their lives by drowning.

[120]Kesubhai Tadvi's house was at the lowest level in Manibeli and it was the first to submerge in Maharashtra.

[121]For details of how Kesubhai's house was demolished and then rebuilt due to the people's struggle, see Kevalsingh's interview.

[122]Just one day before the day of Jalsamarpan, the GoI accepted NBA's demand to review the SSP and the announcement was made by the then Minister of Water Resources, Vidyacharan Shukla. The GoI set up a review committee headed by Jayant Patil. L. C. Jain, Ramaswamy Iyer, Vasant Gowarikar and Kulandai Swami were the other members of the review committee.

[123]The Samarpit Dal remained underground to avoid arrest till the announcement of the review of SSP was made.

[124]Lakhs of rupees were spent on the publicity of the project by the state including holding such camps to promote the image of SSP. Advertisement firms like Lintas were hired to advertise the project.

[125]Navagam, a village near the dam site in Gujarat.

[126]Prabhubhai Tadvi is a senior NBA activist and his whole family is active in the NBA. His land in village Waghadia was acquired for the construction of Kevadia Colony. His home was one of the main centres of NBA for many years.

[127]Baliben Tadvi was a firebrand woman leader of NBA whose lands were acquired for the project colony at village Kothi, Gujarat. Her house was the nerve centre of NBA for many years against severe hostility from the GoG.

[128]Rehmal Punya Vasave, a teenage adivasi boy was shot dead in the police firing while protesting the forcible survey in his village.

[129]Vadchhil is the resettlement site located near Shahada in the Nandurbar district of Maharashtra. After Nimgavhan faced submergence, many oustee families were shifted to this R&R site. Keshavbhau is one of them.

[130]The World Bank appointed the Morse Committee to review the SSP in 1991.

[131]The World Bank's withdrawal came as a big victory for the NBA because it vindicated the NBA. Secondly, the World Bank's involvement had given a lot of credibility to the project; its withdrawal therefore put a question mark on the SSP, the role of the Bank as well as that of the government and the model of development they were collectively promoting.

[132]This refers to the R&R sites established in these villages for the PAPs of Maharashtra.

[133]The host communities often opposed the arrival of the Narmada oustees near their villages as they were afraid that additional population would put further pressure on the already scarce resources. Tensions in the host communities ran high. Opposition to the coming in of Narmada oustees was therefore strong. At one point, Dhanibai, an adivasi woman from one of the host areas in Taloda, Maharashtra, was shot by the police as she opposed the R&R sites in her area.

[134]The stay by the SC was only on that portion of the dam wall that could cause submergence. All the other project-related works, including the construction of the canal, were never stayed by the SC, and yet these remain incomplete even today.

[135]The proposal that at a dam height of 107 metres all the benefits of Sardar Sarovar could not only be preserved but increased manifold, displacement be brought down drastically, and the lion's share of the benefits go to Kutch, Saurashtra and North Gujarat, had been put forward in the beginning of the 1990s and presented later in greater detail by engineer Suhas Paranjape and K. J. Joy in their 1995 book titled, *Sustainable Technology: Making the Sardar Sarovar Project Viable*. See: https://www.ceeindia.org/books.php. A later paper revisiting the alternative is available on the NBA website at http://www.narmada.org/ALTERNATIVES/AltSSP/Ssppaper.html (accessed 20 October 2021).

[136]Even today, the GoG has not been able to fully utilise the waters stored in the dam as the canal network remains incomplete due to lack of funds.

[137]The NBA had filed a Public Interest Litigation (PIL) in 1994 in the Supreme Court of India to stop the SSP on the grounds that Article 21 of the Constitution had been violated. The final judgement of the Supreme Court in the case in October 2000 was a split judgement. One of the three judges, Justice Bharucha gave a dissenting judgment and clearly stated that 'Until environmental clearance to the Project is accorded by the Committee of Experts as aforesaid, further construction work on the dam shall cease.' The operative majority judgement too clearly states that 'Further rising of the height will be only *pari passu* with the implementation of the relief and rehabilitation and on the clearance by the Relief and Rehabilitation Sub-group. The Rehabilitation Sub-group will give clearance of further construction after consulting the three Grievances Redressal Authorities.' See: http://www.narmada.org/sardar-sarovar/sc.ruling/nba.comments.html (accessed 20 October 2021).

[138]A Grievance Redressal Authority (GRA) was set up in each state as per the order of the Supreme Court to look into the R&R problems.

[139]Retired Justice S. P. Kurdukar was appointed head of the GRA, Maharashtra.

[140]Loknivada, a programme taken up by the NBA in which every house in the submergence zone was identified and counted to show that most of the households had not shifted to R&R sites as claimed by the government.

[141]Instead of giving PAPs lands of their choice, the government simply allocated land without their consent. This is called ex parte allocation.

[142]As a result of the Andolan, the Government of Maharashtra (GoM) had to appoint a task force to look into the issues of R&R.

[143]Chunibhai Vaidya, senior Gandhian, had led the fight for the riparian rights of those living downstream of the Dantiwada and Sipu dams in Gujarat. Surprisingly, along with many other eminent Gandhians in Gujarat, he too became a great proponent of the Narmada project and joined the government in opposing the NBA. It was senior Gandhians like Chunibhai Vaidya who brought the required credibility to the SSP, which the government under Chimanbhai Patel could not have done.

[144]Dr Baba Adhav, a veteran trade unionist in Maharashtra, established the Hamal Panchayat in Pune in 1955 for the rights of the workers in the unorganised sector. Baba Adhav has also led the organisation of the dam-displaced people in Maharashtra named Maharashtra Rajya Dharangrasta ani Prakalpa Grasta Shetkari Parishad. This struggle which was built on the principle of rehabilitation before dam construction, led to the Maharashtra Resettlement of Project Displaced Persons Act, 1976, one of the first acts of its kind in the country.

[145]NBA activists and village leaders personally went to different movements/organisations to seek support. This helped increase the NBA base far and wide.

[146]People fought year after year through satyagraha against illegal submergence by declaring that they would not move, in the process even allowing their possessions, lands and houses to drown. The epitome of this protest was when the people stood risking their lives in the cold waters of the dam that entered their homes with the slogan *Doobenge, Par Hatenge Nahi* (We Will Drown, But We Will Not Move).

[147]Medha Patkar.

[148]What Keshavbhau wants to say here is that though Medha Patkar was part of the NBA's Samarpit Dal, the people of the Narmada Valley were not ready to let her drown.

[149]The NBA took up the issue of villages other than those falling in the submergence zone of SSP in Akrani Tehsil as these other villages were also considered forest villages, which meant that people there were denied the right to legally own the lands that they had been tilling for decades. This also helped in broadening the base of the NBA locally.

[150]These lands were also more fertile.

[151]The lands tilled by the people for generations remained forestlands and people did not get legal ownership of these lands.

[152]In the PIL filed by the NBA, some of the top lawyers of the country represented different parties in the SC. Renowned lawyer Shanti Bhushan (former Law Minister, GoI) and his son, senior

lawyer, human rights and anti-corruption activist Prashant Bhushan represented the NBA for several years pro bono.

[153]After the Supreme Court of India lifted its stay on the construction of Sardar Sarovar Dam in 2000, the height of the dam was increased in phases from 2000–2014. The Supreme Court in its majority judgement had clearly ruled that the dam height could be increased 'only pari passu with the implementation of the relief and rehabilitation', that is only after rehabilitation of oustees was assured at that height and the necessary permissions were obtained from the NCA. In 2000, the height (EL, or elevation level above mean sea level) of the dam was 85 metres. Subsequently, the NCA states, 'The raising of Sardar Sarovar Dam (SSD) height upto EL 121.92m was to be completed by June 2004 as per the time frame/Action Plan of NCA but due to additional task of R&R works in Madhya Pradesh and Maharashtra after the judgment of Hon'ble Supreme Court dated 15.3.2005 in the Writ Petition (Civil) 328 of 2005, it could not be achieved.' Due to poor R&R of oustees already displaced, the protests by NBA continued; and yet, in March 2006, NCA gave permission to increase the dam height from 110.64 metres to 121.92 metres, which the Gujarat government accomplished by December 2006. It is important to note that the height of 121.92 is the crest level of the concrete wall of the dam. After that comes the installation of the gates of the dam of approximately 18 metres. Thus, after 121.92 metres, the remaining increase in height would come from the gates and at one go, lead to large-scale and complete submergence of all the villages at full reservoir level. In 2007 the NBA filed a petition in the M.P. High Court highlighting large-scale corruption and violations in the rehabilitation of oustees in the 193 villages of M.P. The High Court ordered that a commission be appointed by the Government of M.P. to probe into these irregularities in R&R. The commission appointed in November 2008 was called the Jha Commission after Justice S. S. Jha, who headed it. With such protests by the NBA, the appointment of the Jha Commission, and the inability of respective governments to rehabilitate people displaced at 121.92 metres dam height, the dam construction, which included spillway piers and installation of gates, remained suspended for approximately eight years. It was in June 2014, after Narendra Modi was sworn in as the Prime Minister of India on 26 May 2014, that the GoG got the necessary approvals from the NCA to complete the dam with installation of gates to its full height of 138.68 metres. The erection and installation of the gates was to take three years. Finally, as stated by the NCA, 'The Narmada Control Authority in its 89th Emergency meeting held on 16th June 2017 granted permission of Phase-II proposal (of) "Lowering down of the gates and impounding water in the reservoir to Full Reservoir

Lever to EL 138.68m" of Sardar Sarovar Dam (SSD)'. The 'Emergency' meeting of the NCA was convened so that PM Modi could dedicate the dam to the nation on his birthday on 17 September 2017. Thus, the work on the dam was completed 56 years after its foundation was laid, leading to large-scale submergence in the Narmada Valley even as the rehabilitation of oustees remained incomplete. Even the Supreme Court of India, in violation of the NWDT guidelines of land-based rehabilitation, allowed disbursement of cash to the displaced oustees for the completion of the dam. The NCA notes, 'Government of Madhya Pradesh through its Grievance Redressal Authorities (GRAs) has made payments of compensation as per direction of Hon'ble Supreme Court dated 08.02.2017 in Writ Petition No. 328 of 2002...'. It is important to note that the canal network of the project remains incomplete even today as this is being written in October 2021, although there was never any stay by the Supreme Court on the construction of the canals. Rehabilitation of displaced people also remains incomplete and the struggle continues. For more details of permissions given by NCA to increase the dam height, see: http://nca.gov.in/rnr_index.htm (accessed 20 October 2021).

[154]Bawa Mahariya, Jalsindhi, M.P.

[155]Though the people were affected by the same project, the rehabilitation policy of each state differs.

[156]Normally the police in Maharashtra forcibly arrested those on satyagraha when the waters rose, but this year the police was not responding to the satyagrahis.

[157]The hillock close to the satyagraha tent/hut in Domkhedi village where the NBA satyagrahis were staging the protest.

[158]What Keshavbhau means here is that people had to take the decision to pull the satyagrahis out of the water themselves because unlike in the past, this year in Domkhedi the police did not come to pull them out, arrest them and take them away.

[159]It is generally believed that following the SC's permission to raise the dam height, the administration/police, who normally pulled out the satyagrahis from the rising waters, were no longer interested in saving them.

[160]What Keshavbhau means by saying, 'But to answer...', is that he had to go and hold a press conference to counter the allegations being made by the government and opponents of the movement that the NBA and its Samarpit Dal were not serious about the strategy of Jalsamarpan.

[161]*Panchnama* of the loss due to illegal submergence was done so that the PAFs could be compensated by the GoM.

[162]By 'they', Keshavbhau probably means the members of the panch along with the officials.

[163]The evidence of the submergence and destruction caused by the SSP of homes, temples, forests, including the submergence of the homes of Keshavbhau and Kevalsingh can be viewed here: http://www.narmada.org/images/satyagraha2003/ (accessed 20 October 2021).

[164]There is a serious issue of secondary displacement in a project like SSP as there are not enough unused/unclaimed lands to resettle the large number of people displaced by the project. By resettling the SSP oustees it has led to additional pressure on lands and common property resources belonging to the original/host villages and communities, often resulting in tension and conflict between the host community, government and even the SSP oustees. Keshavbhau here refers to the conflict that emerged with the host communities, their political representatives, organisations representing them and the government, as the government wanted to transfer to the SSP oustees, the lands and resources over which, already a lot of people, including adivasis were dependent from earlier times.

[165]Keshavbhau refers here to the protests by the local adivasis against the arrival of the Narmada oustees. Some supported the claims of the local people who opposed the Narmada oustees from occupying the forestlands.

[166]There seems to be some mix-up in the date here.

[167]SSP being an irrigation project, the NWDT award made it mandatory that the PAPs be resettled in the command area of the project or be given irrigable lands. However, this clause of the tribunal has been violated, like many others, by the government.

[168]As per the tribunal award, the adult son of a PAP is to be considered a separate family and entitled to all benefits of R&R. However only those adult sons who were 18 years of age in 1987 were considered eligible for R&R as that was the cut-off year declared by the state. This arbitrary cut-off date, years before the actual displacement took place, and the absence of birth records deprived hundreds of eligible adult sons from receiving full R&R benefits.

[169]Shobhanagar is named after Shobha Wagh, a full-time NBA activist who died tragically due to drowning in the backwaters of the SSP. Her demise left a deep vacuum in the Andolan.

[170]Ever since the SSP was planned, most of the developmental work in the submergence areas had come to a standstill. It was the policy of the state not to provide infrastructure facilities so that people would be forced to move out. *Jeevan Shala*s were the schools started by the NBA in the valley. The details and Kevalsingh's role as a founding member come later in the interview.

[171]Yogini Khanolkar, an activist of NBA in Maharashtra, is the recipient of the Maharashtra Foundation Award for the year 2010 for

social work. Yogini's main work is with the oustees of Maharashtra in the R&R sites and those not yet provided rehabilitation and living in partially submerged villages against great odds.

[172]Chetan Salve is an activist of the NBA as well as a film maker with video volunteers. Chetan's main work is with the oustees of Maharashtra in the R&R sites and those not yet provided rehabilitation and living in partially submerged villages against great odds.

[173]Command area of the dam.

[174]Land entitlement papers.

[175]The Jan Sahyog Trust was formed with the Right Livelihood Award funds received by Keshavbhau along with Medha Patkar on behalf of NBA. After Keshavbhau resigned from the Trust, it does not have any adivasi activist/leader from the Narmada Valley (NBA) as a trustee.

[176]For a description of the NBA's Karbhar Samiti or executive committee, see pp. 32–33, and p. 169.

[177]The NBA had state-level committees with people belonging to the submergence and affected villages in the state and full-time activists working in those villages. These state-level committees met regularly to carry out the functioning of the NBA and take local and state-level decisions. But when important decisions or big programmes were to be taken up, concerning the entire movement, there would be meetings of senior representatives of all the three states. Besides this, to discuss the working of the movement and take important decisions concerning the entire movement, discussions were periodically held in the meetings of the *samanvay samiti,* that included senior and steadfast supporters of the NBA spread across the country. The many members of the samanvay samiti, although not based in the Narmada Valley, worked in their state regions for the NBA, some even full-time.

[178]The main issue here is that the lands with land titles in old villages were few. Although people had been cultivating a lot of other land for a long time, these were not registered in their names. This was because land records were not upgraded in these remote adivasi villages by the revenue department of the government. Even those lands transferred to inheritors were not recorded properly. This often led to confusion over ownership, particularly because most families cultivated lands jointly. But when it came to rehabilitation, it became mandatory to have clear land records and land titles, which the adivasi families did not possess.

[179]Though the adivasi families cultivated large tracts of forestland and paid fines for it, these were never transferred to the people in spite of entitlement as per the law.

[180]The NBA with the help of engineers from the People's School of Energy, Kerala, had built a micro hydel project in Bilgaon village, Maharashtra, to demonstrate alternate means of energy generation that are decentralised, sustainable and produced with the people's participation. The construction of the Bilgaon micro hydel electric project was started in the year 2002 and was inaugurated in January 2003. It provided electricity to some of the villages falling in the submergence zone of the SSP and those that had never received electricity since India's independence.

[181]The withdrawal of the World Bank from the SSP.

[182]Instead of toilet paper, the adivasi people use more environment-friendly material like leaves or stones.

[183]The large number of sit-ins, rallies and demonstrations by NBA kept people on the roads for long periods of time, and it put an enormous strain on the people of the valley, particularly the women.

[184]Vesta from village Sikka has played a very important role in the Narmada struggle.

[185]Dr Sugan Baranth, a senior Gandhian, has been an active supporter of the NBA as part of the Malegaon support group.

[186]Nagesh Hatkar, a senior activist of Bhoomi Sena, has been a staunch supporter of NBA from its formative years.

[187]To deter people from participating in the movement, fabricated cases are registered en masse, and so if one person does not appear for the hearing, the case is adjourned and drags on, putting enormous strain on the andolankaris as they have to keep appearing on the date of the hearings in the court situated in towns and cities far away from their villages.

[188]People opposed the government programme of compensatory afforestation as the project itself was being questioned. Large numbers of cases were registered against the people of the Narmada Valley for having opposed the submergence of good forest on one hand and diverting cultivable land for compensatory afforestation programmes on the other.

[189]The R&R policy did not consider providing common property resources like grazing lands, forests, river, etc., that the people had in their original villages. Not providing common property resources affected the oustees adversely in the R&R sites.

[190]Punarvasan Sangharsh Samiti is an organisation in Maharashtra working on the issues of R&R of SSP oustees.

[191]What Keshavbhau wants to say is that the acceptance of R&R by the people of Nimgavhan and changing the stance from 'We will drown but we will not move' was not taken well by the NBA leadership.

[192]What Keshavbhau implies here is that in face of large-scale submergence, the strategy of *Doobenge Par Hatenge Nahi* was not sustainable.

[193]Any pledge taken with the holy Narmada water in hand is considered irrevocable. It was near impossible to back out from a pledge taken with the sacred waters of the Narmada.

[194]The Bagul Committee was appointed by the government to look into the claims of the oustees.

[195]Pratibha Shinde, a firebrand activist of the Lok Sangharsha Morcha, has been at the forefront of struggles around the issue of adivasi rights in Maharashtra and Gujarat. She is the founder of the Punarvasan Sangharsh Samiti in Maharashtra. Pratibha first came to the Manibeli Satyagraha as a student, and has been part of the NBA ever since.

II

A CONVERSATION WITH **KEVALSINGH VASAVE**

My full name is Kevalsingh Badal Vasave. I was born in 1965. I will tell you the history of my village. I have been a part of the Andolan from its beginning. I will also tell you about the various struggles the Andolan has fought.

According to Hindu religion, the Mahabharat war lasted only eighteen days. Yet, that eighteen-day war became the largest compiled epic in India. Our battle has already lasted twenty-two years. If one were to write or recount the history of this struggle, it would take another twenty-two years. Many aspects of the struggle are now well known. In all the various media, in the news, the first thing mentioned is that this is a struggle of the adivasis. Most of those submerged are adivasis. Yet very little is known about the local activists from the adivasi areas who have been actively engaged in the struggle.

The name of my village is Nimgavhan. The name came into being because the first village patil was Nimba Patil. Hence the village was named Nimgavhan. And if we go into our adivasi lore of Devapari, Raja Phanta and Ganda Thakur are two adivasi gods, who are known as Dev Dablya. When Ahal and Kumbha came to abduct Kunj Rana's sister, they corralled their horses at Domkhedi; hence the name of that village Domkhedi. They slept in Nimgavhan, and the name of the village may also be derived from that.

In the beginning, Nimgavhan was the village of three elders. The first was Banya. He had three children named Nimba, Supa and Sikka. Sikka's son is Badal, my father, named Badal Sikka Vasave. The progeny of the three elders now number almost seven hundred. That means this is a very old village. In government records Nimgavhan has always remained an encroachers' village. In spite of being so old, it was never made a revenue village.

So, this village was a kind of a family and everyone in the village lived like one. Never a quarrel, nothing.

Nimgavhan is right on the banks of the Narmada and at the foothills of the seventh mountain of the Satpura ranges. We have been brought up drinking Narmada water. In my childhood we bathed and frolicked in the Narmada every day, and if we felt cold, we used to lie down in the warm sands on her bank. We used to climb onto the huge black rocks on her banks and jump into the stream. That was how we spent our childhood. In our house, we had cows and bullocks and goats, and we used to take them to the forest for grazing. All day long we would climb trees, jump about, play hide and seek. We loved the forest streams. They flowed only during the monsoon. We went around with our friends hunting for crabs in those streams.

Our village has two big streams. One is the Khad River which is the largest tributary of the Narmada in Maharashtra. Our village is situated on the banks of the Khad. On the east is a stream that is named Jumaninala. All through the year it slowly collects water, which is why it is called Jumaninala. In the monsoon, this stream is a beautiful sight. Extremely clean water, high waterfalls, the water like sparkling silver! Near our village there are high mountains which are home to a variety of trees, birds and animals with whom we shared our lives.

On the opposite side of Nimgavhan in Maharashtra is Madhya Pradesh. A bit towards the west is Gujarat. So, our village is at the border of three states, but we have never divided our people or considered any boundaries, saying that you belong to Maharashtra, you to Gujarat and you to Madhya Pradesh. We treat all the three states as a single family. We interdine and intermarry freely. The name of the tribe differs in each state; they are known as Bhilalas in Madhya Pradesh, Pawras in Maharashtra and Rathawas in Gujarat. But the community is one. Of course, those in Gujarat considered themselves above the others, and those in Madhya Pradesh also used to feel somewhat like that. But ever since the Narmada Andolan began, all that disappeared and interdining and intermarriage became commonplace over the years.

We had a friendly and cordial relationship with the surrounding villages. For example, we used to feel that the Narmada had separated Jalsindhi and Nimgavhan, but today even though Jalsindhi has stayed on, we still have bonds of love and friendship with them.[1]

Our relationship is one of cooperation. If anyone of us wants to construct a house, we invite people over for *laha*,[2] where people would be given one meal in the day, and within a day the house would be built. If grass had to be cut or weeding to be done, then too, the entire village would be called for laha, and the work would get done. From marriages and festivals to worship rituals to dance, music, songs and drums, our cultural traditions have continued.

Adivasi people are so hospitable that if anyone comes to their house, they will call him in and give him water. Whether they know the person or not, they will treat him with affection. Our houses have makeshift, often straw doors, which we can shut and go anywhere at any time. We don't have permanent heavy doors or locks. No one gets robbed. However, now, day by day those communities who consider themselves civilised and educated, those who can read and write, they come and spoil all these things.

The farmland in our old villages was partly in the plains and partly on the mountain slopes. We never used an iron plough. We used only wooden ploughs. We used to plough the land, and once it rained, we used to grow jowar, maize, *bhadi* and *banti*[3] among many others. In the water courses we grew onion, garlic and watermelon. Except for sugarcane and banana, we grew all kinds of crops on our land and that too without using any fertilisers.

The land in the villages appears to be less fertile, but what we did was organic farming, natural farming where chemical fertilisers are never used. All our farming is fully based on manure and leaf litter. And even though our productivity was low, we had a comfortable life twelve months of the year. There would be grain left over after meeting all our family needs. Of the pulses we produced, we kept some for our own consumption and took some to the market to procure our clothing and other needs.

In our old villages, we never used too many clothes. Nor did we get too many things from the market. One or two steel utensils, some salt and a few clothes – that is all. The rest of our needs were fulfilled within the village. We extracted oil from the til seeds we produced. Another source of oil was the seed from our mahua trees.

Our Narmada was our greatest gift. All year she would provide us with green vegetables. *Chiwali*, which we loved to put in our dal, was one such green that this dam has managed to destroy completely. We caught fish whenever we wanted to eat any. We got all the wood we needed without paying anything because we owned the forest. The government has been saying that the forest belongs to them, but when has it ever been theirs? It was always ours. The cattle had plenty of fodder in the forest. The cattle as well as the goats! We lived a happy and rich life in our small village.

For the people, Narmada is a goddess. People come to Jalsindhi, the village opposite ours, from all over India to worship her, just to get a glimpse of her, the sacred and mighty Narmada. Our goddess Rani Kajal is right there, in front of Jalsindhi, where we worship the *Akhada*.[4] We pray to her and recite all her names sitting atop that Akhada. Even the Akhada is situated on the sacred sands of the Narmada. We adivasis have lived on her banks for as long as we can remember. We consider the Narmada our mother and ourselves her children. When the Sardar Sarovar Dam brought her waters into my house,[5] I offered a pooja to her. The Narmada, whose valley was so deep it used to take us three quarters of an hour to climb down and reach her waters, that river had come to my house. So I worshipped her. I have the same feeling towards her as I do for my mother. I cannot describe it, cannot put it in words. Today I live in Vadchhil. But whatever I saw then, I still see vividly before my eyes. It seems like a dream. But what could I do? The government has finally forced us to live our lives in this way. We struggled for twenty-two years to stay at that place. Not that the battle hasn't given us anything. Had we not struggled, we would not have got what we have now. But in the end, we had to do all this to save the river.

Nandini: The river water entered your house, submerged it, and yet you worshipped the Narmada?

Kevalsingh: Yes, I worshipped her. The water stayed in my house for eight days. My house was completely submerged, but I never let myself think that Narmada had drowned my house. I worshipped her. I offered her a coconut. And we stayed submerged in the water for eight days. Such is the

Narmada. Who can adequately describe her? It is very difficult to describe her.

Nandini: Water entered your house; you lost your house! Weren't you angry?

Kevalsingh: Earlier, we had to climb down a long way from our house, almost 100–150 metres from the mountain, to reach the Narmada. Now if the same Narmada has come to our doorstep, what else could we do but worship her? How could we be angry? Ultimately, was it Narmada's fault? No, the fault was ours. It was human powers that had forced her to act this way: she was obstructed, so she drowned the land. How can we fault her?

The Narmada is considered a goddess by the people. If a woman is without child she will go to the Narmada with an offering. There are thousands of examples of couples who got a child after an offering to the Narmada and those who have been granted the happiness and prosperity they asked for. Since we stay on her banks, we worship the Narmada every day. If we go fishing, we request her, 'O Narmada Mother, give us fish,' and offer her a coconut, an incense stick or *sindoor*. In the twelve months of the year, everyone performs at least one pooja for her. On Akshaya Tritiya most of the adivasis make it a point to worship the Narmada. Offering and breaking a coconut and taking a bath in the waters is also a form of worship.

The Akhada which is worshipped on the sands of the Narmada is a place for all—a collective place. If there are no rains that year or the monsoon is late, then people from surrounding villages come together with their *damroos*.[6] The whole night people sing the stories of all the adivasi gods and goddesses from Raja Phanta to Rani Kajal in the form of *gayanas*. The *Bodwa*,[7] the medicine man who collects herbs, sits in front of the people. People keep on singing gayanas until the Bodwa enters a trance. Then they ask the Bodwa questions: When will the rains come? And the Bodwa tells them, maybe in two days or maybe three days. In some years the questioning makes people run because it begins to rain right there and then! Such is the singing of gayanas. If the rains start and then stop after a month, or if the rains stop altogether, or the crop is in danger—in such situations, the Akhada may be worshipped every year. Only a knowledgeable person who knows the story of that particular village can sing the gayana. All the people sitting in front of him then follow his singing. In our village there was an elder named Sata Pisu. He used to sing them for a number of years. Pankya Karbhari also used to sing them. Nowadays some young people also sing the gayana. All through the night! They sing the whole night!

There is a lot of difference between the adivasi culture and other cultures. Whether it is the gods or the adivasi gayanas or how one worships. There is no temple in adivasi culture. They worship nature. If there is a tree and near the tree is a pile of stones, that stone *palya*[8] itself is worshipped by adivasis.

Adivasis also perform other forms of worship. If we have to eat the new grain that we have grown ourselves, then we have to worship the god Nilowanwa, and if it is a new vegetable or anything new procured from the forest, it is the god Nilpi who has to be worshipped. Worship of God Nilpi is nature worship. We worship rivers, streams, mountains. There is no idol of God in adivasi culture. Adivasis also worship their *khatri* or ancestors; it is only after offerings are made to them that we eat newly harvested grain or vegetables.

The gayanas too mention the names of many mountains, rivers, valleys and animals. Without the worship of Vagh Dev (tiger god) there can be no protection and safety for the village. The worship of animals, of calves and bullocks, is all nature worship. It is not as if there is an idol of a god in a particular place and we go there and worship that idol. The worship of Rani Kajal is worship of the rains. Nobody has seen Raja Phanta and Ganda Thakur. But they are the subject of many songs.

I had gone to Bawangaja where the statue of Kundurana stands. The entire area of Bawangaja identifies him as Kundurana.[9] Other communities worship it as the statue of Adinath. But it is not Adinath's statue. It is Kundurana's statue. And the temple above the statue is that of his father, Kumbhai. Kumbhai has been changed to Kumbhakarna. And Kundurana has been changed to Adinath. That is the way other communities have appropriated adivasi culture.

It is not that I do not love other communities. The Aryans came to our country from outside. Aryans committed aggression and overpowered the people who lived here even though the latter fought back. Those who joined the Aryans changed their religion and stayed with the Aryans. Those who opposed the Aryans went into the forests and into remote valleys and hills. They are the ones now called adivasis. The Stone Age people who used to worship nature were adivasis too. I spread this information among the people.

Because if we forget our history, the next generation will not know anything. We say we must not forget the history of the movement, but how can we forget our own traditions, the customs that have come to us from our forefathers? How will the new generation know all this? We have to protect it. The gayanas are not written anywhere. If we keep singing them just to preserve them, someone else will at least sing them. If no one sings them, the gayanas will be lost. If they are lost, the entire story of the adivasis is lost. If no one worships nature, who will love nature? That will also vanish.

The Bodwa may also be responsible for a lot of hocus pocus and mantra-tantra, but if he stops collecting herbs, who is going to do it? In the end, we will all have to go to the market and buy from others our own medicines made from our own herbs. So, to preserve this we have to talk to people and bring these things to their notice. That is why we need to tell them that we are the owners of this culture, we are fighting to preserve this culture. Yes, I do believe that we should do away with superstition. But not everything is superstition. There is some emotion at play too, isn't it? People sacrifice chickens to the Narmada. That too is a matter of emotion. But I go further and say, the chicken also is a life. Protect that life too. And if you want to eat it, why do it in the name of something else? Just go ahead and eat it.

If people do not understand what they are doing, it is our duty to tell them—that they are worshipping water and stones, and forests and tigers, and cows and goats—and also explain to them the significance of it. That these are all entities of nature. We worship nature. And in all this worship, isn't there the issue of the environment? This means simply that we love all of nature and the environment. That we adivasis are the true environmentalists. In Jalsindhi village we had organised a gayana. The Khedut Mazdoor Chetna Sangath (KMCS) people started singing gayanas in every village for two days and nights. Hundreds of people came for that. Similarly, at the time of satyagraha, we organised two to three Akhadas as well. All the people participated in them. Each village also has a *govan*, or cattle shed, which is worshipped when the gayana singing is on. The entire village comes together and the message automatically reaches other people.

Nandini: Can you tell us about your education?

Kevalsingh: Near our village, in Roshmal, an ashramshala was established in 1975. After two years, that is, in 1977, I went there to enrol myself. My friends used to attend that school, and when they went away, I too felt I must get educated. One day, I asked my father, 'Baba, I want to go to school.' My father took me to the school. The headmaster of that school said, 'Your son is above age and cannot be admitted in this school.' After eight days I visited the school on my own, and I tried to tell the teachers a number of times that I wanted to study, I wanted to learn. But it was of no use. I was very upset and came back home. I couldn't sleep. I used to tell my mother, 'Mother, do whatever you can, but please put me in some school somewhere. I want to learn.' But my poor mother, what could she have done? She had never even seen the inside of a school.

One day I thought, I will leave home and go away to wherever I can go to school. About that time, our Dagadu Maharaj[10] had finished one *parikrama* of the Narmada and embarked on his second one. I met him and told him that I wanted to learn and was willing to go anywhere and asked if he would help me? He took me to Baidali in Shahada Tehsil. There again, I could not get enrolled in the school. Then he told me that I will take you to Alandi. So after he finished his parikrama, he came and fetched me. I went with him to Alandi. There was no school nearby. The only school was in Dhadgaon, 25 kilometres away. In our village there were only two literate people, Keshavkaka and Murlidharkaka. They had also gone to school in Alandi. The very same teacher who taught them was now taking me to Alandi. At Alandi he put me in a dharmashala. There we had to ask for our food by going on rounds for madhukari, and attend school.

In Alandi they enrolled me in the second standard. The teacher was very strict. I did not speak Marathi.[11] Left alone in such a faraway place, I was very unhappy. All the people around me spoke pure Marathi. Not one of our kind of people could be seen anywhere. I stayed there for four consecutive years from first standard to the fourth. When I came back home after four years, I could not speak my own language. Living among all those Marathi speakers, I had forgotten my own language! By then those of my friends who were my age had already dropped out of school. However, I studied upto the tenth standard at Alandi.

When I was a child, my family was in very bad shape. From time to time, there used to be a drought. The fields yielded very little. To fill our stomachs, we used to go into the forest along with my father or mother. We would dig out roots and tubers, soak them overnight in water, steam them next morning and eat them. It was important for small children like us to graze the cattle and goats. At that time, we used to sell another forest produce called *kadai cheek*, the gum yielded by a shrub named *kadai*, which we extracted and sold in the market in Kavant, and with that money bought food grains and other stuff. My life has been full of hardship. But now this hybrid grain that has come has boosted farm productivity. Earlier there was only the tall jowar, which used to give a good crop only if there were good rains.

I always helped my parents. My main responsibility was grazing the cattle.

My mother is from Surung village and her name is Pawalibai. We got educated only because of her. In our village, ours is the only family where, except for one of my brothers, all of us are educated. All my brothers are younger than me. All of them have studied up to the twelfth and thirteenth standard. It is my mother who constantly urged us to go to school and created an atmosphere conducive to learning. My mother has also participated in the Andolan. In 1999–2000 when Domkhedi was submerged, my mother stood in the water alongside Medhatai for twenty-seven hours. Later, when people were arrested, she was in Dhule jail for fifteen days.[12] And just after her jail term was over and she came home, she died. At that time my youngest brother was not attending school. She had caught hold of him and was urging him to go to school. That same day she expired. Financially we were in such dire straits, I tell you! We could not continue our education because we had no money. In the end, whatever happiness, whatever love we wanted to give her, we could not give her in her lifetime. Today, all of us have built our own houses, have our own families and are leading lives in much better circumstances, but she is not there to enjoy and share that happiness.

Nandini: What was your daily routine like at Alandi?

Kevalsingh: The *Varkari* visiting Alandi and the children who come there to learn, all of them have to ask for madhukari. In his childhood, the saint Dnyaneshwar also used to beg for food when he was in Alandi. He was made an outcast by his community and by social miscreants. So Dnyaneshwar had to beg for his food. Finally, he took samadhi in the same place. That 700–800-year-old tradition of begging for food is still carried on.

School used to start at eleven in the morning. But before that, I used to collect my food from a few specific houses. It was a municipal school, so there was no other help it offered us. The slates, books and notebooks, down to our clothes—we had to buy everything from our own pocket. If you were late to school, once in a while you would get a beating.

Dagadu Maharaj put me in a dharmashala in Alandi and left. I was all alone. I could not even talk to anyone, could I? I couldn't manage the language they spoke. In school, there was this teacher with a long and thick moustache. His name was Bhosle. Oh my, was he strict! He used to call out, 'Vasave, get up.' And immediately I had to stand up. I was taller and older than the others, and he used to say, 'Such a grown-up boy, and you still can't read or write!' I had to suffer his abuse all the time. In this manner, a month passed. And I began to regret having gone there. 'Oh, dear! What a strange world they have put me in! I can't even speak to anyone. And I go to school only to get abused. Should I just go back home?' But even though I had these thoughts, somehow or the other, I started studying.

Some days, the teacher would tell me, 'Here, take this. Write it down and bring it to me tomorrow. If you don't, you will get a good thrashing.' And then all through the night, I would struggle to read the book and to write it down. At times, if I could not calm down, I used to go and bang my head on Dnyaneshwar's samadhi. I lived this kind of life for the first four years. Then I managed to become a better student than my classmates. From then, up to the tenth standard, I was as good as a big boss in class. The reason was Jadhav Sir, who taught us from the seventh standard onward. He was from Nashik. He was a communist. He said he had once met Medhatai in Aurangabad and told her, 'One of my students is from Nimgavhan. Have you met him?'

Medhatai asked, 'What is his name?'

He said, 'Kevalsingh.'

'Oh! He is an activist, my own activist,' she said.

Jadhav Sir is an adivasi. He is very close to Vaharu Sonavane,[13] who has been active in organisations like the Adivasi Ekta Parishad as well as the Shramik Sanghatana. Jadhav Sir and Vaharu Sonavane have been in continuous contact with each other. Jadhav Sir had taken me on his visits to all the adivasi regions from Nashik to Thane districts.

He used to tell people to abandon superstition, stop caste discrimination, come together and unite, because only if we united would we succeed in getting our demands fulfilled. He even knew Kaluram Dodhade;[14] such was his reach. Kaluram Dodhade is the main leader of the Bhoomi Sena. It was along with Jadhav Sir that I met Kaluram Dodhade for the first time.

We used to travel during vacations or holidays. On Sundays or festival holidays he used to take me along with him.

I knew Vaharu Sonavane from earlier times. When I told Jadhav Sir this, he said, 'Oh, my! Vaharu is a good friend of mine. Because of Vaharu Sonavane he became very close to me. I had read Vaharu's poems and his articles in the newspapers. Vaharu Sonavane was also an adivasi from Shahada Tehsil and so I felt I was very close to him too. I had also met him at Shahada. A protest morcha had been organised by Vaharu Sonavane and the Shramik Sanghatana in front of the tehsil office at Shahada. At that time, I had come home on vacation. I heard him speak at that morcha. After the programme was over, I went up to him and told him, 'I am from Nimgavhan. I stay at Alandi in such and such a place.'

Then on his own he told me, 'You know, one of my friends is also in Alandi. His name is Jadhav and he is a teacher. He is my friend.'

'Oh, he is my teacher. He teaches me,' I told Vaharu. On my return I related this to Jadhav Sir. After this introduction, Jadhav Sir used to take me along with him wherever he went. He never got married. I was with him from the seventh to the tenth standard. In fact, from the seventh onward, I stayed with him in his room. So from then on, I never had to go around for madhukari. All I had to do was cook meals for both of us, that's all!

Nandini: In those three years what influenced you most? You said Jadhav Sir was a communist. Did that influence you?

Kevalsingh: The main influence was the realisation that if we had to work and achieve anything, organisation was most important. To struggle for people's rights, the only way was to get organised. Later, when the organisation was formed here, I got an opportunity to do exactly that. Even while I was in school, I had seen morchas being taken out here in Shahada and in Thane district. I had also seen various kinds of appeals and demands being presented to the government. Even at that time, I could see that it would be no use working alone and that only if we all came together could we get something done.

I came to know Vaharu Sonavane at the time the Narmada Dharangrast Samiti (NDS) was formed. Earlier, in Akkalkuwa Tehsil there was this scandal at Bamani,[15] in which a number of young children had died due to gastro (gastroenteritis). At that time, Vaharu had gone there and collected the complete information of that incident. He wrote poems and articles on the Bamani scandal. From then on we became very close. Then in 1986–87, for the first time, the big Dhadgaon Magani Parishad (Dhadgaon Demand Conference) was organised. Vaharu gave a speech at the Parishad. He helped the NDS many times. He participated in our programmes and we in turn took part in the programmes of his organisation. These days he has changed his affiliation somewhat. He is with the Adivasi Ekta Parishad. For some time now, he is engaged in a different kind of work. Otherwise, he used to work along with us.

Nandini: Why could you not continue your education beyond the tenth standard?

Kevalsingh: I did want to continue my studies. The main constraint was financial. I also thought that given the community I belonged to, and the work I wanted to carry on, I had studied enough. I became a full-time activist of the NDS after my tenth standard, so my studies were abandoned. While I was in school, Vasudha Dhagamwar, a woman from Delhi, came to our village. She was asking the people, 'What will happen to you after the Sardar Sarovar is built? Will you accept rehabilitation?' In 1985, when Medhatai had not yet come, I had walked with Vasudhatai from my village up to Badwani,[16] and I saw for the first time the middle strip of land in Madhya Pradesh, running from Kharya Bhadal to Borkhedi and from Kakrana to Dharamrai—the region where only adivasis lived; they had absolutely no contact with any city. I was greatly affected by what I saw in that region and felt that I must serve these people. I had never before encountered such extreme backwardness. The rest of the region where we lived was not too bad. You would meet some educated people here and there from time to time, but there was nothing in that area. I was in the ninth standard then.

After I reached school, our teacher asked us to write an essay on 'What do you wish to do in your life?' I wrote about what I had seen and said that I wished to do something for my people. I got a prize for the essay. That visit influenced me greatly, and I began to feel strongly that I should go among the people in my area and serve them, awaken them. In the very same year Medhatai visited our village as she travelled from village to village in our area.

Nandini: Why had Vasudha Dhagamwar come to Nimgavhan, and why did you join her?

Kevalsingh: Vasudha Dhagamwar was walking from village to village from the Sardar Sarovar Dam site. She had come to make a study of how many villages and how many people were getting submerged by the dam. When she came to Nimgavhan there was no one to accompany her further. That is why she took me along with her to the other villages. When Vasudha Dhagamwar went from one village to the next, people got to know, for the first time, that a dam was being constructed and that we are going to be submerged by it.

Nandini: Till that time, no one knew? Not even you?

Kevalsingh: No, no. When I was young, we used to sing a song sitting on the swing:

Akkalkuwa dharan, Navagaon dharan, dharan bandhariyav,
Navagaon dharan, dharan bandhariyav, madaliyayi Jodi.

Akkalkuwa Dam, Navagaon Dam, the dam is being built,
Navagaon Dam, the dam is being built, sings the duo.

But where was this Navagaon? Where was that dam? We did not know anything. But we must have heard something from somewhere, that is why that song must have been created, naturally, on its own! 'Navagaon Dam, the dam is being built'—that just means somewhere there is a Navagaon and a dam is going to be built there. After that I wrote so many different songs. When the organisation was formed, this same song was expanded further.[17]

Nandini: So right from your childhood, you knew about the dam?

Kevalsingh: Yes, generally speaking, I knew about the dam. But it was not known in the entire adivasi belt on the banks of the Narmada, was it? Other people were not aware of it. Medhatai and Vasudha Dhagamwar had visited the area together. Maybe they knew each other. It was then that there was a feeling that something needed to be done for the people. Medhatai was working somewhere in Gujarat at that time. The name of her organisation was SETU, I think.

I had come back to Nimgavhan during my summer vacation when I was introduced to Vasudhatai. When Vasudhatai told us that she wanted to visit the adivasi villages in Madhya Pradesh and pressed me to accompany her, I went with her. In each village she would stay only with the important persons such as the patil or the karbhari or some representative. And then she would put the responsibility on that person: she would tell the patil that she wanted to discuss something and would ask him if he could get a few people of the village together for the discussion. The patil would call the other people in the village. Vasudhatai used to discuss everything fully. 'Are you aware of the Sardar Sarovar? Your village is going to get submerged.

Are you willing to accept rehabilitation or what? I have come here to collect all this information from you.'

In response to this, people used to laugh. They thought, this dam is going to be built so far away, why would the water reach so far? Our village is surely not going to be submerged, is it? So some people would just laugh and walk away. But other people began thinking: the government can hardly be trusted. Who knows, once the dam is built, maybe it will submerge us. And then they started to demand rehabilitation. 'If the village is going to be submerged, the government must give us land. If land is offered by the government, then we should accept it.'

We used to have such discussions in every village, and then we would go on to the next village. Borkhedi is the last village in the adivasi belt in Madhya Pradesh, and we went that far. Beyond that is the Nimad region.[18] There we crossed the Narmada. There is a village by the name of Dharamrai where you can catch a bus. We went there and took the bus to Badwani. We slept in a lodge. In the morning Vasudhatai put me on a Dhadgaon-bound bus and left for Dhule. That was my first meeting with her.

After her, Medhatai used to visit every village to collect information. Earlier, we had a lot of trouble with the forest department people. Because if they happened to catch someone with wood, it was trouble for the entire village—they would extort money or beat up people or ask for chicken or liquor. So Tai told us, in detail, how to fight the forestwalas. Many a time she herself managed to catch the forestwalas red-handed. Tai went to the extent of telling us to completely stop paying them any kind of money or fine or whatever else we used to pay them. She would stay in a village, get introduced to the people so that she could understand what was happening in their homes, what the situation in the village was, who was doing what in the village, what kind of development work had or had not taken place, and so on. From roads to schools and dispensaries—all the issues were discussed. And when, in these discussions, the issue of getting organised would come up, we would talk about how we must unite if we wanted to achieve all the things we had discussed. In every village, we would be there along with Medhatai.

After reaching out to all thirty-three villages of Maharashtra, a small committee was formed. It was named the *Karbhar Samiti* (executive committee). Four or five people from every *pada* of a village were chosen to be part of it. When all these people had been chosen, the first meeting of the executive committee took place at Nimgavhan. I was there at that meeting. After we discussed all the issues from the dam to the forestwalas, the issue that remained was: what name should we give our organisation. It was unanimously decided it would be called 'Narmada Dharangrast Samiti'. It would carry out whatever its subcommittee—the executive committee—would decide. If that committee said, take out a morcha, everyone would work towards taking out a morcha. The demands of the morcha would be decided by the executive committee. All decisions would be the responsibility of this committee, including decisions about the future action and programmes of the organisation. It was decided that on certain days of the month, full moon night or new moon night, a committee meeting would be held because, even if all the people could not come together very often, some selected people could meet once a month. In that meeting all the information about the villages that were part of the organisation would be collected.

Nandini: Please tell us about the work you did in NBA in the beginning.

Kevalsingh: I think, it was around May 1985 that Medhatai had come, and that was our first contact with her. At that time, we used to feel: this girl from Mumbai, how will she be able to stay in our hills? She was young—at that time her hair was not yet grey—but she was giving us good guidance. That is why we joined her. I travelled to Badwani the second time along with Tai. At that time, no one from Badwani participated in our programmes. We used to sit near the Rajghat temple. Two to four representatives used to join us, and we would have a discussion with them for the whole day and then return to Maharashtra.

Tai asked me which region I would select for my work. I selected the eleven villages from Kharya Bhadal to Borkhedi and Dharamrai to Kakrana. No one from the organisation had reached that part of the valley till then. The language of these people was different than mine, so I took KMCS activist Khemla[19] along with me and we visited each village, surveyed the people, talked to and discussed issues with them, played and laughed with them and created a kind of intimate bond with them. I explained to the people how to build an organisation and that if we wanted to get anything, we would have to come together. Khemla came with me on two of my visits, and then I started working on my own.

After the formation of the NDS in Maharashtra, the activists were allotted different areas for their work. Akkalkuwa region was to be the responsibility of Arundhati[20] and Himanshu.[21] Medhatai had taken up the responsibility of Akrani herself. Thinking about how to expand the work in Madhya Pradesh, I was given the responsibility of ten or eleven villages and was sent to get information from Kharya Bhadal, Kutbandhani, Korai, Kooli, Ghongasa, Borkhedi, Dharamrai and Kakrana. When I first visited those villages, no one in the village was bothered about the dam. These villages were given to me because I had visited them with Vasudhatai and had some knowledge about them. To develop some sort of bond with the people, I used to run and pick up toddlers with running noses. Or if I saw a woman at work, I would talk to her. Or if I saw an old man, I would go, sit with him and talk to him. I would ask, what crop have you sown? How much did it yield, etc.? After he became interested, I would tell him, 'Oh, we are all headed for a big loss. A dam is going to be built on the river. Are you aware that this dam will submerge our village, submerge our houses?' After giving him all this information, I would ask, 'What is to be done? If we want rehabilitation, we will have to fight for it. We will have to get organised. That means we must come together, unite. If there are any action programmes, we need to participate in these programmes.'

I like singing. Have always liked it! So, to bring people out, I would sing. Immediately, girls and young men would gather around me. In this way, I used to attract the people in the villages I visited.

First it was one village, and then, one by one more and more villages came in contact with us and our interaction increased. Then we told them we would have to form a samiti the way the NDS had been formed in Maharashtra. And so, in 1988, the Narmada Ghati Navnirman Samiti (NGNS) was formed in Madhya Pradesh.[22] And this entire adivasi region came together under this committee.

Nandini: Was there any organisation working with the adivasis in the submergence zone?

Kevalsingh: There was the KMCS in Alirajpur region in Madhya Pradesh. But it was restricted only to the Alirajpur Tehsil. Khemla and Shankar Tadval[23] were their two main activists. By then Medhatai had found out that a lot of the area in Madhya Pradesh was not listed in the submergence zone.[24] Since I had visited the area earlier, I was asked to go there, so I went, and ended up building an organisation!

Nandini: How did you manage to do all this? Where did you stay, how did you work?

Kevalsingh: First, I had no fixed place to stay. Suppose I was to visit a village on the opposite bank, say Kakrana, which is a big village. Unlike Vasudhatai I could hardly go to the patil's house and tell him to go get some people, could I? Instead, I visited every house—I talked to the people there. Then in the course of my talk I would tell them, 'Why don't you come there? We can talk, sing, dance, play.' In this way I brought people together. Secondly, whatever difficulties I faced I used to face on my first visit. When I came the second time, if I said, 'Come to our meeting', people used to come on their own.

Or they would come simply because they had heard that this person had come to their village.

But, while building the organisation, I observed that there was a divide. Whether it was a Maharashtra village or a Madhya Pradesh village, since the patils and the karbharis were government people, there was a divide between them and the rest of the village. The rest of the village would readily join the organisation. However, the patil and village head and those close to them or working under them used to be in two minds whether to join or not. And in the end, it was the patils and the village heads who broke the organisation, didn't they!

I stayed in these ten–twelve villages for one and a half years. In the beginning I took help from Khemla and Manglya.[25] Both of them could speak the language of the people in the villages. Later I also learnt their language. Also, it turned out that a number of Khemla's relatives stayed in the area. Khemla is from Umrali.[26] Umrali and Kakrana are adjacent villages, and so, many people recognised him. It is also possible that people had seen Khemla in some of the KMCS programmes and rallies. During those days, KMCS used to hold very large rallies. Khemla was very useful to me. Khemla's organisation was much older than the NDS. Rahul and Amit were its founders. Khemla was there as an activist right from the beginning, and so he had a lot of experience with organisation building. He knew how to speak to people and what actions to take, and that was very useful to me in the villages. I learnt from him, and I started working in the other villages based on that experience.

Manglya became a very close friend. He stayed with me like a full-timer. His wife used to say to him, 'You move around with him all the time; who will look after the house?' But Manglya did not listen to her. He learnt a lot moving around with me. He can now read and write. Today he speaks in front of thousands of people. He has become a full-fledged activist, hasn't he?

Later on, I felt the need for another activist to visit the area and so I told Medhatai, 'Tai, I will organise a meeting over here, and you should personally attend it.' The meeting was held in the village of Dharamrai. People from all the villages gathered there. The meeting continued all day. But that day we could not get lunch over there. The people of the village belonged to the Naik tribe. They felt that we would not eat food prepared by them, and so they did not offer us any food! Next day as it was a big market day in Dahi,[27] we organised a public meeting. I gave my first public speech at the meeting. I did not know their language, but I spoke for more than ten minutes. Tai gave all the information about the action programme and the dam. In this way, these eleven Madhya Pradesh villages were included in the government list of affected villages. Otherwise, these villages were not recognised as part of the submergence zone.

After working for almost one and a half years in this area, I worked for a year in seven to eight villages of Maharashtra, from Bhadal to Bhusha. But I had Manglya with me. Because Manglya was of my age, he loved going around with me. Manglya had only one condition—I should teach him to write the way I did. I used to write down the alphabet wherever we found a stone surface. I would write his name too. We would use whatever surface we found on our travels to write something. And he would ask me all the time, 'What is this? Tell me what that is.' Within a year Manglya could read an entire book on his own. Manglya was my first student! After a year of working in this area, Arundhati Dhuru requested me to join her because she was the lone activist in the Akkalkuwa region. So, I took up work in Akkalkuwa.

In the beginning, the NDS demanded answers to many questions from the government. Are we going to get land in exchange for our submerged land? Are we going to be rehabilitated? If so, where? So right after the organisation was formed, we decided to have a conference in Dhadgaon. An executive committee meeting was held prior to this conference where we worked out our charter of demands. Since Dhadgaon was the tehsil headquarters, we also decided on how many people should gather there to show our strength. We chalked out what slogans we would use, how to shout the slogans, how to speak at the meeting and how we would maintain discipline. We taught people everything, from shouting slogans to singing songs. This was necessary because the people hardly knew what slogans were meant for. And if we were going to gather in such a large number, we should at least be able to shout our slogans properly. From Maharashtra, Medhatai, Arundhati, myself, Keshavbhau, Jahangir Pawra and Dnyaneshwar Patil, who were all part of the executive samiti anyway, were there, and from each village about four or five persons would also be present. These were people who the others listened to and followed. Once the decisions were taken, it was the responsibility of the concerned activists to implement them and take them to the people.

I will give you an example. Medhatai had written a song in Marathi, 'The Dam has come, The Dam has come!' But to translate it into Pawri, she took our help. The song became very popular because it put forward our demands to the government and also challenged it. That song represented everything that was to happen, didn't it! The entire village would be assembled for a meeting, and then we would sing it, and everyone would sing it after us. People were unaware of slogans, for example, 'Fulfil Our Demand Or Vacate Your Office'. They cannot speak Marathi. So we were the ones who had to do it the first time, isn't it! Otherwise people would have laughed at us.

In the beginning I wrote a lot of songs. As time passed and the struggle progressed, songs kept being written! What those songs were, even I will not be able to recall now! My songs became very popular. When there was a meeting being held at Rajpipla, and we took out a big rally to the dam site, I had written a song, '*Gunthanikhasli, teri ran***odai...*' It became so popular at that rally, you won't believe it! About 6,000–7,000 people from all over Maharashtra had gathered there, and all of them sang that song. It became such a hit even the police would laugh out loud listening to them! At Ferkuva there was another one. In every struggle we had one such new song. Amit's songs were also very popular and became famous. He wrote, '*Bandhe Bandhe...*' And later '*Jago re Bhila, jago Bhilala...*'

Later on, there was '*Zindabad Karevo...*' This song was created inside the jail in the year 1999 when they had rounded up all of us and had jailed us in Dhule. We sang '*Zindabad Karevo...*' all night! Kailash,[28] four or five others and I wrote that song. This song became so popular in jail that Dhule Jail felt like a cinema hall. All the prisoners used to come and watch us. 'Are you in jail or are you just having fun?' is what they used to say.

'*Navagaon Dharan Bandhiriyva...*' is a song that goes straight to your heart. It is in Bhilori and so Pawri speakers can't handle it well. Still the song became very popular in the Akkalkuwa area. I cannot recall it now; it is not my habit to write down things, so that song was never written down.

The songs I had written till now,[29] the songs I wrote for the Jeevan Shala—all these songs had become very popular. The children of this school have performed these plays and have sung these songs and have won prizes every year. I write my own plays. I stage them along with the children. We had organised eight *Bal Melawa*s (children's fairs) for the Narmada Jeevan Shala. In five of those fairs, children from this school won first prizes for singing and performing plays. And all those plays and songs were written by me.

Nandini: Please tell us more about the organisational processes and action programmes of the early days.

Kevalsingh: The first public programme took place in Dhadgaon. People came from their villages from a variety of directions, and all of Dhadgaon reverberated with their slogans. Some slogans from this side, some other slogans from that side—people converged on Dhadgaon from all sides, and oh my, such an atmosphere it created! It must have been the first time that Dhadgaon town had seen such a huge gathering of people. No one had taken out as much as a morcha before this. We were about 6,000–7,000 people, and an equal number of people had come to see this gathering. We presented our thirty-six demands to the government. They ranged from rehabilitation to essential services. These same demands were then communicated to the tehsil, district, state and central levels of the government. And finally, the central government declared that we would not get any forestland. It was at this time in August 1988 that a three-day shibir (workshop) was held in the Dhadgaon school. I participated in that shibir. For three days, the representatives of three states[30] and the activists sat together and discussed with full seriousness what was to be done. Whatever we were asking for was being denied, we were told.

So, in that shibir we decided that come what may, we would oppose Sardar Sarovar. In August 1988 when this resolution was passed, the three states of Maharashtra, Gujarat and Madhya Pradesh had three different committees. It was decided, in this shibir, that instead of having three different committees we would have a single organisation. That was how the Narmada Bachao Andolan came into being and the dam itself began to be opposed.

Nandini: Three days! So much thinking and discussion?

Kevalsingh: Tremendous! There were 150 to 200 people. It was a time that demanded very serious thinking, didn't it? Discussions had been held everywhere; at Kevadia discussions had been held with the Narmada Control Authority (NCA). They yielded nothing. In Maharashtra discussions had been held with officials as well as ministers. No solution had emerged. Nothing had happened in Bhopal and Madhya Pradesh too. The Gujarat government was not even prepared to listen. Nor the central government. So, what was to be done? Could the construction of the dam be stopped? How to stop aid from the World Bank? At that time, we thought that if financial aid stopped, construction would automatically stop. There was serious discussion about whether it was possible to do all these things. In the end we felt that the only alternative was to oppose the dam. We would get something only if we opposed the dam, otherwise we would get nothing. That was the stark realisation in the shibir and so we decided to oppose the dam.

After that, we wondered: what was this animal called the law? People knew nothing about the law. What are our rights in this independent country? This was discussed many times. Lotan Sangana Pawra, the sarpanch for the last thirty years was opposing us all the time. Ours is a remote area and our people should therefore not be allowed to become literate—these were the kind of unjust ideas he kept thrusting on us. We felt that at a minimum, the gram panchayat needed to pass a resolution reiterating the demands raised by the NDS. To pass that resolution, we had to have our own sarpanch. So, after this discussion we decided that our members should fight the coming panchayat election. In the group gram panchayat there were ten villages which were in the submergence zone, and from those ten villages we could have easily elected eight or nine of our people.

But the problem was that many people were not even enrolled as voters. So, first we started enrolling the voters. We invited the officers and gramsevaks and completed the voters list. We also saw to it that everyone had their house tax receipts because to be a candidate for election, your name had to be in the list of those who paid house tax and had names in the voters list. We managed to fill the forms for thirteen of our candidates for the election.

In each village, there were many people who had never voted. They did not know how to vote. We had allotted the responsibility of specific villages to specific people to see that people were not left out of the voting. I was given the responsibility of villages from Bharad to Keli, Thuvani, Atthi, Selagada and Pimpalchop, because my name had become well known in those villages. I prepared dummy ballot papers and went from hamlet to hamlet, organising meetings of the prospective voters in each hamlet. And we had to explain to them that this was our symbol and this was how you put a cross against our symbol. That is why we won a majority of the votes. It is likely that if people had not understood the process, we might not have got elected.

After eight of our candidates got elected, when it was time to elect the sarpanch, we were attending a shibir in Dhule. We returned to Roshmal to participate in the election of the sarpanch. But our opponents had brought together a lot of people by bribing them. And all those people were armed. All the officers had been bribed too. The police sided with our opponents. We were unaware of all these happenings when we reached Roshmal unannounced.[31]

The officers asked us, 'Where are your people? The time for election is running out.'

'How would we know? They were supposed to be there in time.' Milind Murugkar[32] is a learned person who knows his way around. But even he was not allowed to speak. We said, 'Okay, if it is getting late, we will just go out and see what the matter is.' When we went a little ahead, we found a battle raging in the Khad River, and the four of us were captured.

They said, 'Now that we got hold of them, we will not leave without killing them.' These were people who had always opposed us, and they continued their dire threats. Perhaps they would really have killed us.

Dongarsingh Jodha was also there. He got scared. He knew that our organisation was very strong, and if I was killed, there would be strong retaliation. So, Dongarsingh managed to take us to the foothills by stealth. But everywhere we found people searching for us. We hid ourselves in the thick forest of a valley. It was also raining. There were a lot of mosquitoes. We were now hiding in a deep gorge. I was telling the others, 'You hide over here; I will run away. They will not be able to find me.'

But they said, 'No, no. We all should stay together.'

We sat there till midnight. Where were all the people? They must have returned home. The only sound was that of dogs barking. So we decided to leave the valley. It was a dark night.

Meanwhile, in our village, the people from the ten villages had gathered. They had plans to celebrate our victory at leisure after getting our sarpanch elected. They would play the drums, dance, eat and drink and make merry. That was what they wanted. But right at that time, we had been caught by our opponents and it became a matter of major concern. No one had eaten since then. A woman from Roshmal had married into our village. They sent her to find out about us. No one gave her any information. She began to have her doubts and thought that they must surely have killed us because it was clear the Roshmal people were lying.

She returned home and told everyone that no one had given her any information. So, it was likely that they had killed us. Everybody became even more worried. They decided to go to Roshmal and take revenge. All of them had taken up weapons and were marching to Roshmal when at about one in the morning we met them on the road. We shouted, 'We have reached safely, do not go anywhere.' Everyone came running to us, and we narrated the whole story to them.

Messages that the other two with us, Ajit and Jahangir, had been killed in the battle of electing the Roshmal sarpanch had reached the respective villages of Bilgaon and Savaria. The people in these villages were also very angry, and they had marched to Dhadgaon taking a different route. After seeing we were safe, they joined us, and together we climbed the mountain and reached Dhadgaon. It was four in the evening. The shopkeepers of Dhadgaon closed their shops. Within five minutes Dhadgaon town fell silent. The staff at the police station was scared.

We registered a case at the police station and filed an application with the tehsildar. We went to Dhule and narrated the incident to the collector. We managed to win the case in the courts. After this, the election of the sarpanch took place in peaceful manner. Murlidharbhau became sarpanch. This, in a way, can be called a victory of the Andolan. From that time onward, those people who used to have only bad words for us and who used to say, 'These people? They are brainless idiots' as well as the local political leaders—all of them fell silent.

Nandini: How was it decided that you will work in the Akkalkuwa region? What were your responsibilities?

Kevalsingh: The decision was taken by Arundhati. She said, 'I cannot handle all the work by myself. I need an activist to work with me.' I worked for five years in the Akkalkuwa region. Arundhati and I worked together for four years.[33] We had to face all kinds of trouble because the people from the Tadvi clan in Akkalkuwa get scared somewhat easily. One reason for it is that they could see the height of Sardar Sarovar increasing every day in front of their eyes.[34] They were of the opinion that they should accept rehabilitation at any cost and had decided to break away from the Andolan. We had to work very hard to convince them to stay with us.

The Dhadgaon 'Demands Conference' of 1987 where 6,000–7,000 people from Maharashtra gathered at one place for the first time and in a way questioned the government, was a big programme, and it raised issues of all kinds, from schools to dispensaries to complete rehabilitation. Baba Adhav was the chief guest at the programme. After that conference, the responsibilities of the Andolan increased manifold. Whether it was a demand for work in the village, or health issues or a matter of writing applications and letters, we were involved in it all. In the beginning we conducted surveys of village after village in Akkalkuwa. How many families are there in the village? How many of the families have been declared as project affected? How many of them hold land? How many are not included, etc. This survey was necessary because even the government did not have the actual numbers of people who would be affected. Nor did we. It was essential to put forth the actual number while putting forward our demands, and so we carried out a survey in all the thirty-three villages of Maharashtra. It took us one year. We had to do a lot of surveys. From time to time, again and again.

There are heaps and heaps of those papers. A few of them lying at the Vadodara office were burnt and thrown away.[35] Back then we could not get educated people to do the survey. We activists had to do everything. We had to travel on foot. There was no boat, no train, no roads. I used to walk from Bhadal to Manibeli in a day—that is, 80 kilometres! The first large rally held in Rajpipla had 11,000 people, from

Maharashtra and Madhya Pradesh put together. At that time, I travelled from Bhadal to Manibeli in one day. When there was submergence, we had to survey from Dandiya to Kambli to Kamthi (house poles, pillars in different shapes and sizes used for foundation, roofs, etc. in traditional houses of wood and clay). We had to keep a record of everything, writing it all down.[36] Heaps and heaps of paper!

Look, suppose, Kesubhai's house is going to get submerged. Then, how much wood does it have and how many poles? How many chickens does he have? How many goats, cows and bullocks? All this information, collected through surveys will be lying there somewhere today. Some people like Milind[37] from Pune used to come and go, helping us with the records as there were no literate people locally available. Now there is a list of everything. We had to work one and a half years for the Maharashtra Task Force. We filled in people's information in detail. An activist like Shobha[38] had to give one and half years of her life to conduct this survey. Just for one such task!

When we decide to take up a big programme, we need to do so much preparation and planning, I tell you; it is horrendous! I will give you an example of Harsud. We had to put in huge efforts to take people out from the eight villages in Akkalkuwa. Our people were going out of their own area for the first time. The people had seen only the towns of Dhadgaon, Kavant and Akkalkuwa and nothing beyond that! They were travelling by train for the first time, and so we were totally responsible for them! If someone got lost, or some mishap happened to anyone—it was a big responsibility, I tell you! In our later rallies and programmes two to four people went missing. We have not been able to find them. The work activists have to do is full of risk.[39]

The new activists who joined later are unaware of all of this. Who asks us, what work did you do? No one asks us! Today Nandinitai is asking for this information for the first time. Otherwise, till today no one has asked us anything. Who got beaten up and how much? How many were in jail, how many times and how long? Are those people living or dead? Nobody is concerned today. How much work has Noorji or

Jatarbhai put in? No one is bothered. Only Medhatai knows all this, but all she does is cry for some time and walk away.

The people because of whom this Andolan arose, who helped to make its voice heard all over the world—are these people alive or dead? That's the least we can try to find out. But even that is not happening. Many a time if a person like me thinks of writing about it, they feel, 'Let it go. Who is going to read it?' But if its history is written down, future generations will benefit from it. Because every battle is lost before it is won. People may feel that we have lost, but we haven't. I keep saying this all the time! The dam has been completed, so be it. But we carried out our responsibility and fulfilled our duty. We did it till our death. And if the organisation is standing today and the Andolan is continuing—this could only have happened because people have remained with it and sustained the struggle. Otherwise, there would be nothing, not even a sign of the Andolan would be left behind.

The biggest programme we had undertaken was the Harsud rally held in 1989. All the activists from Maharashtra worked very hard for this rally. It was the first time we undertook such a long journey by bus and train. We had discussions for hours to plan and organise people's participation. We planned for it almost two or three months in advance. There were many activists at that time; there was Arundhati, Mahesh,[40] Keshavkaka, Medhatai and myself. We had to do all the work, right from visiting the villages. I had even gone outside the area we lived in and worked to canvass for the rally. I had travelled to Jawhar and Palghar in Thane district and to Pune district too to contact different organisations and invite them to the rally. We felt, if so many people come together, our victory would be assured, and so I went about trying to get support for it.

The Bhoomi Sena and the Kashtakari Sanghatan were invited, and it was my responsibility to invite them. For Madhya Pradesh and Gujarat, other activists had taken the responsibility of invitations. Ishwarbhai[41] and others had taken the responsibility of Gujarat. And for Madhya Pradesh, Silvytai[42] took the responsibility. More than 10,000 people from Maharashtra attended the Harsud rally. We went from Dhadgaon to Dondaiche in twenty-eight big trucks. Then from there we travelled to Bhusawal in not one, but three train loads! We changed trains at Bhusawal. From Bhusawal, we boarded the train going to Khandwa and reached Harsud. All the people with us were first-time travellers. From Dondaiche to Harsud we went by passenger trains, and it took us twelve hours to reach Harsud. At every change of train each of us took care of their own people. From time to time, we went around asking each main person of the village, 'Are all the people of your village on board? Check. Has anyone been left behind?' Whenever the train stopped at a station, we would go running around making sure everyone was safe.

We were prepared to spend eight days away from home. People had got *shira* made with roasted jaggery and maize *rawa*. The porters at the railway stations helped us a lot. They helped people board the train and if required, stopped the train till they had done so. At Bhusawal railway station, many of the staff helped us too. Even today, the porters help us during our programmes. They give us breakfast and tea as well.

We stayed in Harsud almost for two days. The people liked the meals served at the rally very much because they were provided free of cost to people from the adivasi areas.

(Here, Kevalsingh explains that to reach Harsud in Madhya Pradesh from their villages in Maharashtra, the journey first began on foot for them.) It takes five to six hours to reach Molgi from Manibeli. Distances to other villages are similar. Molgi village is far from the banks of the Narmada—about 30 kilometres away. Some people took five hours to walk to Molgi. Some took six hours. In Akrani Tehsil it took the same time for people to reach Dhadgaon. There is no bus or jeep, and so people had to walk all the way to Dhadgaon.

The programme gave us lot of courage. People carried a bit of soil from their own farms and that soil was made into a symbol of the battle in Harsud. People from all over India had got soil from their lands. A kind of statue was built from that soil. People saw that the soil of our country is the same all over. Everyone should preserve their land and soil. For the first time people saw a gathering 50,000–60,000 strong, and it affected everyone. So many people! Oh, my! Also, everyone enjoyed it there. They had a lot of fun. People danced a lot as if they were at a marriage. They had carried their own drums. They danced as if it was a Holi or Diwali celebration. And they gained tremendous courage! They felt that they were not alone. There were so many people with them. Later, on their return to their respective villages, people fought many different kinds of battles.

A trainful of people came from Thane district also. All the fisherfolk had come. They are also fighting for their land. Mumbai is the nearest city for them. Industry is growing there. The big heroes and heroines (of the film industry) are planning to buy up the land of these adivasi people. In addition, the government is planning to sell adivasi land to big contractors and builders. These people are struggling against all this. Their struggle is the same as ours.

Nandini: So this Harsud rally was not undertaken only for the Narmada?

Kevalsingh: No, in this rally, a new people's slogan was coined. 'We Want Development And Not Destruction'. We will allow projects only for development. But if they lead to destruction, they will be opposed by all.

At the village level there are always small programmes going on. From conducting meetings and carrying out surveys to writing letters and applications of various kinds related to people's demands. After Harsud there was the programme at Khalghat,[43] Baba Amte's programme. The plan to block the road for thirty-six hours was a challenge to the Madhya Pradesh government. Patwa was the CM. He made all kinds of promises but it was of no use.[44] The programme was very important. Many people from Maharashtra had gone to participate in it. After that, we decided to take out a Sangharsh Yatra to the dam site in Gujarat, but it was stopped at the border of Gujarat by the government. But we had worked very hard for that programme too. The activists had to organise a people's *fala,* a contribution to meet those expenses.

When we decided to undertake the march, the financial situation of the Andolan was bad. We had one or two months to organise the programme. It was important to enrol members into the organisation. One rupee per month, so twelve rupees a year was the membership fee. We printed the receipts for this. The activists and some others took up the task of going to each and every house and collecting membership fees. We also called on everyone to join the Sangharsh Yatra. At that time the young boys and girls in Akkalkuwa had built a strong organisation under my leadership. Hundreds of young people came for the Yatra. It started from Manibeli and went from village to village with the people singing, playing the drums, dancing and singing songs all night at every village we stayed for the night until we reached Domkhedi. From Domkhedi the Yatra went to Jalsindhi and Mathwad, then onwards to Umrali and Alirajpur.

There was such enthusiasm in the Yatra. Tremendous! The atmosphere was charged and because I was young, many young people got drawn to it. Whatever you want to say, say it without hesitation; that was what I told them. I used to organise meetings for them too. The youth must come forward; not only young men but young women too. In the people's Sangharsh Yatra there were more women than men, and this needs to be specially mentioned. If you watch that film again on TV or cassette, you can see this for yourself.[45] It was in the Yatra that for the first time women participated in such large numbers.

Nandini: What was the reason that so many young people got attracted?

Kevalsingh: Song is the main reason. I used to invite young people and tell them, 'Today we are going to dance; come with your drums.' And then when the young people came with their instruments and the singing would start, everyone would gather there. Then we would have a little discussion about the meeting. That is why they got drawn in, didn't they? It could be movement songs, marriage songs, romantic songs, sorrowful songs—it could be any kind of songs! It was through drums, dance and songs that we managed to reach out and propagate awareness of the movement. And dancing meant that all the young boys and girls would come. This is how the young people got organised.

Once the organisation decided that a programme would be taken up, we would have a lengthy discussion about it and agree that we must attend that programme. It would involve a long journey that would probably take many days. In such a situation, we would ask the old people to stay behind and let the youth come forward to join the action. When we had the programme at Ferkuva, it was winter and it was very cold. You can't imagine how cold it was. But people stayed on for thirty-six days.

At that time, I was the only activist from Manibeli because even Arundhati was not able to walk that much. People from the adivasi region of all the three states gathered at Jalsindhi. On the very same day! How beautifully it must have been planned! That night all the people gathered together and danced through the night. There was so much enthusiasm in that programme. It was just tremendous!

From Jalsindhi we went directly to Umrali. Umrali was almost 25 kilometres away. The first night's stay was in Umrali. The 3,000 people from Maharashtra had walked all that distance. The second night was at Alirajpur. The third night I do not remember the name of the village where we stayed, and the fourth was at Ferkuva.

So, this is about the thirty-six-day Ferkuva Sangharsh Yatra.

At the Gujarat border the government had mobilised thousands of police. The group under Baba Amte's leadership crossed the border and went ahead (but this group too was stopped just as they crossed the border and was not allowed to go any further both by the police and the people of Gujarat brought in by the GoG to block the road. Attempts continued to be made to enter Gujarat by different teams, but the large police force deployed on the Gujarat border thwarted each attempt by arresting the NBA people). But the rest of the people were stopped at the border. We sat there in expectation that they would allow us to go ahead. We tried to cross the border one group after another group with tied hands. Many activists were beaten up. Then there was a lathicharge. I think Silvytai was one of the persons who got beaten up. After that there was a fast. Medhatai fasted for twenty-two days and was joined by the others right there on the border. The battle went on for thirty-six days in the severe cold—right in front of the huge police force, but the people did not waver. In the end, we decided that no government person would be allowed to enter our villages. People returned to their villages with a resolve to implement 'Our Village, Our Rule!' With that battle, people became even stronger.

Since they had not allowed us to enter Gujarat, we decided we would organise a programme in one of the villages in Gujarat itself (this programme was organised by the NBA once the people returned to the valley from the Gujarat border at Ferkuva). So, we organised a programme in front of the Hapeshwar Mandir in Gujarat (Hapeshwar village and the temple are both in the submergence zone of SSP located in Gujarat on the opposite bank of the submergence villages in Maharashtra), and all night long we danced to the beat of the drums as if it was Diwali and showed the Gujarat government that we had won. And it is there that people resolved that they would not leave the Narmada, would not leave their villages.

Nandini: You were in Ferkuva for thirty-six days. What were your main responsibilities?

Kevalsingh: Compering and coordination, organising programmes all day round, in between singing songs and shouting slogans and welcoming and looking after invited guests. Sometimes people like Nirmalbhai from Chikhalda[46] would share the work of calling the guests on stage while I was compering. But most of the time it was Bhadra[47] and I who were on the mike system for the thirty days. Meanwhile, from time to time we also joined the groups trying to enter Gujarat and got beaten up. We were arrested and taken to Dahod.

Nandini: Why is it that the mike and compering was entrusted to you and Bhadra?

Kevalsingh: That I wouldn't be able to say, but I am reasonably good at compering and coordinating, and Bhadra is a good singer. Most of the time Bhadra and I would sing the songs. When conducting a meeting, I can speak a bit of Hindi, and I can speak Gujarati too, and because there are so many adivasis it is necessary to speak the adivasi languages and also translate. That is why the mike has become my life for the last twenty years. In every programme I was the one who used to compere and conduct the programme. Whether it was in Madhya Pradesh or in Maharashtra.

People from the Nimad region helped us a lot. All the people used to be inside one huge tent; thousands could sleep and stay inside it. They took care of the food, from cereals to pulses. All our eating and drinking! After all, it was part of our battle. We used to say, if we left, it would look like we had accepted defeat. On one side were the people who were on a fast, and on the other, there were the police and the people from Gujarat. They would have made fun of us saying, we ran away, wouldn't they? Therefore, we sat there with lot of determination, and that is why we won such a big victory. It was our victory that the World Bank appointed the Morse Committee and decided to withdraw from the Sardar Sarovar Project.

There were problems too because there is so much to be done on the farm; in the house too. But our resolve and sense of the struggle gave us the strength to come away from our homes. People did that and that is why this struggle has continued for twenty-two years. Even now people are not tired and are still fighting courageously.

Nandini: When you first started working in Akkalkuwa, what was the situation there like?

Kevalsingh: In the beginning, the organisation was very strong in that area. Till 1990 all the villages were united. The Vasavas and Tadvis were different but as a village they were united. But after 1990, the government managed to wean away people like the Patils and Karbharis. They were bribed with huge amounts. Those corrupt people then split away and they in turn took away even more people with them. In the beginning, there were only these four or five villages—Chimalkhedi, Manibeli, Danel, and Sinduri. In Sinduri, Narayanbhai was a good person. Very religious too. But he split away very early and managed to take the Tadvi families with him. Later on Danel's karbhari, who was a government servant, took some people away. Then in Bamani, the kamdar was a government servant too and he managed to take with him the families around him. In Chimalkehdi, Ambalal was very good. But he split away around this time, and in Manibeli, Ukhadbhai managed to take some people with him. Gill who was the rehabilitation collector—he was responsible for splitting up all these villages. But the people who stayed behind were very strong people. They explained to the government, that we were not opposing the people who were leaving. Our opposition was only to ensure that the government allowed them to lead a happy life. The government should give them all that is due to them. As for us, we would not leave the village. We may get submerged, but we would oppose the dam. It was with this determination that people stayed till the end.

I stayed in the Akkalkuwa region for four to five years from 1989 to 1994. I would stay the night in whichever house I used to be in. I ate whatever they ate. I felt that I belonged. And the people in the houses where I stayed felt I was like another of their sons and a part of the house. I should tell you about one particular incident that happened to me in 1991. (Some) Tadvi families were opting for rehabilitation at that time, and we were trying to tell them to wait and that we should all get rehabilitated together. We should fight on, at least for some more time. We had to oppose the dam. Some Tadvi families did not agree with me and they began to think that they were not getting rehabilitation because of our opposition.

One day Nava from Bamani and I were returning to Sinduri from a meeting in Chimalkhedi. On our way five or six young men armed with knives and other weapons confronted us. Nava got scared and ran away, leaving me alone. They surrounded me, abused me and asked me, 'Why are you opposing the dam? We are losing out because of you.' They brandished their knives and weapons at me.

I told them, 'Why would we oppose you? If you wish to accept rehabilitation, go ahead. We are not forcing you to stay on. You can always go. I am not scared of getting killed. If you have the courage, take me to your village, and kill me in front of everyone. You will kill me on the sly and make some poor fellow the scapegoat and get him arrested. That will not do.'

I left the men and reached their homes. I waited for them, but they did not come. But the women from their families were good. They talked to me in Gujarati and smiled and laughed. I did not tell them that their men had attacked me. They served me tea.

I walked on to Sinduri. On the way, I met people from Mukhadi and Danel. They said, 'Nava told us that they might have killed you and that is why we have come.'

I said, 'Nothing has happened to me. Such incidents do happen sometimes. I feel they happen because of the government's instigation.'

In 1988 some 11,000 people had managed to take over the dam site. They managed to stop the construction for one to one and a half hours. They were arrested and taken to Rajpipla. Some people were also lathicharged. The police brought government vehicles and buses, picked up people and scattered them.[48] For the first time, people got beaten up, and they realised, 'So we may also get beaten up in such programmes.' But then people started fighting back in the villages, unafraid of the government. In this way, each programme took us ahead step by step. People started saying, 'If you beat us up when we come there, then we will not allow you to enter our villages.'

Soon after, the officers working on the dam were not allowed to enter the villages. Then the government tried to send other types of employees, like teachers, doctors, etc., and through them, tried to break the people's unity.

The activists had to be ever vigilant. The officers used to take thumb impressions of people on blank paper. People wondered why there was nothing written on the paper. Later the officers used to write on the blank paper that the people who had signed were willing to accept rehabilitation and pointed to the thumb impressions. Activists visited every house in every village and gathered this information. Then in 1991 when the satyagraha started, people said that they were getting fooled because they were illiterate and that they must at least learn to sign.

During the satyagraha, the literate people started teaching the representatives how to read and write, starting with how to sign. With us were Bhagwanbhai[49] of Nimad, Kamalatai,[50] Mahesh who had worked for four to five years and was a full-time activist in Maharashtra and other activists. We used to sit and discuss issues all day, and in the night, we would teach. Some representatives used to say, 'Whatever we have learnt is over and done with, but now let our children learn.' But that meant we had to have schools for our children. So, in 1991 the executive committee passed a resolution and the *Jeevan Shala* was started. We never felt the school programme would expand so much. We just thought our children should learn something, and so on 6 August 1992 we started the Jeevan Shalas.

For five years I worked in Akkalkuwa tehsil. Many times, I confronted the police. I was underground, remained hidden and still fought. We fought the way Shivaji fought, using guerrilla tactics. We opposed the breaking apart of villages and the cutting down of forests. When the forest was being cut down in the submergence zone, we brought school children together and fought it Chipko Andolan style.[51] We did not allow the Manibeli forest to be cut. It is submerged, but it is still there.

I was kept very busy by many different programmes. Visiting Delhi, going to Mumbai, taking people with me for one and half months, coming back and organising meetings in the villages, finding out what the situation was in each of the villages, which officer visited which village, who signed on the blank paper—all this was going on. After 1991 there was an ongoing struggle in that area—the break-up of Manibeli, the bulldozers and the many people who were getting beaten up for opposing their use![52]

In Manibeli the whole village had become a police camp.[53] Kesubhai Tadvi's house was dismantled.[54] At that time, half of the people of the village had gone with Baba Amte to Delhi. Many activists were in jail. Mahesh and I were the only two left in Manibeli.

The day Kesubhai's house was to be demolished we were around but we were underground. Had we been spotted, we would have been arrested. We were hiding in village Kaker in Gujarat, opposite Manibeli. They had completely encircled Kesubhai's house. There was no way we could enter it. The patrolling was very strict. Nevertheless, we managed to send Kunta[55] inside. She stayed there the whole night. Then we managed to send Guman who was physically challenged.[56] He entered the house but the police were totally unaware of him. Then Pratibha and Sanjay, the students, went in. 'Go and oppose them,' we told the students. Kunta fought with the police all alone. In the end, they arrested her. Then they broke the house down and carried it away. Later on, Medhatai started a fast in Mumbai.

'You broke the house against everyone's wishes. You must rethink everything. Rethink the dam.' Those were the demands.

When pressure was brought on the government, it had to agree to reconstruct Kesubhai's house and restore it. At that time, there was a meeting held at Monga Patil's house at Dhankhedi between Collector Gill and the engineers of Sardar Sarovar. I was hiding there. The collector had asked the engineers, 'If we have to bring back and rebuild Kesubhai's house, how can we do it?' The engineers had an easy answer to that, 'What is there to build in an adivasi house? Put up two poles here, and put some wood over it there. That's all there is to it.'

When Kesubhai's home was rebuilt, I was right there. They called in sixty labourers from Gujarat. It took them three days just to dig the pit. Then they started erecting the poles. One pole would turn out to be longer than the other. They were unable to erect the poles. Four to five days passed. I used to sit there every day and watch. I did not utter a single word. In the end, those labourers could not manage anything. There was an engineer named Chaudhari. I knew him well. He said to me, 'Kevalsinghbhau, the labourers are unable to build this house. Please try and help.'

I told him, 'You people are building this huge Sardar Sarovar dam; how is it possible that you are not able to build a simple house with two poles? You told the collector that all it takes to build an adivasi's hut is two poles. I was there at that time in Monga Patil's house! Why did you say that to the collector? And why are you now searching for a senior engineer to help you out?'

'No, no. These labourers are unable to build it. We are only engineers who make the drawings. We don't build the things that we draw.'

I said, 'Okay, how much will you pay me?'

We called Vitthalbhai.[57] 'They are asking us to build this house. How much should we ask for?'

Vitthalbhai said, 'Seven thousand.'

The engineer said, 'No, no. Not that much.'

We said, 'Give us 5,000 rupees.'

They had already dug the pits. We constructed the house within half a day.

This was the same engineer who had worked out the levels of the Narmada in 1993 and had told us that Kesubhai's house would not be submerged. And right then I had told him, 'Chaudhari Sahib, your calculation is wrong; this house is going to be submerged.'

He said to me, 'How do you know? Are you an engineer?'

I said, 'We have been living in this area for so many years. Who knows how much the water rises, we or you?'

'No, no. You have no brains,' he had said.

Kesubhai's house that was rebuilt—it got washed away that same year! Such are these engineers and officers; we had to fight with each one of them. When I was carrying out a survey of our village—a levelling survey—we looked at the base levels for each of the houses and found that all the levels were wrong.

I told them, 'Keep your maps aside. Throw away your binoculars. I will tell you the level of this house in metres.'

He got angry and said, 'Okay, tell me, tell me what level it is at.'

I said, 'This Jeevan Shala is at 108 metres. Do you want to measure it? Go ahead, measure it.'

They measured it and it was actually at 108 metres.

At that time, they were saying that the school would not be submerged. I said, 'Sahib, your calculations are all wrong. The height of the dam is 95 metres and you are saying that the school at 108 metres will not be submerged? The backwater will rise up to 117 metres. Even if it rises to 110, the school is bound to be submerged. I will give this in writing.' But they did not listen. That year all the houses were submerged.

The study that engineers carry out can only be done by the village people. The big city colleges will not provide you that learning. Which meteorologist can tell you how much rainfall there would be in a year? Our people will tell you by looking at the constellations. And what kind of engineers are these? They just study whatever is written in the books. The one who puts in labour, the one who has the experience of living in this region for years together, he is the one who knows what is going to happen here.[58]

Each and every story is important. I gave you just a small example from Manibeli, that of Kesubhai's house. Of all the adivasi areas, the biggest and most serious struggles have taken place in Akkalkuwa. After that, when Rehmal was shot and became a martyr, from 1994 the struggle spread to Akrani. But before 1994, police camps had been set up in each village of Akkalkuwa. Activists moved about hiding from the police because they had bound the people by enforcing IPC 144. But even in such adverse conditions people managed to communicate messages to the right places. This was done by the boatmen Rama and Movarya.[59] And even small children. 'Go, take this note to that place,' we would tell them.

When the *Jalsamarpan* was to take place in Manibeli, the village was full of police. All our grain was stored in Jatarbhai's house. It was raining heavily. Even in that rain, some 600 of us were hiding in the forest. On the day of the Jalsamarpan, the police came to know that we were hiding. People managed to enter the caves of tigers to hide, brushing even the tiger aside! What the police were doing, where people were hiding, what was to be done next—we used to pass on every little bit of information to the outside world. Whether it was night or day, whether the streams were full or not, we managed to do it, and that is why this Andolan was sustained. It was sustained not only by people here but by the support from organisations and individuals all over the country.

But (many among) the Tadvi community did not stay with us. They accepted rehabilitation. That too, incomplete rehabilitation! The Andolan thought they should get the full rights given to them by the Award.[60] But the Tadvi did not think about it, and later on, they really landed in huge trouble. Two to three years after they had accepted rehabilitation, they came back to us and said, 'We were wrong. Pardon us. Help us to get our rights.' We took them back with us and fought for them too.

In 1991, the first house to get submerged was that of Bhulabhai (in village Vadgam, Gujarat).[61] Land in Maharashtra would also be submerged; that is why it was decided to make Manibeli the centre of the satyagraha. The satyagrahas started with the first one held in Manibeli in 1991. Then the Gujarat government took up the campaign of *Manibeli Hatao*.[62] At that time, we had to struggle on many fronts. Arundhati and I along with representatives from each village gathered at Manibeli in a show of solidarity to strengthen the resolve of the Manibeli people.

In 1991, the Maharashtra government sent bulldozers to demolish Manibeli. We had to take all kinds of action including lying in front of the bulldozers. We were beaten up very badly at that time. My waist was badly hurt, and even today I cannot sit properly. Arundhati Dhuru was also very badly beaten. Rama and four or five other people were horribly beaten. They demolished some houses in Manibeli only through police repression. But there are nearly forty-five families that have not left and are still living in Manibeli without rehabilitation. Their houses have been submerged two or three times. First, the whole village was submerged. So they built their houses further up on the hillside, but even those houses were submerged. Now they don't even have a proper place to build their new houses, yet they continue to stay on in Manibeli.

Despite many warnings, the government kept raising the height of the dam. The lower gate was plugged. Finally, the water rose to levels that submerged the village. Submerging people's lands and houses without rehabilitating them was blatantly unjust. So we went on satyagraha with the slogan, 'Neither We Nor Our Houses Shall Be Moved. *Doobenge, Par Hatenge Nahi* (We Will Drown, But We Will Not Move).'

When they tried to displace Manibeli, I was arrested and put in Rajpipla jail. There were forty-odd people with me. They released us the next day. Then they slapped a number of cases on me. The 1993 case is still going on. There is still a warrant out for me. I am said to be 'absconding'. I keep visiting the police station, but the very same police will come to me the next day and tell me, 'You are absconding. Please appear in Court.' There are cases against Kailash, Mahesh, Vitthalbhai, Kunta, and me; the police have charged us with an attempt to murder them. There is no judgement given in the case as yet. In short, such cases abound! When the Domkhedi satyagraha was going on in Akrani, I was put in Dhule jail for eight days the first time, fourteen days the second and six days the third time.

When Rehmal died in the Chichkhedi firing, we had gone to Dhule in protest. We organised a rally in Dhule and the police lathicharged the thousands of participants. Almost 180 people were injured. We were all arrested and were in jail for fourteen days. At the time of the satyagraha, the police would arrest us, take us to Dhadgaon and release us. Later, when Section 144 had been declared in Dhadgaon, we held a *mashal*[63] rally in the night during the Ganpati festival. The police said we had broken the law so they brought a criminal charge against us. Then too, we were in jail for fourteen days. The third time, when a road was being built with bulldozers in Domkhedi, we lay down in front of the bulldozers. At that time, we were sent to jail for six days. I was also jailed in Madhya Pradesh, for a day in Badwani and for another day in Bhopal. The government kept putting us in jail, saying we violated this or that section of the law.

There were so many cases against us. The worry was, if we were caught, who would be there in the villages? The first time I was underground for a month when Kesubhai's house was being demolished. The second time, when Jalsamarpan was announced, I was underground for ten days in pouring rain, hiding in the hills.

Underground meant we stayed out of sight of the police. Anyway, people's houses were at quite a distance from each other. We could go and eat at anyone's house or they would send us food. But during the Jalsamarpan, things were very difficult. From taking food to 600 people in the pouring rain, to making sleeping arrangements for them, we had to look after everything. We had built many small huts for this purpose. All the food was in the custody of the police. However, some people would manage to get some food grains out quietly. The children would then bring them to us, avoiding the police by stealth, and we would cook it while it was raining and eat!

We were 600 people in the forests of Manibeli. There was huge police presence! There must have been 3,000–4,000 of them. The highest-ranking police officer in all of Maharashtra had also gone there. And helicopters flew overhead to search for people and their hiding places. In the forest, we cut small poles of wood, built small huts, covered them with teak leaves and made them into makeshift sleeping places. We stayed for ten days in this manner. The activists staying there were,

Mahesh, Rehmat,[64] Sukhdev[65] and Chogalal[66] from Nimad. And there was Shashank.[67] That's it! Finally, on the day of the Jalsamarpan, we held a rally. There were police battalions after police battalions! They had placed battalions wherever people could go. We pushed them aside, one by one, and reached the river. Just then, we got the message: our demands had been met. Do not perform Jalsamarpan. Had the message come five minutes later, we would all have jumped into the river.[68] We came that close. The police couldn't have held us back.

Nandini: Were you really prepared to sacrifice your lives?

Kevalsingh: Yes, we certainly were! This Mehersingh from Genda, he was about to jump into the river. The rest of us had been stopped by the police, but he had managed to reach the river. Then we shouted to him, 'Come back, the message has reached us.' Even then the police were very scared. They took the people to each of their villages by boat and dropped them off.

Those who had declared Jalsamarpan were not too many. Medhatai, Arundhati, Devrambhai and Sitaram Kaka—there must have been six or seven people. But had it actually taken place; thousands would have jumped into the river from every village. Such was the atmosphere at that time!

Nandini: You named those in the Jalsamarpan batch, but why was there no one from the adivasi areas, those which were the first to be submerged, who pledged Jalsamarpan?

Kevalsingh: The adivasis were there, but it was just that their names had not been declared. If that batch had really performed Jalsamarpan, thousands would have jumped into the river, right in front of everyone's eyes. It was surely not a matter of adivasis being scared or that they were not willing. At that time in Manibeli some 4,000 of us were hiding in the forest. I was leading them. When the day for Jalsamarpan came, we broke up into small batches and ran towards the river. Some were stopped by the police; some reached the river. Had we not received the message, 'our demands have been met, don't do anything now', I am sure the people would have done something drastic. It happened right in front of my eyes.

Our demand for review had been accepted. A committee was established to review the dam. After all these incidents, the committee began its work.

Nandini: Could you talk about the submergence in Manibeli?

Kevalsingh: It was in 1993. We were all fast asleep. The night of 16 August, I can never forget. That night the water rose fast! It rose so very fast that people could not even leave their houses and got waterlocked in their own homes! Then the police came and forcibly evacuated everyone. Such a horrific submergence it was! Kesubhai's house was washed away, right in front of our eyes. Milind, Mahesh and I, we were there.

The police had to pull everyone out of their houses. The current was so strong, it washed away everything. Almost the entire hamlet of Manibeli and Wamipada—completely washed away. Yes, that was in 1993. How can I ever forget? I had seen it with my own eyes.[69]

Such was the horrendous submergence of 1993.[70] Twenty-two houses were simply washed away in Bharad, and thirty to forty in Pimpalchop. From Mukhadi onward, eight villages were washed away.[71] After a *panchnama*, some compensation was paid.

The police had built a shed and the people were shifted into it. Since it was night time, there could have been a loss of lives. We stayed in the temple near Narayanbhai's house because 'Narmadaai'[72] house had already been washed away. The next year we stayed in a house at a higher level. But after this, every year it would be flooded! As the dam was built higher and higher, more and more houses were flooded.

In 1994 there was a fast in Bhopal around two issues—asking for the dam to be stopped and the findings of the Review Committee to be made public. Around the same time, a case had been filed in the Supreme Court. The fast went on for about twenty-seven days. I too fasted for sixteen or seventeen days. I had taken the place of Luharya.[73] Chief Minister Digvijay Singh[74] himself came and visited the fast, and I broke my fast (NBA withdrew the fast as its demand was met). Digvijay Singh gave a speech and said that he would remember the young man (me) all his life. I had fallen so ill that even the CM was concerned. After that twenty-seven-day fast, the report was made public, and the Supreme Court stayed the dam construction. The stay on dam construction was to continue for six years.

Nandini: You fasted for seventeen days! What was it like?

Kevalsingh: Luharya was fasting on behalf of the adivasi region. He was taken to hospital because he fell ill. So, I asked everyone from the adivasi areas if there was anyone who would take his place. No one was ready to do so. Medhatai opposed my fast on the grounds of my ill health. She said, 'Do not fast.'

But I said, 'Fast I will!' Then on the seventeenth day of the fast our demands were met.

I had lost blood, I had lost my appetite, and I used to feel dizzy. I had lost 11 kg when they forcibly took me to hospital. They couldn't find my pulse. They had to call in a specialist doctor from Mumbai to find it. Only after that could they start me on saline to force-feed me. They used all kinds of machines to force-feed us because we refused food. It was because of the Bhopal fast that the dam construction was stayed for six years. Thus, the Andolan was fought, step by step. I feel that at no step were we defeated. If finally the Supreme Court allowed the dam construction in its judgement, that really is a defeat for the Supreme Court, and for the government. It is because the government did not give due respect to the Supreme Court. Ultimately, the government is violating the Supreme Court orders. Because the Supreme Court had said, the dam construction should be in step with rehabilitation. Today even though rehabilitation is incomplete the government has filed a false affidavit saying that it is completed, and obtained permission to raise the dam height.

So, this is how the struggle has gone on for 22 years. During this time, I went on a fast only once. Rama Atya, Kelabhai, Mathurbhai, Luharya, Himmatsingh and Dakhalsingh from the adivasi area were on fast in Mumbai. Himmatsingh Sildar Pawra from Mal village and Dakhalsingh Jangalya Pawra from Genda village had fasted for eleven days. Rama Atya fasted twice—in the very beginning, with Arundhati Dhuru in Mumbai and then in Ferkuva. Ranjit from Domkhedi had fasted for eight days along with Medhabehen in the Domkhedi satyagraha. Khajyabhai Pawra was from Sawaria Digar; a very simple and straightforward person, he fasted for 22 days in Ferkuva. He is no more.

In 1992 when we started the Manibeli satyagraha, it was also the time when we began the Jeevan Shalas. At Vadgam in Gujarat, on 15 August, we had the first Jeevan Shala flag hoisting. After that the Vadgam people were arrested.[75] Their houses were forcibly demolished. Then, when they saw that the water levels were rising, the police arrested all the satyagrahis. After this, the police demolished Narmadaai, which housed the office of the satyagraha.

At that time, I was underground in Manibeli. Many people were arrested, including teachers and even students of the Jeevan Shala. They were kept in Dhule jail for a number of days. At that time, Manibeli was the main centre of the Andolan, and the government kept a close eye on it. Manibeli was the first village to be submerged in Maharashtra. Houses were being demolished in the presence of thousands of police. People from Akrani to Nimad came to the satyagraha to oppose these acts. However, when Medhatai was present, the police refrained from action.

I travelled with Medhatai to the villages above Chimalkhedi. We saw that the police had badly beaten up Arundhatitai and Rama. They could barely stand, it was that bad. People who had witnessed it told us in detail what had happened. We were very angry. We kept firing questions at the police officers: Why did you do this? But the officers are police people too. What answer would they give? A few policemen had chased some girls for quite a distance. They even molested two girls from Selakda. When we tried to find out who the perpetrators were, we realised that the chief police officer was one of them. We filed a case against him, but we do not know whether any action was taken against him.

Gujarat police were no different from their Maharashtra counterparts. They raped 'Durgaben' from village 'A' in Gujarat. She could not bear it and committed suicide by jumping into the river.[76] All the local women, young and old and even children had to struggle against such circumstances. They had to stand up and fight against these attacks on their dignity.

In 1994 after the fast at Bhopal, the Supreme Court directed that construction which submerged people should be stopped. That brought some relief and peace to the Andolan. In this period of peace, the Andolan conducted shibirs for young people on how to take up development activity, such as how to improve farming, how to stop topsoil erosion with bunds and a number of similar issues. Though work on the dam had been suspended, the satyagraha continued. Because though the Supreme Court had prohibited further work, whatever construction had already taken place continued to submerge the villages. That is why the struggle against the water, and the strategy of Jalsamarpan continued from 1994 to 1999.

In 1993 there was the issue of the villages of Akrani. The Andolan had raised the question: did the government know the number of people who would be submerged? The administration was caught napping. So, the officers accompanied by the police tried to enter the villages forcibly or on the pretext of conducting surveys. All this happened in 1993.

Nimgavhan and Domkhedi had become the main villages of the Andolan. The government realised that these were the villages they needed to break first. To put pressure on the people, the GoM planned a systematic programme—they sent thousands of police along with government officers and their survey equipment into the villages.

At that time the Latur earthquake occurred.[77] I stayed in Latur for eight days to help people there. When I returned from Latur, I came to know that the government was making preparations, and the police were being trained for the past eight days in Dhadgaon. There would be a separate contingent of officers for each village, and each would be accompanied by 250 police personnel equipped with guns. When we came to hear of this, the people of four villages—Domkhedi, Surung, Nimgavhan and Bharad—came together, saw that the road to these four villages had to pass through Chichkhedi and decided to block that road.

We had already warned the collector that they would have to put us all in jail if they tried to enter our villages. I myself wrote those applications for all the villages and handed them over to whosoever was collector at that time. Our supporters from Dhule, Dr Choudhary, Tatyaji and others were there. Because of this warning, there were even more police in the contingent which was coming to our village. From the children to the elderly, all of us gathered unarmed on the roads and began to block them from morning to evening. Using our mike, we warned the police, 'Do not come forward. We will not allow you to enter the village. We may die here, but we will not budge.'

But in spite of our warnings, the police came anyway. The people managed to block those thousands of police at the boundary of the village. There was a bit of a fight. The police tried to use force and intimidation, but people did not budge. When the police realised that the people were not going to move, they started firing. To start with they shot in the air. When they saw that people were still not willing to move, they began firing at people. They fired forty-eight rounds, and in the end, one policeman directly targeted Rehmal and fired at him. In that skirmish, Rehmal became the first martyr of the Andolan. Milind Kothawade was with us, and so was Mahesh. Medhatai had gone out somewhere. But as soon as she got the message, she came and joined us.

We witnessed that most difficult struggle with our own eyes. We went to Dhadgaon for Rehmal's postmortem. After we had performed his last rites, we took a protest march to Dhule to ask why, when the people were unarmed and resisting peacefully, did the police fire? When we gathered in Dhule to seek answers, Collector Kunte straightaway ordered a lathicharge. Within five minutes the 1,000–1,100 people vanished without a trace. It was such a fierce lathicharge that State Transport bus drivers jumped out of their running buses. We saw this with our own eyes. It must have been the most brutal lathicharge ever on the Andolan. About 180 people were injured. The rest could hardly find a way out of the scuffle. With great difficulty, we managed to regroup with about 300 to 350 people. We conducted a programme at the same place, and we were arrested and sent to jail for fourteen days. This was the biggest struggle in Akrani.

Perhaps one can say that the 1993 struggle at Akrani was the biggest struggle in the history of the Andolan. We know that horses and horse riders (mounted police) were mobilised against the Andolan. We also know that at Anjanwada[78] police targeted people and there was firing. But Chichkhedi was a most shameful act of firing. And then the lathicharge in Dhule! Even today, if you watch the CD by Seema Dhuru[79] that captures it, you will get goose flesh. Many people had head injuries, many had fractured hands, feet and legs.

Nandini: Your marriage had been arranged, and on the day of your marriage, your fiancé was in jail with Arundhati didi!

Kevalsingh: After those four years in Akkalkuwa, I got married. My wife's name is Vaharibai. Yes, she was in jail the day we were to marry. After she was released, a new date for the marriage was fixed! And in 1991, the month when Arundhatitai was beaten up badly was the month we got married. My wife and I stayed in Manibeli for two years and managed the satyagraha there. There was one house of the Andolan in Bamani too. We also managed that for a year.

I used to go out for a meeting or some other work. But my wife, with the help of a girl in the village, used to take care of the Andolan home. I will give you a small example.

All the people from Manibeli were in jail. There were so many police at Manibeli! During that period my wife managed the satyagraha. We used to be in hiding. At that time, the police brought some labourers from Gujarat and began to forcibly cut down the forest. The police watched over them from a distance. I climbed down and walked up to the labourers on the hill and told them, 'Brothers, your struggle and our struggle are the same. We have fought very hard to retain this forest and these trees. Think twice before you cut these trees. If you do not want to listen to me, I will call the people here. Then it is between you and them.' And all the labourers just ran away!

The police asked, 'Where are you going?'

'We are leaving. Why are you involving us in a matter of life and death? We adivasis are brothers,' said the labourers, and they left.

Then twenty to twenty-five policemen came and arrested me. It was May, and in the hot afternoon sun, they encircled me. 'Why did you send the labourers back?'

'Don't you know why we are fighting? Why are you forcibly cutting down these trees? We are opposing the dam; do you think we will allow you to cut the trees?'

'If you want to talk about this, talk to our superiors.' I talked with their superior on the phone. He was staying at the Shoolpaneshwar Camp.[80] They kept me surrounded until he arrived.

I asked them, 'Can you please give me water? You have immobilised me. The river is nearby. Please get me some water to drink.'

The police said, 'We can't. What will we bring it in? We don't have a container.'

'Get it however you want. I am in your hands. I want water, and it is your duty to give me water. If you can't, then come with me to the river.'

'Go, go. Drink your water, but come back soon.'

I left. I drank the water and right away jumped into the river and swam straight towards Gujarat! After reaching shore I said, 'Bye, bye! Tata!' and off I went. Vaharibai, my wife, saw them (the police) and thought they must have taken me to jail.

In the night, I would visit my wife in secret and leave. 'Do not be scared. I am fine,' I told her. In this way I managed to save the forest. But that forest is submerged today.

Nandini: After marriage you remained busy with the struggle. Didn't your wife have problems with that?

Kevalsingh: No, her friends were also part of the struggle. The two girls who were molested in Manibeli were her friends. They were from her village. All the girls from Selakda had joined the struggle, you know! The one you see in this photograph (points to a photograph at the interview spot) is a woman from Selakda. Hers was a militant village. All the girls from her *mohrya* (parents' village) were fighters. Why would she be scared? She was part of the fight from the beginning. Whether it was Manibeli, Pimpalchop or Domkhedi, she has participated in all the satyagrahas and big programmes.

In the rainy season people used to stay in the office. So when the rains began, we could not leave the house just like that. The people would keep their belongings there, and we used to take care of them. Whenever visitors came, we would serve them food.

Kevalsingh's wife Vaharibai talks about her work: When there is a meeting, the women do not come together very easily, I can tell you! I would go from house to house, not once or twice but many times and call them, 'Come, come.' If we have to go for a satyagraha, it was necessary to put away the work one was doing. I would say, 'Come for the meeting. These are outsiders; how can they come every day for us?' Some woman may even abuse you, but one has to be patient and not lose one's temper. Finally, one has to think, it is our own work. Outsiders come because we are going to be submerged; they come for us. In this way, by explaining it to them, I used to get them together and conduct the meetings.

Kevalsingh: Fifty per cent and more of the strength in the Andolan was that of women. In the beginning, there were very few women, but later on, they came out in large numbers. And they fought! There were many young girls from Danel village. It is difficult to remember their names now. In Akrani, women from the villages of Selakda, Keli, Thuvani, Atthi, Nimgavhan and Domkhedi were at the forefront—of being beaten up and also fighting with the police.

Nevalibai of Atthi village and Pinjaribai of Mal village, both of them were women's leaders. In our village, Murlidhar kaka's wife Tarabai was the main leader of the women. There were some women from Selakda too. Whenever there was a programme, they would get the women of their villages to come and participate. They used to tell the women, 'We have to fight this battle, and so we must go and take part.' They would put forward their views before the men too. Pinjaribai was even part of the Jalsamarpan group. Dedlibai was beaten up very badly and she was in jail a number of times. The Domkhedi satyagraha was very well carried out by the women. Khiyali from Domkhedi played a large part in the Andolan. Pinjaribai, Nevalibai and Dedlibai were in the executive committee too.

When the Chichkhedi firing took place, there were more women than men, I tell you. That is why the police were forced to stop and fall back from the village boundary. Thousands of police were there, but they were not allowed to enter the village.

One does not know from where people got that kind of energy and strength! People were shouting without restraint, 'Kill us, kill us! If you want to kill us, kill us!' There was a large number of policewomen too. Also, CID officers. They said, 'Your women are no match for ours. Look at our women, one policewoman can easily tackle two or three of your women.' That made our women so angry, I tell you! They just gave a slap on the hand and the policewomen ran away. There was a bit of a physical tussle. After all, the people were very angry. The police were at a lower height, and the people were on the hills. If they wanted, the people could have pelted them with small stones or even rolled down large boulders on them, and the police would have been crushed. People might have been thinking that way, but the activists reached there in time and spoke to the people. Milind and I said, 'Don't do anything now; let bygones be bygones.' So, the people turned back. If people had not listened to us, that would have been the end of the Andolan. It would have become aggressive and violent. They would have said we had become Naxalites, wouldn't they?

Nandini: There were many programmes held in Delhi, Mumbai and Bhopal. Was it difficult for people to camp there? What did your work involve?

Kevalsingh: As an activist, I had to shoulder the responsibility of taking many people from the Narmada Valley to cities like Mumbai. We had to see to so many things like making sure that other travellers did not trouble our people. Huge cities like Mumbai are full of people and vehicles. In that chaos, we had to walk properly, maintain lines, stop the vehicles when people wanted to cross, and other such things. On top of it, our people disliked going into the brick-and-mortar toilets. The number of our people was also not small. Thousand, two thousand at one time. Where do we send them to relieve themselves? How to make those arrangements without dirtying anyone else's habitations? We had to see to all that. From time to time, prominent people would want to have discussions with our people. They would speak Marathi, Hindi or English. English, I do not know, but when people spoke in Marathi and Hindi, I was the one who would always have to translate it into Pawri and Bhili. Yet in spite of working responsibly for the last twenty years, there are three people of the Andolan who went missing and have not been found so far. They should be declared martyrs of the Andolan.

A boy from Domkhedi was going to Delhi from Vadodara and got off at some station and did not manage to get back on to the train. He has been missing since then. Another was from Dehbramal. The third one, a woman, also from a village outside the submergence zone went missing during the 2006 programme in Delhi. We circulated her photograph, put it on Doordarshan too, but she has still not been found.[81]

In big cities like Mumbai and Delhi we used to stay, sleep, eat and drink wherever the programme would take place. In Mumbai, groups that sympathised with us used to organise food for the people. As for shelter, people used to stay on the roads. Many a time there were problems. There would be no water, not for a bath, nor to go relieve oneself. It used to be very difficult for the people. All these programmes were a success only because people endured all these difficulties.

You take people who are used to airy, open spaces and put them into congested, crowded places like Mumbai, and they are very likely to fall ill. Also, the people were seeing the city for the first time, and so they went a little mad too! To take them safely back to their villages was a job of great responsibility. Anyway, it was good they did not stay mad after leaving the city. By the time they reached their homes, they were back to their earlier selves.

We also met with people from various organisations. We gave them the complete information on the issues we were fighting, and told them that the struggles they were involved in were no different from ours. So, why didn't we unite and fight, or support each other? Each activist has brought people into the Andolan. I conducted two or three programmes in Pune where the Andolan has a support group. They organise programmes in Pune too. I gave short speeches during the programmes, which motivated people greatly. I used to tell them straight—come, visit the valley and see for yourself. Even if today the government is claiming that rehabilitation is complete and the dam is about to be completed, there are still thousands of people who have been displaced and who have not been rehabilitated. How can we simply abandon such people?

We used to call for financial support for the Andolan. It could be in the form of grain, clothes or actually coming to the valley and working for the Andolan. People helped us then, financially or in whatever way they could.

After the Supreme Court judgement, prominent people from all over India like Arundhati Roy,[82] well-known judges, artists, our lawyers—all came together in Delhi. And once again we had to explain to everyone what the situation was like in the Narmada Valley.

People from the valley attended a programme of the oustees of the Enron power project. There was a lathicharge. People were arrested and put in Yeravada jail for eight days.

We also attended the programmes held by organisations working with adivasis in Thane district and had discussions with them. Gosikhurd is a big dam in Maharashtra where the people sorely needed support, which we gave them. Their movement had been inspired by the struggles of the Narmada Valley. So our people and activists have gone wherever people's struggles are taking place in the country.

I have gone to the programmes at Bargi Dam. The participation of our people strengthened the Bargi struggle.[83] If they had not gone and visited the people of the Bargi struggle and supported them with information, the struggle would have gone nowhere. People like Rajkumarbhai[84] came here (to the struggle area against the Sardar Sarovar Dam), gained experience and then went back to Bargi and built the movement there. People who were with me like Ranya Dahya and Noorjibhai went as far as Kolkata. They took up the slogan '*Desh Banao, Desh Bachao!*' (Build the Country, Save the Country).

At the Domkhedi satyagraha,[85] the main strategy of the satyagraha was to gather together all the representatives of the Andolan and deal with the rising waters. We used to do lot of *nirman* (construction work) and conduct shibirs while the satyagraha was going on. The people who came with the Kerala group worked and built a small powerhouse at Domkhedi.[86] If we stay at one place and build a satyagraha centre there, people all over the world can come to know that a programme is going on in that place. All the reporters and supporters can come there. From morning to evening we can work, contribute labour, conduct meetings and perform street plays. We can send people in batches to various villages to carry out a survey, gather information and conduct meetings of the village people.

My main responsibility was to coordinate the programmes, conduct meetings, prepare and send people in batches for the satyagraha.

In the work of nirman, the study of herbs and roots was my responsibility. I have created a number of medicines. I used to train the people who attended the shibirs in how to use herbs and roots, how to prepare medicines, which illness can be cured by which medicine, etc. We used to prepare tooth powder from a tree called the Beheda. Tablets made from its fruit can be used for stomach ache. Now the entire area from where we used to get the herbs and roots is submerged. *Shatavari* (a medicinal herb) can be sold for 110 rupees per kg. You get it only near particular streams and water bodies. Those sources are submerged now. All this information, I used to give to the people.

My other area of study is that of adivasi culture. Adivasis are nature worshippers. I tried to explain this to people at the time of the satyagrahas.

After Manibeli, Domkhedi became the centre of the Andolan and the satyagrahas in Maharashtra. Domkhedi satyagrahas continued from 1995 till 2000. In the first two years of the satyagraha, the water had yet not reached up to the hut. Very big programmes took place. Supporters from all over India came and visited. All the people from Narmada Valley gathered there. We used to stay there throughout the rainy season and plan for our struggle ahead. In 1997 the water rose till the necks of people. That time we stood in water for twenty-seven hours. Women and girls were there in large numbers. The water kept rising higher, but no one came out of the hut. We had also divided ourselves into batches. One batch comes out and gets arrested; the second batch is ready to stand in the water. The police were there in large numbers. From time to time, they informed each other on wireless about how far the water level had risen. They had a barge, so they could have come any time to arrest us. After twenty-seven hours, when the water rose up to the necks of people, hundreds of police stormed the hut, and the first batch was arrested. They were taken to Dhadgaon and released.

That was how we spent the 1997 rainy season. In 1998, the water level increased further and the house where we used to stand for the satyagraha was completely submerged. Then people stood in Bhola Dahya's house. At that time, Mansoor Khan,[87] Amir Khan's uncle, was standing in front of us with his camera. We began to think that even in Bhola Dahya's house, the water would rise above our heads. Even then the police did not come. Nobody even checked what was happening.[88] We went to Jugi's house, thinking that Bhola Dahya's house would collapse. Then we realised that Jugi's house would also get submerged, and so we shifted to Bhajyakaka's house. That was the last house where we used to cook our evening meals. That house was also on the verge of collapsing but the satygrahis were not willing to leave. In 1998 everything went under water. That was the year that all the villages from Nimgavhan onward got completely submerged, wasn't it! We felt that truly we would perform Jalsamarpan. There were no government officials around. At that time, people from the villages took the decision that to continue the fight, we needed the people to live.

That is why we dragged leaders like Medhatai out of the water. At that time, Medhatai was very upset. She cried a lot. The police started saying, 'This is all a drama. First, they stand in the water on their own, and then they drag themselves out!' They tried to spread this propaganda. But we were sure that if we had to keep the fight alive, we needed the people who would fight. And so, we made that one mistake. So, this is how the fight over the Domkhedi satyagraha took place. And from that same year onward, the satyagraha was over so far as Domkhedi was concerned.

After that, we offered satyagraha in Chimalkhedi for two years. In 2000, the satyagraha was simply to monitor the water levels; that means it was clear that we would not get ourselves drowned. But the government was telling us all the time that the water level would not rise very much; so we were monitoring the actual water levels and gauging the losses incurred. We performed this monitoring satyagraha in Nimgavhan for one year. After that, the height of the dam kept on increasing, and more and more villages were submerged. Then in 2003, people inspected and accepted the lands and shifted our houses here, to Vadchhil.

Until the height of the dam reached 100 metres, our village did not get submerged. Only some people's land used to get submerged. In the 1999 monsoon, our entire village was submerged. It kept getting submerged every year for the next three or four years, that is 1999, 2000, 2001, 2002. Then we shifted to the upper reaches. But how long could we stay there? Our productive farmland was completely under water. Only having a house above water was not going to feed us, was it?

We never had the least bit of expectation from the Andolan that they would give us grains like the way they gave to the other villages.[89] We never said give us grains. Government officials came and carried out a panchnama for one or two years. Whatever compensation we got from the government, we accepted. People like us could not afford replacing our houses and all the wood washed away in three years. It had also become difficult to find the material and wood for house construction.[90] From Bharad to Manibeli, so many people's houses were washed away; there is no record of their names and no compensation. In the end, even bare survival was difficult, people thought. The cows, the cattle, the people—they could not even reach the river. There was water all around, but we had no water to drink![91] Because there was so much *khishad* (muck). All was marshland now! It was difficult to live there.

For two years, the houses remained under water during the monsoon. After the dam height was increased to 110 metres, people had constructed small huts in the upper reaches and used to stay there. The houses were in terrible shape, weren't they? The side walls and the wood had all rotted, and much of the loose wood that was collected had been washed away. Only the vertical structure remained. Finally, when the dam height reached 110 metres, people thought that now nothing could be salvaged. That is why they dismantled their houses and from 2004, in view of all this, they thought of rehabilitation and began to accept land and shift.

Whatever we could grow in the upper reaches was all we had. After two years of bitter struggle, the government provided some help. Someone got 10,000 rupees and someone else got 20,000, and on that we survived for two years. Would the government keep giving us compensation every year? After all, did the Akkalkuwa people get anything? No! 'You do not shift your houses and then carry out a panchnama!'[92] That is the language the government used. They also made it clear, 'We gave you compensation for two years, but from now on, no more compensation.' The government thought if they gave compensation every year, people would not move at all. Every year they would get submerged and carry out a panchnama. Manibeli and all the other villages that were completely submerged, have they got any compensation? Till now they have not!

From the beginning, our village was the one that fought. People have endured horrendous beatings. The people who went to jail have mainly been from Nimgavhan and Domkhedi. We are the ones who have stood in the waters, and we are the ones who pulled Medhatai out of the water when it reached up to her head. 'Tai, do not perform Jalsamarpan,' we said. 'We are there to carry on the fight.' It is the people from our village who gave Medhatai hope and strength and saved her life. In Maharashtra the biggest strength of the Andolan came mainly from these two or three villages. We faced gunfire, we faced the lathicharge in Dhule and people let their means of livelihood drown and suffered the consequences for two to three years. And after that, even when we shifted to higher parts, we knew that land was also going to get submerged. It was a very difficult situation to live in.

If we had waited more, it was certain that the village would have been split into many small pieces. A village that was so united would not today have been split into Amlibari, Rojva, Gopalpura and Vadchhil rehabilitation sites. Had we waited a little more, it would certainly have been split into four more sites and the people would have been completely scattered. In the end, left with no alternative, and with everyone's consent, we accepted rehabilitation at Vadchhil. We didn't accept it individually, separately, one by one. The government could not divide us. We fought with the government to get this rehabilitation. Some people left because they were scared and some because they were greedy and wanted money. At least our village is not like that. Our village is a village of fighters and educated young people and finally we have managed to get rehabilitation together.

While leaving our village we cried a lot; when we shifted our houses, we cried; we looked at the river and we cried. We cried for the people left behind. We cried for Bababhai who would now be left alone in Jalsindhi, the village opposite us on the other bank. What could they do? Yes, we felt in the end, we had to accept rehabilitation because there was no alternative. To get this much also we had to fight. Otherwise, we would have remained there suffering hardship. And just because we have accepted rehabilitation, it does not mean we have cut off relations with the people who have remained behind. I myself have visited people from Bhadal to Manibeli, and have talked to them, listened to what they feel.

The reason for accepting rehabilitation is that the government submerged our villages and homes year after year for two to three years. After having submerged our homes and letting all our wood rot, how long could we go on? And if we were to truly ask for the land that was our right, and if we were to accept rehabilitation, then we must get whatever is rightfully ours.

How long are we to go around shouting, 'O, give us. Give us our compensation. Give us …?'

People were also saying all kinds of things, weren't they? 'You have become used to begging. Because the government gives freely, you sit there and keep submerging your village yourself.' All around Dhadgaon, people were saying this. So, we thought, rather than allowing our homes and land to be submerged every year, it is better that we accept rehabilitation which is rightfully ours, and so, we accepted rehabilitation.

We lived like kings there, enjoying all the amenities. Here, we have no natural resources. It is true that we have bright electric lights and many comforts, but we are not happy here because the land the local farmers have sold us has lost its productivity. They have ruined it completely with the use of fertilisers and pesticides. In spite of the hard work we have put in to improve the land over the last four years, it has not got any better. We are forced to use the same amount of fertilisers as the farmers did. Only if we spend on the very expensive fertilisers and seeds can we earn something. And only if we get a good crop can we return the loan we have taken. The old and the new villages are as different as the earth and the sky.

In this village there are 130 undeclared sons. If these sons, who are themselves fathers of three or four children, do not get land here, there will be no alternative but to go back to the old village and take over whatever land is remaining there. When the government brought us here it told us, 'Get your children with you; we will include them as affected persons.' They had independent houses there, but here they do not even have a plot of land to build a house or a piece of land for farming. Out of the 130 sons, if even fifty per cent of the sons are included, that would be a big relief for the households. These are adult sons and the government has made them landless. And the reason for our demand is that the Supreme Court judgement states that each adult son needs to be given 5 acres in his own name. The GoM officials have turned these educated youths into landless persons. What a game the government has played! If we do not do something about the undeclared sons right now, it will be very difficult to do anything later. What is happening now is this: for any flimsy reason the claim is being rejected straightaway—you don't fit the criteria, you are not an adult, there is no evidence you are the son of a landholder. It is the responsibility of the Andolan to insist, to collect and show the government the evidence that a particular person's father is a landholder, so how then even though he is a landholder's son have they shown him as landless?

They had promised to give us irrigated land. Borewells have been dug but they are not functioning. Or else the earlier owners have taken away the motor pumps. They showed us water circulating through the water channels when the land was purchased by the government. But there is no water now. So, we should get water for the land along with a motor pump set. That requirement has not been met. In this region groundwater levels are very deep. To bring the water levels up, a lot of work is needed. Firstly, we are asking for the hill opposite us. On those 50–52 acres we can plant trees. There are small streams which we will train and build bunds on. After that, automatically, water and land will be conserved.

Then, there is no proper delineation of boundaries and settlement of area. They say they have given a person a 5-acre piece of land, but people are not sure, whether it is 4 acres or 5 acres. It is important to get proper delineation done.

If we are to get land in the command area, we need that to be recorded on the 7/12 form. If it remains in the name of the earlier owner, he can do all kinds of mischief. We may end up in the same situation as in Gujarat.[93]

In the process of planning this village, the road is at a high level and the plots at a lower level, and so, during the monsoon, the plots get waterlogged. The plots need to be raised.

In the old village, the entire village would come together and help one another. Houses were built collectively by all the people of the village. The traditional practice of helping each other has vanished in this new settlement. Here we cannot get anything done without money. You need to give a whole day's wages for farm work. In the old village, one good meal counted as a full day's wage.

Here we have to work throughout the year. There we had to work only for four months, and we could eat for twelve months. Whatever was produced in the rainy season was sufficient for one family. In between, if needed, we would go to the forest and collect gum, extract lac, or pick some fruits and sell them in the market. People could do small things like these to support themselves. Catch fish, eat what you wanted, and if some was left over, go and sell it. Here we have to plough the land fully even before the monsoon if we want to get a good monsoon crop. If the monsoon crop has been harvested, and oh, there is water still available, then sow the winter crop. If there is still some water left, then, come on, let us sow cotton in May as a summer crop. In this way we have to work all through the year in this settlement; only then can you get something.

In our old village, people always had some money with them. Here, even if you have 1,000 rupees, they get spent within a day. To entertain one guest, we have to spend 400–500 rupees. There, we could easily provide liquor for a guest because we used to brew our own.[94] Here, we have to go to Shahada and get some. We also have to buy expensive chicken from Shahada. There, we could find chicken and fish within the village.[95] There, if we had stored tendu leaves, we could roll our own bidis. Here, rehabilitated people have raised their status, so we have to buy cigarette packets for the guests. Such are these fashions! To maintain that status, we have to spend money.

Even if the government is claiming that this is model rehabilitation, according to our accounting, there is a lot that the government still owes us. One mahua tree gives us an income of 3,000–4,000 rupees per year. The lifetime of a mahua tree is about fifty to sixty years. Has anyone paid us for the loss of that mahua tree? Has anyone paid us the price of the land we have lost? No one has! If we have to get something, we have to stand up and fight collectively over here too. We will fight. Whether the activists of the Andolan are with us or not, we will fight. We are fighters. We will fight till the end and get what we are owed.

Nandini: What is the situation now of the people who have not been rehabilitated and who have remained behind in their original village?

Kevalsingh: The people from Akkalkuwa have not accepted agricultural land that had been bought. They are demanding forestland for rehabilitation. If we make all the calculations, the GoM had sanctioned 4,200 hectares of land, out of which 1,500 has turned out to be bad land or land lost to streams. So, the people are saying, since all that is unusable land, in its stead they want good forestland which the government has itself sanctioned. But the government is not releasing that land as yet. In Akkalkuwa, there are more than 300 landholders declared as affected. In Akrani there are more than 200. But if we add together those declared as affected, adult sons who have not got land yet and the landless, all together they comprise 1,100 or more persons. All these people have still not got land.

Nandini: What is their condition? The submergence has already taken place.

Kevalsingh: At present, they are being given food grains from Jan Sahyog. All the responsibility for it is being taken by Suhastai.[96] It's been two years now; food is distributed once every three months.

The fight is going on. This year too there was a satyagraha in Chimalkhedi, but the enthusiasm of earlier times is missing. The activists themselves find it difficult to reach there.

At present there is very little work being done in the submergence zone. What I mean is that there is a lot of work to be done in the submergence zone, but what is being done is a little inadequate. By the beginning of the rainy season, the work of showing land to the people and taking possession should have been completed. Even the Andolan activists have not done it. Now if the dam gates are closed, the whole of the adivasi belt and the Nimad region will be destroyed.[97] The villages of Alirajpur opposite Maharashtra will not survive. By the next monsoon all these things should be completed, but that is not happening. Now when the issue was to search for land, we ourselves went and selected the land. How many late nights we spent! Medhabehen was also there at that time. The process, right from buying land onwards, was decided in front of the collector, but in the last few days, it has all gone into cold storage.

Earlier, there used to be a meeting every month. In Nandurbar, the village representatives, the activists of the Andolan and the officials used to have a meeting. But for the last three months no meeting has been conducted. How far has the work proceeded? If it is not proceeding, why is it not? These were some questions discussed at the meeting. There used to be spot surveys carried out—for the islanded zones too, but that has also stopped. That should have happened by now.[98] The officials have begun to feel that there is no one chasing after them any longer. Somehow or the other the pressure has lightened. Yogini (Khanolkar) is a little too young. To place the responsibility of all the rehabilitation work in Maharashtra on her—it is not as if she carries much weight with the officials. She may be respected as an activist of the Andolan. But the officers from Maharashtra are skilled in sweet talk and you would think you had a very good discussion, and that the work will get done, and walk away from the meeting. But after that you find out that the decisions taken at the meeting have not been implemented. Then you get on to the mobile phone and ask, 'Why has that not been done?'

'There are no orders from above. What can we do?' That is the language that will be used.

Look, Yogini, works with commitment, but if she takes up the responsibility only of the agitations and the organisation, it will greatly reduce her work load. But if alongside, she also takes on the running of the school, then work for the school will be half-done, and the responsibility of the Andolan will also be weakened.

Nandini: But you people are there, aren't you?

Kevalsingh: Yes, we are, and there are many of us. But that is what I have been repeating all the time—we must be included in the decision-making.

The decision-making process is not like it used to be. Earlier, if anything had to be done, it used to be done with the people's consensus. Now, we have to do whatever the activists tell us to do. The methods of working are different now, I am telling you. They have changed a lot.

Earlier, we used to organise a meeting in the village. The representatives in the executive committee would take a decision, and it had to be accepted. If we happened to go to Mumbai and the minister or the officials were not ready to have discussions, we would have a small meeting right there. 'We have travelled such a long distance, and they are not even bothered to meet us. So, what do we do? Shall we wait for some more days, or shall we carry out a *Rasta Roko*? Or should we start a fast?' The people themselves suggested ways to put pressure on the government. But nowadays, things do not happen this way. There are no meetings at all! If only to ensure that people come and join, a meeting of four to five villages could at least be organised to discuss everything. Now only those who can be contacted on mobile phones are contacted. How many people do you expect will come and join you this way? Things should not get decided in a meeting of a few activists; they should be decided by a people's consensus. After all, it is the people who have to fight.

Before, whenever a big programme was organised, the representatives of the three states used to take decisions together. Suppose Medhabehen was to start a fast, there would be long hours of discussion and thinking that would go into it. What would be the effect of such a fast? If a similar fast had been undertaken a few times earlier, should we undertake it now or not, and for how many days? You also had to plan a programme fully including deciding on where people would get their food? One or two people cannot decide such issues. We have to think about it in all seriousness and get a complete consensus; only then will people stay with you in the struggle. The decision-making of the organisation is very important. And the activists' position mainly should be that when people are prepared to fight, activists can support them and provide the necessary strength. As far as leadership is concerned, an activist can take up the role of leader for a particular programme. But whatever happens at village level must be decided by the people from that village. Because whenever people take a decision, they become committed to carrying it out. You can say, 'See, you said so, that is why this programme is being taken up.' Otherwise, if you say, 'Come with me,' and take a person with you for a day and keep him for a month, the next day they would say, 'You lie to people, and take them with you.' That is why an organisation that reaches out to people, talks to them, listens to them and plans in accordance with them is a better organisation. If people are sidelined and only activists take decisions, then there can be a bit of trouble.

There have been many activists in the Andolan. Right in the beginning there was a person named Shirke. He worked in Madhya Pradesh. He did not stay long but he did very good work. After him there were Himanshu, Arundhati, Silvytai and Nandinitai,[99] Shripadbhai,[100] Sanjay,[101] Alokbhai[102] and Joe bhai.[103] They worked closely with people and with commitment and sincerity. Then there was Milind. He was such a good activist. He stayed only for a short while, but he formed a strong relationship with the people by working with them and speaking with them in their own language. At the local level there were activists like Mahesh, Chogalal and Rehmat. In Maharashtra, there were Ajit, Keshavkaka, Vesta and myself. Such were the activists created at that time. They formed a solid steel flank to the Andolan. The local activists and the activists who came from outside had very good rapport. Their methods of working together were robust and strong. It is because of this close bond that the Andolan could achieve what it did! The activists who came from outside did very good work. Some wrote, and some stood with the people and faced the beatings along with them. Amit wrote powerful songs for the Andolan. Those songs are sung today all over the valley.

Among all of them, it was Medhatai who assumed the leadership role. I would not say that Tai has completely abandoned the area from where she began her work. But the hustle and bustle of work she has now taken up, that too right at the international level, seems to have caused some neglect of the areas from where she started her work—whether it is the submergence zone or the Sardar Sarovar area or the Bargi area.

Then there was Ranya Dahya—the main representative of village Mukhadi. The whole village used to follow his leadership. Noorjibhai from Danel—he was also the leader of his entire village. Vankabhau from Danel looked after the health issues within the Andolan. There was Mathurbhai in Sindhuri and also Seshara Dahya and Narayanbhai. All these people were wonderfully cooperative and their entire village used to listen to them. Chimalkhedi's Bija Jugliya—he has even been to America.[104] Udaysinghbhau from Dhankhedi has led his entire village and has kept it going strong. What can I say about Manibeli? Manibeli's women from Champa to Kunta—all young women! Narayanbhai, Vitthalbhai, Jatarbhai—all of them played important roles, and that is why Manibeli became a central battleground.

Manglya from Bhadal became the fieriest speaker among the youth. In Madhya Pradesh, there was a batch of activists like Bababhai, Khajan and Vaniya. In the Nimad region, there were activists like Champalal[105] and Ashish among others. Ashish[106] looks after the Badwani office now, and also Rehmat. All of them carried out their responsibilities very well. All of them, whether individually or collectively, are still active.

In Maharashtra, there were Ajit Pawra, Keshavkaka and me; only the three of us were full-time activists. Others were representatives of their respective villages, and they would assume the leadership of their villages whenever it was needed for the big programmes. Rama Atya worked for two or three years, as a boatman. Then there was Luharya. Ajit was there too but only for a few years. Keshavkaka and myself have been there all the time, and we continue even now.

Nandini: What Andolan work do you do now after moving to the Vadchhil resettlement site?

Kevalsingh: We are running the Jeevan Shala, which is a part of the Andolan. When we go to Nandurbar, speak to the officials and put forth our position, when we hold discussions within the village, all that too is Andolan work. The 'encroachers' from the adivasi areas of Shahada Tehsil are interested in becoming part of the organisation, but we cannot reach them. However, we are giving them complete information about the Andolan. We write applications for people; we accompany them to the police station or the tehsil office.

Nimgavhan and Domkhedi are two villages which banned liquor for a very long time when we were in our old villages.

After we have come to Vadchhil, no one has sold liquor till date. The people around us say, 'We are all old educated families, why would we sell liquor? We will follow your teaching and ban liquor.'

Whenever we have to meet a minister or visit the Mantralaya or present our issues to an official, from the chief minister to the prime minister, I have presented our issues. I have presented our concerns before Vishwanath Pratap Singh.[107] When Sushilkumar Shinde[108] was the CM, and Medhabehen had undertaken a fast in Mumbai, I presented our issues to him too. I did the same in the presence of R. R. Patil[109] and Rehabilitation Minister Patangrao Kadam. From the secretary to the collector and from the level of the tehsil to that of the commissioner, I have put forward our position many times.

It is difficult to remember everything. But I will tell you about one particular incident I can never forget. It was the rainy season. There was a meeting in Chimalkhedi in the evening. Vesta, Dama Pawra, myself and Medhabehen were on our way on foot from Manibeli to attend the meeting. Somewhere between Chimalkhedi and Dhankhedi, it began to rain heavily. Everything went totally dark. There was no sign that the rain would stop. We had not packed any clothes, nor did we have a torch with us. We couldn't see even one step ahead of us. We were all sopping wet and shivering with cold. If there had been a flood in the river at that time, no one knows what would have happened! The big streams were roaring. We just stopped and sat there the whole night. But even in that torrential rain, Medhabehen peacefully went to sleep! I cannot imagine how she could have slept through that night! Then she gets up in the morning and says, 'Oh, my! Weren't we supposed to reach in the evening? I just fell asleep.'

Till today, I have not been scared of anything. I was never scared of any officer, nor was I scared of death.

Nandini: Were you scared at the time of your fast?

Kevalsingh: Never. On the contrary I thought if I die because of the fast, it is good. I was never scared of dying.

By the year 1994–95, my household responsibility had also increased. I was the first married son. There were other sons, but my mother was after me to take on some responsibility of the household. That is why my travel outside the village got curtailed. I told Medhabehen that I would not be able to take on a lot of work outside the village, but I could stay in my village and work there. I asked them, 'Why don't you make me a teacher in the school?' Everyone agreed.

I have been teaching from 1996 up to the present. I am a trustee of Narmada Navnirman Abhiyan representing all the adivasi teachers. Keshavkaka, Noorjibhai, Mohanbhai[110] from the Nimad region, Kailash and Ashish and a few people from Pune, Mumbai and Dhule are also trustees. At the moment my responsibilities are to train the teachers, go to the schools and monitor how the children are being taught in those schools. Twice a week, I have to go and train the teachers and assess what kind of teaching the children need. Every month all these things are discussed in our meetings.

The thinking behind the Jeevan Shala was our own, meaning that the main representatives Noorjibhai, Vestabhai, and a few other people were the ones who thought that there must be a school for children. Today the schools have expanded greatly. In the beginning, we only enrolled children from Chimalkhedi; there were no outsiders. And because the children were from the same village, they used to have their meals at home and come to school.

The school building was built by the villagers. When we decided that the school would run full time, we also decided that the parents would contribute six months of food, and the Andolan would somehow manage to get food for the rest of the six months. After that, the second school was opened in Nimgavhan. Giridhar Guruji worked at this school from the beginning along with a young man named Batesingh from Dhankhedi.[111] Today there are thirteen schools with a total enrolment of 1,500 students.

In the beginning, we used whatever methods had been used to teach us when we were in school because we had no experience of any kind. But later on, when we became more experienced, we began to use different methods for teaching. We thought about whether we should use only government school textbooks or if we should add something of our own to the syllabus? And so we introduced farming studies, the study of trees, herbal and medicinal plants, the study of the environment, and the study of people's movements—not just the NBA, but all the movements that took place all over the country—from the freedom struggle onward. We thought about how children should speak out and express themselves, and how they could sing and perform plays. We also incorporated knowledge about health. Adivasi children love sports and games.[112] We thought of how to impart teaching through games. So, we planned all of our teaching to make sure that children would learn to be self-sufficient and stand on their own feet. That is why the school was named 'Jeevan Shala', the school of life.

Rohit from Rajasthan came to train our teachers. Krishna Kumarji,[113] the prominent educationist, visited each and every school, and gave teachers study material of different kinds. Our teachers visited Eklavya[114] in Madhya Pradesh, Aksharnandan[115] in Pune and also some Kolhapur schools. They observed and learnt different methods of teaching. In these schools they use methods that rely on locally available resources for teaching. Take for example, geography; it is so easy to teach. Rivers, valleys, hills and mountains, the distance between two villages, the direction in which they lie—these are all subjects in geography. How to grow a particular crop? What are the types of soil? Our children have seen all this, so that learning resource has already been created within them. We taught them how to identify and collect herbs and make medicines out of them. We managed to prepare medicine for scabies.

Then we taught them about our own culture, our gayanas, the stories which have not been written down, those that parents and elders tell children. We invited storytellers and told them: today, just talk with the children, tell them stories. This is how we taught our children. To follow these methods here at this rehabilitation site is difficult.[116]

For one thing, our local spoken languages are not part of our education. We usually try to teach children in some other language—like Marathi, Hindi or English. But in the Jeevan Shalas, until children learn these other languages, we teach them in our own language. By the fourth standard, children have to appear for the government exam. Keeping this in mind, we follow the government syllabus because children must clear that exam.

Today our children participate in sports up to the national level. Most of the students who have completed school with us are now studying in Pune, Ahmednagar, Aurangabad, Akola; one boy has gone as far as Chandrapur. Since 1992, 700 students have passed out from our schools. The first student of this school is in the third year of college.

This December we will have a 'Walk and Talk' shibir[117] for the teachers. We are organising a special ST bus.[118] We will start from Shahada and Dhadgaon and go up to Kolhapur, which distance we will cover in eight days. We have invited different educationists to guide our teachers. The responsibility of the shibir has been taken up by Sunititai. Earlier it was done by Hiraman Jadhav, one year by Geetanjali, and one year by Rohan.[119] Now Yogini has decided to do it too.

There are two shibirs a year, one in the Diwali vacation and another in the summer holidays.

Once we travelled from Bawangaja to Maheshwar and the Mandav area in Madhya Pradesh. We also visited most of the villages of the Sardar Sarovar submergence zone. Baba[120] was with us at that time. I have his photograph too. We visited Ajanta-Ellora and Aurangabad too. After that trip, we could not do more trips due to financial difficulties. Over the last fifteen years, we organised eight Bal Melavas. This year the ninth Melava will be held. We will organise it at Dhadgaon, at the tehsil office. The government school teachers from Dhadgaon just take their salaries every year without doing any work. They do not attend their school duties. Let them at least know what a Jeevan Shala is like.

There are now forty-two teachers and sixty to sixty-five *mavashis* and *kamathis*[121]—a staff of almost 110 in the Jeevan

Shalas. The schools are not only in Maharashtra; the Kharya Bhadal, Bhitada, and Jalsindhi schools are in Madhya Pradesh. At present, the teachers are from the local community. In Madhya Pradesh there are some teachers from outside too. Some teachers have been our own students who have passed out from our school. Sidiya-Siyaram[122] is our first student. He looks after the schools and is also an Andolan activist.

I first worked as a full-time activist of the Andolan. Then from 1996, I started working as a teacher and even today I continue to do so. Running fifteen schools is no simple task. Conducting meetings, carrying out inspections at every school—it is a lot of responsibility. So, we have assigned that task exclusively to Batesingh Guruji and Giridhar Guruji. Paperwork may be done by Yogini. But we want that the main task of supervision and conducting meetings should be done by Giridhar Guruji and Batesingh Guruji.

But I wish to say this—there is very little faith in us. (*Laughs.*) We had fights over this issue many times. The fights over distribution of work and responsibility have given us somewhat of a bad name. There is no problem in carrying out the work. But there must be a collective consensus—that is very important.

Nandini: Do you think local teachers can successfully shoulder the responsibility of running the Jeevan Shalas?

Kevalsingh: Very much so! That is why Batesingh and Giridhar Guruji are there. But even they say that while they were working, they were not given sufficient responsibility, which also means that they too have been somewhat sidelined. I have told them (the senior leaders of the movement and the activists looking into the working of the Jeevan Shalas) a number of times—entrust the main people with full responsibility.

Now the school budget has increased so much because we are buying everything from the market. Until now we used to buy whatever we needed from within the village. This was a good thing for several reasons. The poor villagers earn some money. The price is lower than the market price and you save on transport. The budget for school used to be around 20,000–21,000 rupees. Now that we are buying from the market, the budget has increased to more than 35,000 rupees. Till now the budget was based on material bought within the village. If you prepare a budget based on buying things from the market, the budget is bound to increase.

If money is available during the harvest season, we can buy our requirements for twelve months at one go, can't we? Now, in this village almost 1,000 quintals of jowar must have been sold, and that too at Rs 7.50 to Rs 8/kg. Why spend Rs 1,000 per quintal and bring jowar from the market? Udad and moong are grown here, and very soon tur dal will be harvested. If we can organise funds, we can buy things in the village itself. People sold udad at Rs 14/kg in the market. I had told Yogini, 'Yogini, do not buy the grains there.' Moong was being sold for Rs 1,800/quintal.

But Yogini did not listen to me. Last month she went to the market and bought moong for Rs 2,100 or 2,200/quintal. She bought tur dal for Rs 3,200/quintal. We could have saved Rs 500 to Rs 600 for every quintal. And then she asks me, 'Oh my God! How did it increase so much?'

I said, 'If you do not listen to us, then it is bound to increase.' But in the meeting, they keep insisting on a 'proper bill'. Perhaps they buy from the shops just so they can have a proper bill.

Nandini: Running the Jeevan Shala for so many years, you must have faced problems too.

Kevalsingh: The government put a lot of pressure on us. For the government, it was a kind of a challenge. In these extremely remote areas, the externally appointed teachers did not come to these schools, so the schools remained on paper, and the teachers kept withdrawing their salaries and enjoying the benefits. Even after several complaints and the suspension of a number of teachers, the government could not manage to run proper schools in these areas. We even undertook a fast of one or two days saying, 'Do not allow all that money to go waste. Do not appoint teachers who do not reside in the village. If you have to run the school, only appoint local teachers from that area.'

When we realised that the government was not going to let our children learn, we were forced to start a Jeevan Shala. Then the government started putting pressure on the Jeevan Shala teachers saying that the school we run is illegal. Also, since we are not registered, our students will not be allowed to appear for exams. They keep insisting that our school must get attached to the Zilla Parishad schools. Every year we have to go and fight with the education officer at Nandurbar and get him to accept the Form No. 17 and allow our fourth standard students to appear for their exams. This has been happening for the last fifteen years.

It is difficult to find teachers in this area where illiteracy is so high. And when we do, you know how education works these days. The tenth and twelfth standard students clear their exams by copying. If we ask a question, even the teacher cannot answer it. So how do we train someone we want to appoint as a teacher?

We, of course, had to face financial difficulties. Even today, the government does not recognise our schools. That is why this year we are planning to organise a Bal Melava of 1,500 students at the tehsil headquarters to show them how strong our students are and what we teach them compared to what they teach their students.

Nandini: What have you thought about the future of the Andolan?

Kevalsingh: If we gather together the people who have fought these battles for twenty years, the struggle can certainly be revived. It is most important to take into confidence the people who have got cut off. Those people have got cut off because of the many problems they faced. But this understanding is not there in the present-day activists because this is the mobile age. Mobiles have reached here too. A mobile is never going to build a movement. If we have to build the Andolan once again, we have to go amongst the people, we have to understand their issues, we have to find tasks at the local level that people can take up. Only then will the movement become as strong as it was before. But if I stay put in one place and say, 'Come, I will write the application for you, your work will get done,' it is never going to be built. Writing applications is the work of an organisation; it is office work. The Andolan is a movement, it is not an organisation. It is a power that emerges from the participation of the people. We have to reach out to the people and revive the spirit that has weakened. We have to awaken their resolve and strength to fight against injustice. Only then will the people rise up again. We have to work so that the activists who have been cut off can stand up once again. If that cannot be done, then the Andolan will exist only in name.

Rehabilitation does not mean people have become rich. If we have fought such a long battle and finally succeeded in providing land to people, then the struggle should not end until they get everything that is declared as their right by the Narmada Award. We have to fight to get those rights. And if we have to fight we have to reach out to the people. Only then will we know that this Andolan is alive. Just meeting a few people here and there, or meeting officials and telling them that this and that remains to be done is not going to work. We have to take to the streets and fight. Otherwise, the propaganda and general perception in Maharashtra is: 'Oh my, the government has given the adivasis so much! So much of land and irrigation facilities. Why, even their houses were transported!'

The government has not given us a bounty. People have been given land according to what they had earlier. But we had so much more than just land. We had our forest, our river, our own trees. Has the government paid us the value of the trees we have lost? Who is going to pay that? And they have not even given us half of what they had promised. To get all that is rightfully our due, we have to work among the people and with them.

Nandini: Is this not happening today?

Kevalsingh: No. Talking about what remains to be done in a meeting for a few hours in a month and going away is not the way to resolve issues, is it? For that we have to sit down together for a few days.

There is much less leadership now, that's why! Without leadership nothing can happen.

Nandini: By leadership you mean local leadership?

Kevalsingh: Whether it is local or from outside, if the leaders organise and lead the people with foresight, they will succeed. Developing local-level activists is also the responsibility of the other activists, isn't it? We have to take them into confidence, build their trust and work with them. If we tell an activist, 'Go and give this message to that person,' and he or she needs petrol to get there, then we need to make sure the petrol is made available to the activist. But that is not happening. The work is not planned well.

Nandini: Is it possible to develop local activists?

Kevalsingh: Yes, easily! And why not? Nowadays there are so many literate and well-educated young people. We can form a *party-mandal* (group-cum-circle) of youth in every village. In Chimalkhedi, such a youth mandal named Narmada has already been started. But to do that, we need leaders and not just a show of leadership.

Nandini: Are local people no longer coming forward?

Kevalsingh: Local people would come forward, but...I will tell you about myself, okay? I feel like doing a lot of work. This year I visited the Taravat rehabilitation site five or six times, spending from my own pocket. I was given the order by an activist above me: 'Go there and carry out this work.' But if I am not given the petrol for my bike, which I need to get there, it becomes very difficult for me, doesn't it? My financial situation is pretty bad; I have to run the household on whatever honorarium I get from the school because I haven't been able to give full attention to my farm. Then, if some activist eats a leisurely lunch in a Shahada restaurant and presents a bill for it, why shouldn't people like us do that too? Are we supposed to work on a hungry stomach? Their bills are fine, and ours are not? Then what is the use? We are also working for the cause. And if, in such circumstances, someone tells me, 'How do I know why you had gone there? Perhaps you had some personal work,'—then I am afraid, I cannot carry on for very long.

Today the situation is such that almost no meetings have been held over the last three or four years. When Medhatai visits us, people gather together mainly to meet her. Tai asks people, 'What are you doing? What is happening?' But the activists working here do not hold any kind of meeting. I cannot really comment on these activists. They are working hard in their own way. But they should not forget that they are running a people's movement. Medhatai has told them many times—she has named people as examples—that this is the way we must reach out to the villages: after going to a village, do not stay put in one person's house; visit five to ten houses at one go. Find out what problems they are facing.

It will require very, very hard work for the Andolan to be rebuilt.

Nandini: You have spent so many years in the Andolan, you have been an activist and there are many local leaders. Can you all not come together and carry out all the work yourselves?

Kevalsingh: Yes, perhaps we can. But we get the feeling that opinions are divided. Because whatever rehabilitation we accepted was on the basis of a consensus between all the people—activists of the Andolan and everyone else. It was Shobha[123] who first came here for the rehabilitation of this village. She chose the land. She called a meeting of the people. But before the meeting could take place, she tragically drowned while bathing in the river. It is in memory of her resoluteness and fighting spirit that we have named this village 'Shobhanagar'.

So, even though we accepted rehabilitation as a village and as part of the Andolan with a clear consensus among all, we feel that the current lot of activists tends to ignore us somewhat. The area in which the organisation works has moved away from us, which makes it difficult for us to work with them. But if we get some encouragement, we will feel comfortable in doing so.

Whether those differences of opinion actually exist or not is difficult for me to say. But they are related to the issue of acceptance of rehabilitation. A feeling developed in the people who remained behind that they were left behind because the people of Nimgavhan and Domkhedi accepted rehabilitation. People also told us that the Andolan was weakened because we went away. It is possible that activists also feel the same way. But we have not left the Andolan. Whenever we go to any of the officers, we put the entire story of the Andolan before them. We have always demanded rehabilitation not only of all of the Maharashtra villages but also all the Madhya Pradesh villages. Despite this if we are being somewhat isolated, what more can we do? But we are still fighting...

Nandini: What is the most important achievement of the Andolan?

Kevalsingh: The most important achievement is that we pushed out the World Bank. Second, we have put this issue before the world: what is development and what is not? With big dams there is total destruction of the environment. Economically, there is little benefit. On the contrary, they cause huge loss and displacement. We brought all this to the notice of the world, and so, that too is an important achievement. Granted that the Supreme Court has given a judgement against the Andolan, but if among those three judges one has said that all this is wrong, that too is our victory. In this way, one by one these victories have come together and consolidated our achievements. Yes, the Sardar Sarovar will be built, yes it will displace people. But whatever our Andolan has put before the people, those thoughts are very important. The rehabilitation programme that we have presented to the government is extremely beneficial for any organisation. There are people in Maharashtra who have been displaced before Independence, who have still not been given land. They too will fight for rehabilitation and they will tell the government, 'You give land for rehabilitation in the case of one dam, so how can you refuse it in the case of the other?' All these are going to be big achievements in the future.

Nandini: Do you have a sense of loss?

Kevalsingh: No, not loss. But the remaining people should get rehabilitation. I do not think they will stop the construction of the dam now. The gates will be put in place in a month or two. But after such a prolonged struggle, people should get their rights. People dream of heaven, but you have to die to get there.

Some people have improved their situation. Some people's condition is going to worsen greatly—in fact it has already worsened. We will have to stand up and fight once again. Madhya Pradesh will be in very bad shape. If the farmers from Nimad get a lot of money, they will be able to go anywhere, build a house, buy land. But the adivasis cannot survive on money. They will go through the money in no time, and then there will be devastation—they will have to migrate to Surat or Ahmedabad as daily labour. Things should not come to that. Whatever happened in Ukai[124] has happened, but that must not happen again.

In Madhya Pradesh, Sardar Sarovar is not the only dam, there are many dams, and a whole lot of people will be displaced. If we think of all those oustees and rehabilitating all of them, it is going to be very, very difficult.

Finally, some people did get rehabilitated. They are happy, at least they got a piece of land. But what about all those who did not, and who will not get land? This then is a weakness of the Andolan. People will say so, and so will we. We will have to carry on this struggle, without weakening, until they do. In the Sardar Sarovar Project area there are seventy-five per cent adivasis. It is for them that we have fought such a big battle. Otherwise, would Maharashtra have done anything about their rehabilitation?

Nandini: How important is the history of this movement?

Kevalsingh: I consider it to be of great importance. Because the culture of our country is so ancient. In today's scientific age we see only that one dream. But we have to be alert about this scientific age as well. Who knows where and when it will finish us all. So, whatever was our culture, we must retain it by all means.

Firstly, the gayanas should be written down, or recorded on a tape, the way you are doing right now. But if there is no one to sing them, it will be difficult. Except for the couple of times I have spoken on TV, I have never come forward to be photographed. Why should we project ourselves to be larger than this short life that we lead? That is why to this day, I have not written anything down. (*Laughs.*)

I think on my own terms. Not for publicity. Whatever you want to do, do it and move on with your life. (*Laughs.*) We will work so long as our hands and legs will allow us. But I should not expect that I must be recognised and remembered by many. True, I will go to the media according to the needs of the organisation and because I have to tell the full story. But I have no inclination to pose for photographs. Anyway, I must have been photographed many times because I am always at the mike—but until now whatever photos I have seen of the Andolan, there is not a single photograph of mine. That is why I say this! (*Laughs.*)

Nandini: But then, how will the work done by people like you be known outside?

Kevalsingh: That is necessary, no doubt. And that has not happened to the extent it should. Again and again, only a particular set of people keep getting highlighted. We must certainly remember the work they have done for the Andolan and the sacrifices they have made. That must all be remembered.

But for example, Baliben of Antras (village Kothi) and Bhagat from Manibeli—these people have passed away. All their lives no one knew their names. Or even today, the most well-known person putting forward the Andolan's viewpoint, Batu Patil, is struggling with illness at Amalibari. No one makes it a point to go and meet him. Which of the new activists even know who Batu Patil is? This is true even of the old timers; none of them visit him either! Perhaps they cannot spare the time. When a few people meet, they should talk about him, what he was like, what he did.

During the Manibeli and Domkhedi satyagrahas, when the Andolan activists told me to give an interview, I faced the media. I have narrated the complete history of the struggle in the valley in front of the world's media. But the story of living things, the medicinal plants and how to make use of them—that knowledge is not known to the world. Nor has it been recorded. I feel very sorry about that. What you see in front of you now is just a big lake/reservoir. But just how magnificent, how beautiful the Narmada was, how sweetly she burbled as she flowed! The sands of the Narmada, the big black smooth rocks on her floodplains, the very many trees on her banks... it was so green! None of this has been recorded. Her many ghats, waterfalls and pools, all these things that marked her are now lost forever. The unique vegetation on her banks, the herbs and roots, the fishes she held—you won't find them anywhere else in India. Because the Narmada flows entirely through rocky terrain, the fishes which populated her waters have been completely destroyed.

No cassette has ever captured any of this.

If I begin to talk about all this today, people will say, is this really true? No one will believe it anymore! Because today, you cannot see the whole picture. Jalsindhi was such a beautiful, natural place of worship—thousands of people from Gujarat, Madhya Pradesh and Maharashtra would come there to visit the Narmada. There is no idol in Jalsindhi, but people believed it was a godly place. It is said that the Narmada had stopped and stayed a whole night in Jalsindhi. These things may be imaginary, but they are central beliefs of the adivasis. They used to come here and sing the gayanas all through the night and carry on discussions too. If these things had been captured on cassette, whatever we want to say to the world would have been communicated so much better. That has remained undone.

The media reached the valley very late because earlier there was no means of transport. One had to go on foot everywhere. And in all the hustle-bustle of things that were going on, no one paid much attention to the river and her natural elements. But when all of it was lost, then you began to regret, 'Oh, that has got left out,'—how at Pimpli, the Narmada flowed through such a small course, how at Bhadal you could cross the Narmada in a single leap. It was a simply beautiful, natural place. You had to see it to believe it. In her lower reaches, places like Maheshwar became famous because she flowed there in a thousand streams. But all these places in the adivasi region never became known. And now it is all lost forever, isn't it!

Some aspects, like how the village was laid out, have been covered to a certain extent in the shooting done by Seema[125] and others. It has also been covered in *Laha*.[126] But whatever was on the banks of the Narmada has not been covered. Apart from the Narmada, there were other things—what were the houses like in each village, the people's way of life, their relationships with each other, the soil and the crops in each of the hamlets, the beautiful streams that joined the Narmada, the winter crops fed by those streams such as onion, garlic, watermelon, the trees that grew and the various herbs and roots; none of these has been covered in the media. And then, there are the places of worship of the adivasis where the Gaondev or Vaghdev was installed, in places where there would be forest and trees (sacred groves). None of this got covered in the media.

The festivals of the adivasis, like Holi, have been widely covered, but not in the way they should be. They have been captured only in photographs. Every village used to have a *devedani*.[127] One ritual celebration of adivasi worship is known as *Govan*. If a Govan is to take place in any village, you have to invite people. Then the gayana singers come together. They all sit in a row and sing the gayana all night. One story is selected and is narrated fully in the form of gayana. This is the most important tradition. Has it ever been covered in the media?

The adivasi Diwali starts with the main Diwali festival, but then it continues for two to three months. Today it is Diwali for this village, tomorrow it is for another village. Celebrating Diwali collectively in this way has been a very important part of adivasi culture at least till now. That has also never been covered! Indal is a festival that forms a part of the completion of a vow. Once it is decided to celebrate Indal, 100 to 150 people with drums gather together from nearby villages, and they all dance to the rhythm of the drums! This is also a big adivasi festival, and this too has never been captured by any media.

So what we see is that much of adivasi culture has not been recorded or shot on camera. Whatever remains can still be documented by visiting those areas where it has not yet been destroyed. But unfortunately, the part of the Narmada way of life that matters the most does not exist anymore.

I do not think that the full story of the Narmada struggle of the last twenty-two years has been documented anywhere. Whatever has been written is related to particular issues of the struggle that are very specific, like the issues raised by the Andolan related to the environment, or the cost-benefit of the dam, or displacement issues, or the finances for the dam. But the story of activists and people who participated in the struggle, and the story of the fight they waged has not been written anywhere. That story—of the struggle of the people in each village—needs to be told through interviews with them. If this history were to be written, it would be of great help to our future generations. They will come to know how their ancestors fought to save their lands, forests, villages and Narmada Mata. Otherwise, everything will be completely forgotten.

The Andolan has raised many issues under the guidance of activists who have come to the valley from outside, so getting information from them is certainly very important and necessary. These activists too have sacrificed a lot. But those who have given their lives and have created the firm foundation for the struggle are the local activists, so it is vital that they be part of this history.

In short, what I want to say is that those who led the struggle in the local regions have never been in the limelight because only a particular few activists were in the public eye as Andolan activists. Some local activists have been mentioned in relation to certain events, but there is no detailed information about them. For that we will have to reach out to them, get their personal narratives and the nature of the work they have done. Only then will we get to understand all this.

The coming generations must know just how big a struggle their ancestors have waged and how much and what they have sacrificed in this struggle for the society. We can get all this information from people who have been in the struggle for twenty to twenty-two years. Ranya Dahya always gave long speeches. He was what we call an environmentalist, and every time Ranya Dahya spoke, what he said could have won him an award. He would speak about insects and wild animals. No one ever mentions that anywhere! If we have to look for this living history, we will have to reach out to people and gather this knowledge from them. Only then will we get a clear and complete picture of how the battle was waged and how it was sustained.

To preserve all this in adivasi society, leadership is very important. Along with leadership, creating awareness in people is a big responsibility. It is not within the capabilities of a small activist like me. It is necessary that wherever there are adivasis in the country, studies of these communities should be undertaken.

Nandini: You told us that songs play a role in making a strong movement. All those famous songs—some written by you and those that you have sung—have you collected any of them? From where did you learn these songs?

Kevalsingh: Gayana I have not learnt, but whatever songs I have myself written and sung, I have been able to do because of an inner strength. Those songs have written themselves. No one learns how to write a song. Our emotions make the songs. People liked them and then kept singing them. When we were children, we only sang marriage songs. But all those inspiring songs I wrote and composed while working as a key activist of the Andolan. During that time, I wrote a lot of songs. And now that I am part of Jeevan Shala, I have written many different songs for children. Several of them are popular as well.

I have also written a lot of poems. Apart from that, I used to write plays, didn't I! There was one play that the children had written; it dealt with the dam itself. I thought of how to enact that play, and the children did a very good job of it. Another play, which was one I wrote, was about the environment, about how in the name of development, people destroy the Earth. In the Bal Melava we enacted a play on why girls are not sent to school, and there was a song in it too. The song was so good, we won first prize for the play. In the play, a little girl cries and asks her father, 'Why aren't we allowed to go to school? You send only my brother to school and you make us work in the fields, make us stay at home or send us to graze the cattle. Why do you do this? I too have a right to education. I too will study. I too will go to school.' She cries a lot until finally the father relents and sends her to school. Besides these, there is very little that I have written. Only a few articles in book collections. I have not retained any of it for myself.

The Andolan songs would be difficult to sing, but I will sing a couple from the Jeevan Shala.

I too want to run and play,
O Father, send me to school.

The children had sung this song very well indeed in the play. The last lines of the song are important. In the end, the little girl gets irritated with her father and says:

Don't you know of Savitribai?
There was a Rani of Jhansi,
She was a woman too.
Savitribai put her life in danger
and fearlessly ran a school for girls.
I too am a daughter of these brave women.
Let me study, o father, let me study,
and let me fight against injustice.

Another song goes like this:

We are children of the Jeevan Shala, O Father, O Brother...
We will never weaken.
We are brave adivasis, living among the forests and animals for generations...

There are so many songs, but now I remember only a few.

Nandini: A few last questions. Do you think the Andolan should engage in electoral politics?

Kevalsingh: I myself have fought an election as candidate for the Taluka Panchayat Samiti from a constituency of three gram panchayats that included the Andolan villages from Nimgavhan to Pimpalchop. But in such elections, those who do real work get lost. I was fighting this election, so the Andolan activists should have come and campaigned for me. I lost by nine votes. But those who voted for me did it willingly and in all earnestness. But if we get into elections and electoral politics, I don't think it will be possible to work the way we do now, because then we will always be under pressure from someone. There will be ten other people speaking against us, or we may be the only ones speaking up. Or we may put forward our viewpoint, but nothing may be done about the issue.

Geeta has been a sarpanch. We made her a Panchayat Samiti member. She went to the officials so many times with our issues, but the officials refused to do anything, saying, 'That is a submergence zone. What work can we take up there?' Hearing this, people get disheartened. We took so much trouble and got her elected, but none of our issues were addressed. She may make all efforts, but if she does not succeed in getting things done, that would amount to letting the people down. But if, with the organisation behind us, we put pressure and say, 'We have to dig a well here. Tell us, are you going to sanction it or not?' then the work gets done. In Akkalkuwa and Akrani talukas we got about forty to fifty wells dug because of the strength of the Andolan. This the elected sarpanch and panchayat members have not been able to do.

If we work independently, without owing anything to anyone, then we can even catch hold of the collector by his collar. There is definitely a vast difference between the activists of the Andolan and those who work by engaging in electoral politics and winning elections.

Nandini: Some time ago, the Andolan was wondering whether it should declare itself a political party and fight elections.[128]

Kevalsingh: People straightaway told us not to fight elections. Suppose we founded a party and fought the elections – getting one or two members elected to the State Legislative Assembly of Maharashtra with its 248 members would just mean that no one would listen to them. If we have to make a difference, we have to win all the seats. If not, then it is very difficult. People will begin to feel, 'What difference did they make? They are no different.'

I am very clear on this; I think those of us who have been working as Andolan activists should not get into this mess at all.

We can fight a small election that is confined to the region where we have an organisation. Suppose that the village sarpanch is from the Andolan, he can get some work done. Then we can fight an election, but we should not fight to be part of the government. And if we do become part of the government, will we get a cabinet berth or a post? We should think about that. Otherwise, what is the point? We will sit in the opposition and just talk; that is all we will do. It is better if we strengthen our organisations. Then we can raise a voice and reach the government. I don't see that any of those elected over the last twenty years have been very effective. K. C. Padvi has been the MLA from Akrani Tehsil for the last fifteen years. He has supported the Andolan from time to time. He had even given us in writing that he would get people rehabilitated. But now that he is elected, we don't even see his face. How then can we trust anyone?

Nandini: The Andolan has been going on for so long now. Do you see any changes in the decision-making process?

Kevalsingh: Yes, the way things were done and decisions were taken at the executive committee meetings was quite different earlier. I will give you a small example. Suppose someone has undertaken a fast on behalf of the valley. How long should we stretch it? Will we get support? How much pressure would it put on the government and officials? Will the issue be resolved? Now that the person's health is failing, and the government is not ready to listen, what should we do? Should we call off the fast? A very serious discussion on all these things took place in the decision-making committee. Someone would say, 'We should do this!' Someone else would say, 'Yes, we should!' Others would say, 'No, we shouldn't!', and so on, until a consensus was arrived at.

But at present, the executive committee does not even exist. In the first few years of the Andolan, it met every month. In those meetings we would talk about what the situation was in each village, what was taking place in the world outside—everything would be discussed. But, because the committee is no longer there, I don't think decisions are being taken this way. From 1998–99 it almost ceased to function. Some people split away in 1994. Some villages lost their strength—not the strength to fight, but the mental stress took its toll. On the one hand the water had entered the village, on the other no one knew whether rehabilitation would take place or not. This was the feeling that people began to have. And then villages began to be rehabilitated. By 2003, all the executive committee members of the villages had left along with their people.

Presently, once a year a meeting does take place. In the beginning all of us would collect from here and there and attend the meeting every one or two months. We would sit together, and everyone would come to know the current stage of the battle. Now people have been dispersed far and wide. It is difficult to even meet one another, and information about the meeting does not reach everyone.

Nandini: Do you have any regrets?

Kevalsingh: The government tried to entice every activist of the Andolan. Some they offered jobs, some they tempted with bribes. But those who had resolved to serve the people in the true sense did not ever accept any of these. If activists like us had been enticed, the Andolan would never have succeeded. If we had thought only of ourselves, by now we would have built two-storey or four-storey buildings. To tell you the truth, we suffered a lot. We worked for the people even while our families abused us, cursed us. That is why we are still respected wherever we go. If we had done something wrong, who would have known us? Whoever has done good work has had to face the good and the bad. Savitribai had to face beatings. Whether it was Jyotiba Phule, Lokmanya Tilak or Gandhiji, everyone had to make great sacrifices for the movement. These things happen in all movements. That is the history of our country. The people of the valley have also sacrificed a lot, and that is why the Andolan has continued to exist and gain strength.

The only thing I feel sad about is that just as a farmer prepares his land and makes it fertile, we too had made the Andolan fertile and because of that, the activists who came later enjoyed its fruits—but without putting in the effort. We put in a lot of work. We used to write, carry out surveys and do many more things, but someone else used our work to make their name saying, 'Look, this is what I have done!'

We have never been able to tell anyone about all that we did because we are from the submergence zone; why should we boast about it? Whatever effort we put in, we did it for our own people. But we began to feel that those who were working among us were setting us aside. At such times, we think—the Andolan came up because we put in so much work. The new people who come, do they even know what the Andolan is? They don't. Our hearts grow heavy when we see someone working gratis on the base that our labour and sacrifice built. Fine, let anyone come and work. But it would be good if they did so in accordance with the thinking and the decisions of those who have earlier made the sacrifices. That is why I have spoken these few sentences.

Today work is being done. But not the way it used to be done earlier, when we used to take everyone into confidence, asking them what if we did such and such thing? This doesn't happen today. There is a lot of difference in the conditions. We are now in a scientific age. You can communicate from anywhere to anywhere within minutes. But we still have hope; our love is still alive. That is why we want that someone should come to our village, talk to us and listen to how we are living our lives.

What makes us sad is only this (*that no one comes to ask*). I cannot see anything else that is hurtful. We did what we did. We are happy that it has borne fruit.

The following interview is Kevalsingh's second interview, on 2 February 2012, four years after the previous one in 2007.

Nandini: We meet again after four years. The last time, you mentioned a number of problems related to rehabilitation. So after four years, what is the situation now?

Kevalsingh: The issue of the undeclared sons remains as it was. In these four years none of the affected people have got irrigation. This year, in 2011, people are literally going bankrupt because of debts. Eighty-two people have been given land, but for the last seven or eight years they only have possession—their names have not been entered on the 7/12 forms. When we ask the officials about it, they tell us that all those lands are acquired *ex parte*. This is a great injustice.

For one, the original ex parte holder has his house in this village. We had demanded that they show us land in the surrounding areas, but they are not ready to do so. They keep telling us to accept a package, accept money.[129] We are not people who can live on a package. We want land. They are offering ten lakh rupees per hectare. People will simply go through the ten lakhs in a year and then their lives will be completely ruined. No one thinks about it. Even the collector admits, 'We know their lives will be ruined. But what can we do if there is no land to give?' They themselves say this! We told the government, level this land, cover it with silt from some dam, provide proper irrigation, but they are not ready to do that either. All these issues I had told you about four years ago, and none of them has been resolved. People's economic and social situation is deteriorating.

In our old village we practised laha. But after rehabilitation that practice has been abandoned. The practice of helping each other on the farm or helping each other construct our houses is also almost on the verge of extinction.

In our old village we used to drink natural water from our dug wells. We used to drink the water which nurtured our medicinal plants and herbs and after touching their roots, flowed into the streams and wells. After we came here, we find the taste of the water is completely different. In our old village, even food cooked without oil used to be very tasty. Here we use oil, but the food has no taste. Access to healthcare is a little better because the dispensary is nearby, and the doctor comes to the village. But the prevalence of illnesses has increased. The reason for this is to be found in what we eat—hybrid jowar, grains grown with a lot of fertilisers and vegetable with a lot of pesticides. That same poisonous water percolates into the soil and into the groundwater. All these are reasons why people are falling ill so often. Earlier, people used to get well with the use of medicinal herbs and plants. Here they have no alternative but to go to the doctor. For serious illnesses we have to go to Shahada and get admitted into a private hospital, which is very expensive.

Yes, there is one advantage here. There are big established schools nearby, so children have got enrolled there and have started studying. Who knows, but probably because there is less physical work here, it is good for the body.

If we get an adequate and stable income from the farm, we can improve farming. We can take up experimental farming and develop organic farming here. If we put in that kind of effort, then the quality of land will improve and we will spend much less on our farming. But that will take a very long time because these lands have become infertile. How do we make them fertile? That can only happen very slowly. If we face some difficulty in the future and have to sell some land, it will fetch a high price. But even if the land price is high, I do not think other costs will be small. Still, we can think of some development in the future. Today cotton, papaya—all these cash crops demand lot of money. If we stop growing those cash crops and start growing local varieties or jowar, bajra and maize, then we can lead a good life. But to do that it will take us many years.

Nandini: How is the Jeevan Shala functioning at the rehabilitation sites?

Kevalsingh: From the earlier batch of students who have graduated, some of them have done their MA, some MA BEd, some have become primary teachers, some are engineers or have graduated from agricultural colleges, and some have excelled in sports and reached up to the national level in their game. The two Jeevan Shalas, with which we began, have now grown to thirteen or fourteen Jeevan Shalas. More than 5,000 students have graduated from these schools.

I myself was headmaster for ten years. I managed the schools very well during that time. Whether it was singing, theatre or games, the Narmada Jeevan Shala of Nimgavhan always used to get the first prize. But some old teachers left the school—I will not name them—and new teachers joined. The older teachers and I, we used to think differently. Our aim was that of educating children to help them through their life struggle. That dream has remained, but there are no teachers who can identify with the dream. Some of the earlier students are teachers now. Some of them are activists too. They run the school these days. But I left the school last year because we had some differences which I cannot air openly. I can still run an experimental school. But that can happen only if the teachers and I have views and thinking that match.

One works, puts in all that effort and then no one appreciates it, no one loves you. What we think and what others think can be different, but at the least there must be love and affection. I did not leave the school because of work issues. I never wanted to leave because after you have put in so much work, to leave so suddenly is not the right way of doing things. What about the educational loss to the students? What about the students you were trying so hard to shape? I submitted my letter[130] three months before school opened. The decision (on issues raised regarding the functioning of the Jeevan Shalas) should have been taken before the opening of the school. That did not happen. I spent more than ten days thinking about whether I should leave the school. If there were going to be no answers to the issues I had raised, then, in the end, it was better to leave. I left the school because my questions remained unanswered. If we try to go deeper into the reasons, there will be big differences of opinion. So I will not go that deep.

Nandini: What was your honorarium at the Jeevan Shala, to which you gave so many years of your life?

Kevalsingh: There was practically no honorarium to speak of. I worked on an honorarium of Rs 50 in the beginning, and then it went up to Rs 300. Later on, as we managed to get different trustees, it was increased to about Rs 600–700. When I resigned, my honorarium was Rs 1,500. Today if someone asks me, 'What do you do?' and I tell him, 'I am a teacher,' he would say, 'Oh, you are a teacher? You must be earning a handsome salary.' At such moments the smile on my face tends to waver. Because even a junior government teacher who has worked for two to four years gets a salary of Rs 12,000–13,000. But that is fine. We were building a different society. That was the reason we chose to accept the honorarium. Nevertheless, we were doing it at the cost of our farms and our households. Later people began to think, if we are paying you Rs 1,500, you are nothing but our servant. But you can do nothing with Rs 1,500. Everyone knows that only too well.

Nandini: Activists like you are central to every successful movement. As you look back upon it now, what are your views on the different strategies adopted by the Andolan to halt the construction of the dam—especially, '*Doobenge, Par Hatenge Nahi*'?

Kevalsingh: In the early stages of the Andolan, all the discussions about the strategy for further work on every single issue took place in the executive committee, and the decision was taken with everyone's consensus. Coming to *Doobenge, Par Hatenge Nahi*, even before that strategy was adopted, people had fought many big battles. We had taken out several morchas and had met many ministers and officials. We had challenged all the governments saying, 'We are willing to discuss all the issues face to face across the table. However, the questions which need to be answered are: What are the benefits of the dam which is being constructed? What are the disadvantages and costs?' But the governments were not willing to discuss the issues across the table. At the start we had asked for land. That issue was never resolved. It was proved that the government had no land to offer.

The second issue was that of benefit and cost. It was a matter of the country's economy, of its finances. The Andolan had asked that if the government was going to spend crores of rupees to build the dam, and if, even after building the dam, there were going to be no benefits, then why build the dam? Why sacrifice the lives of lakhs of people? In the end, the people warned the government, 'You have not answered our questions; you have not provided us with life support. If we cannot fulfil our right to life, what can we do? If you are going to submerge our village by force, then you have left us with only one alternative—to be drowned!' That was when the people raised the slogan *Doobenge, Par Hatenge Nahi*. The people took up a massive challenge—they had to go to jail many times, they were lathicharged a number of times too. But more than that, people were ready to stand in the rising waters. At that time, the Manibeli satygraha had already started. In 1993 Manibeli was completely submerged. And since 1994 onward, as the height of the dam increased, turn by turn, more and more villages were submerged.

It was natural then for people to think to themselves, 'We said we are willing to get drowned, but now our villages are submerged. If our houses are washed away, the wood is washed away, we will never get it back. So, fine. This is our battle. We will continue the fight. But again, once the houses are washed away, we won't get them back.' So a few people began to move their houses to safer places. Many people also wondered, how many times will we allow our houses to be submerged?[131] And so, some people accepted rehabilitation. At the same time the second stage of the battle began. If you are arresting people for saying *Doobenge, Par Hatenge Nahi* and not allowing them to die, a second strategy was initiated by the people. That was Jalsamarpan. At that time we were trying to get the dam reviewed. A review committee was to be formed, but it did not get formed in time. So one batch of NBA people had warned that they would carry out Jalsamarpan. We got support from all over the world and fought that battle also successfully.

In the end in 1994, because the review committee report was not presented to the people and made public, we had a twenty-seven-day fast in Bhopal. And only after that was the report made public. The report was completely in favour of the people. A case was registered in the Supreme Court and because of the case, the Sardar Sarovar work could be stopped for five to six years. In 1998 when work on Sardar Sarovar restarted one step at a time according to the directive of the Court, once again *Doobenge, Par Hatenge Nahi* became the battle cry in Domkhedi. The struggle began in earnest and continued at Domkhedi till 2003. In the end, the height of Sardar Sarovar was raised to 110 metres, and Domkhedi and Nimgavhan were both submerged. In 2004, people decided to accept land and that was the end of the *Doobenge, Par Hatenge Nahi* strategy. And from there begins the next strategy, that of rehabilitation.

To tell you the truth, once a strategy was planned, the struggles were systematically conducted in accordance with it. But not all people think alike. Later, some people felt that whatever we did was not right, and that we incurred avoidable losses. That if we had accepted the land when the government first offered it to us, they would have given it to us. But when the battle is on, everyone fights. It is only later that people start thinking—was it beneficial or harmful? This continues for a long time after the struggle. Look at the way Anna Hazare's movement is still discussed in the papers after all this time.

Nandini: Many people have raised this issue that a people's movement should not have relied on the court. What do you think?

Kevalsingh: We must respect and show faith in our judicial system. Because the judiciary is for all citizens of India. It is also wrong to think that once a verdict is given, we cannot do anything about it. We can raise our voice against the Supreme Court's decision too. In any case, the Court's judgement is being violated by the government machinery. In its judgement the Court clearly stated that until there is complete rehabilitation of villages (up to a particular height) the government cannot push the construction of the dam (to that particular height).[132] The government is submitting false reports. Moreover, the Court would not give a judgement that is false and completely against us. Because if there are three judges, they are not likely to have the same opinion. We can fight for what is our right through these different opinions too.

Nandini: You have yourself undertaken fasts. What are your views on fasts as a strategy?

Kevalsingh: If people feel that they are left with no weapons to fight with, then one way of battling on is by fasting. It is an important weapon placed in the people's hands by Mahatma Gandhi. I am against using fasts all the time, or using it for minor issues. Ultimately, you also have to see how it affects society. People may begin to feel that as soon as anything happens, these people go on a fast. I am not a person who fasts much. I undertook a fast only once—to demand that the review committee's report be made public. Once the issue was resolved, we ended the fast. If there is a particular issue which is capable of being resolved, we can undertake a fast. But if there is a problem that cannot be resolved, it is no good to undertake a fast and then abandon the fight half way; it does not have a good effect on society at large. There are many ways you can fight. We can court mass arrest; there is *rasta roko*, and there are many other ways. Fasting is not the only way.

Nandini: Jalsamarpan, drowning by water, is many steps ahead of a fast, isn't it?

Kevalsingh: If there is no alternative left, then let people get justice through Jalsamarpan. That was the objective. By Jalsamarpan we would demonstrate the fate of the lakhs of people in the Narmada Valley and in the Sardar Sarovar area. Many fasts had already been undertaken and protest marches and sit-ins too. Finally, what else could we do? It did not mean that all the people in the valley had to undertake Jalsamarpan. A small contingent was ready to do this. Their action would be a message to everyone, because one of the issues in the fight being waged was awakening the government to the consequences. And because the government awakened at the right time, they could stop the Jalsamarpan.

Nandini: In the Narmada region you had started working with the Punarvasan Sangharsh Samiti. What is the status of that organisation today?

Kevalsingh: The Narmada Punarvasan Sangharsh Samiti was formed fifteen years ago as part of the NBA. Pratibha Shinde and Sanjay Mahajan were the two people who had started this organisation. At that time, I was the main activist in Manibeli. In 1992 when Kesubhai's first house was dismantled, thousands of police were mobilised. It was at that time that Pratibha Shinde reached Manibeli and the two of them—Pratibha and Sanjay experienced Aurangabad Jail for the first time. We told her that some people from our villages had accepted rehabilitation and that she should take care of the work at the rehabilitation sites. That is when she established the Punarvasan Sangharsh Samiti. She meticulously worked out how rehabilitation should take place and what people should receive, complete with lists. Initially, five villages accepted rehabilitation. She worked in those villages at every level, from declaring the people eligible for rehabilitation right up to the distribution of land. Even today, her Sangharsh Samiti is active. At the same time, she started 'Lok Morcha', a new organisation active in getting land for encroachers and fighting on other issues in Gujarat villages. In Jalgaon they are fighting for forest landholders. They stay in the villages and work, so local people have faith in them. They get support from other organisations at the national level and their organisations are slowly expanding. They have received many awards for their work.

Nandini: At the time of the Right Livelihood Award, NBA had taken a decision that no individual within the movement would accept awards. After that, NBA activists have received awards. What do you feel about awards?

Kevalsingh: I can point out one difference. Pratibha came here some ten years after the NBA. So far, eight adivasi activists from her organisation have got awards. Till date, not a single local adivasi activist of the NBA has received any award. This does not mean I want one. I have no desire for awards. None whatsoever.

The Right Livelihood Award was given to the Andolan as a whole. That is why Keshavbhau had gone to receive it. Adivasi activists from other organisations have also got awards. But no adivasi from the Andolan has got any award.

Nandini: The last time we spoke, you had many cases filed against you. Where do they stand now?

Kevalsingh: The two or three cases in the Dhadgaon court have already been decided. The judgement has come. But in 1993, a case was registered in which patently false charges of dacoity, breaking a camera, and attempt to kill have been slapped on five of us—Arundhati Dhuru, Mahesh Sharma, Vitthalbhai, Mangibai[133] and myself. Mangibai and Vitthalbhai stayed in jail for one month and were released on bail. I have been shown as absconding for the last eighteen years. Thinking that after eighteen years the case should be finally decided, I have been trying to get anticipatory bail, making many trips to Taloda and Shahada. At that time my lawyer Yogini Khanolkar was abroad, and handed the responsibility to a private lawyer. Private lawyers are after all only interested in earning money.

I went to Shahada and Taloda eleven times and spent 10,000-15,000 rupees from my own pocket. All of the 2010 crop was spent on these cases. By now, I must have spent 70,000-80,000 rupees visiting Dhadgaon, Taloda and Shahada. All from my own pocket—not a paisa from the Andolan. The case is still going on.

Vitthalbhai comes from Gujarat and Mangibai from Amlibari, spending from their own pockets to attend court. We are the three accused. The other accused have not come to court anytime. In fact, all these cases are Andolan cases. Dealing with them should be their responsibility. But no such responsibility is accepted by the Andolan. The only thing is that the Andolan lawyer is fighting the case for us.

Nandini: As activists, how do you deal with financial issues?

Kevalsingh: I know many people and have a large network of relationships. During the day, at least ten to fifteen people visit my house. There is someone or the other from the organisation at home every day. I must be using 1 kg of sugar every day just to prepare tea. My four children stay outside the village for their education. I have to spend on them. If like everyone else, I had insisted on being given good irrigated land, I would have got it.[134] So, I am stuck with this dry land. I only get one crop from it, and only I know how much I get out of it. Day by day, I am getting more and more indebted. My struggle is ongoing. Let us see what comes of it.

I do not speak much about it. I am not saying these things only for the activists working in the Andolan but for all those working across the country. Right from the time of Mahatma Gandhi, the situation has been no different. As a responsible activist, I accept this. A person fighting for truth has to be prepared to undergo hardship. It may appear as if I am praising myself, but that is okay. In all of this, we should not forget our history. And we should not forget our own people who have worked among us.

Nandini: Would you advise the coming generation to be activists like you?

Kevalsingh: Wherever I go, to any office, ten or fifteen people gather around me. 'I have this problem; please write this out for me; please get my work done.'

I always tell today's educated generation, 'Son, you have to stand on your own feet, but while doing so, spare some thought to our community too. Work so that our community progresses.' That is something I will not forget all my life.

Nandini: Four years back you said that many villagers from Alirajpur in Madhya Pradesh, and even from Maharashtra, have remained behind in their old villages, and that they should be rehabilitated before the monsoon. What is the situation now in the old villages?

Kevalsingh: In these four years, rehabilitation should have taken place. It has still not happened. People are staying in the villages in the same conditions. Even today, they are not being offered any land for rehabilitation. If we think only of Maharashtra's submergence zone, there are 300 declared landholders who have not got any land as yet. In Madhya Pradesh, the problems of the people around Jalsindhi and the nearby adivasi belt still remain unresolved. Nimad region has remained the way it was earlier. The government has no land to offer these people. There is no land to be bought either. People are demanding forestland but that too is not yet sanctioned.

The Andolan has earlier provided information many times in their reports about where land is available. But now even the Andolan activists do not have proper communication with the people. So far as Maharashtra is concerned, this issue will be resolved only if 1,000 hectares of land is made available. Today the big issue of undeclared adult sons remains totally ignored. If they are not declared as project-affected, one does not know what they will do in the future. The Andolan needs to do these undeclared sons justice. To get justice, we must continue the struggle, however difficult it might be.

A couple of years ago, the NBA made a big noise about forest landholders. Huge rallies were held and forms were filled out for each person. But today the issue of forest landholders has pretty much taken a back seat. In many villages the land has not even been surveyed. And the issue of who is eligible to get land and who is not has also not been properly resolved. The Andolan needs to work on the issue of forestland holders in a responsible way. But it is being handled in a very careless manner.

Nandini: We discussed this four years ago: after an experience of twenty-five to thirty years in the Andolan, despite there being such capable people, why is it that local leadership has not come up even today?

Kevalsingh: I have been searching for an answer to this question for the last thirty years. And I seem to have failed miserably in this respect. For any sustained struggle to work, leadership is the most important thing. Today, in order to look after the Andolan's work, to do the office work, the paperwork, you need to be educated and you need to know English. To establish communication and make common cause with other mass movements and organisations you need some kind of strength. I think perhaps that is what is lacking.

In areas like Dhadgaon, many small organisations are coming up. If we can take the help of these organisations, it would be good. But why is it that there is no place for local activists in these organisations? I don't think I can answer that question. But I feel that we can start a new, independent organisation. Now there are many educated students who are idle even after getting educated. We need to bring a little awareness to them. And they will need the support and love of the community if we want them to be a part of this new organisation.

The second thing is the financial aspect. That too may be a reason because to work for any cause without money is difficult. Even if all you need is simply a room for an office, you cannot do without money. We need people who can provide financial support. We also need people who can document things and write letters.

We need leadership that can take the local activists along with them. There must be a combination of old experience and new strength. The roots of the Andolan go deep; if the senior and junior activists come together and work together, then there is no need to build a new organisation. The old first-generation activists must stay and they must guide the movement ahead. We talk about the garden of culture. Then elders must be respected. The old people must stay. We have to take from their experience and learn from what they did. But somewhere, this is going wrong, and that is also why local activists are being alienated. This is all I have to say.

Nandini: It has now been many years since you left Nimgavhan and came here to Vadchhil. When people settle in a new place, after a few years they make it their home. Do you now see Vadchhil as your own place...as home?

Kevalsingh: The mother who gives birth to you is your mother. Whether the child is dark or fair, she loves the child. Now about the place where we accepted rehabilitation—I can discern which is my mother and which my *mavashi*.[135] A mavashi is a mavashi. If a father has two wives, the mother is the one who gives birth to you, and the other woman becomes a mavashi after she marries the father. Even today, my village is the village where I was born. Today it has been submerged, but it is still my village—the place where I grew up, and the one I will see with my mind's eyes however old I may become.

Here we may slog as much as we may. Fine. We may even progress a bit, that's true. But like all human beings we look to the future. This land I feel is not going to give us much happiness. The hardship here, it is cruel. Day by day, our expenses are increasing. And at times I think, is this piece of land even going to remain in my hands? Because if in some years there is little rain or no crop, we have still sunk 60,000–70,000 rupees into these 5 acres of ours. And if we fail to get even that much from the land, who knows, in the future, a moneylender would likely snatch it away from us.

In our hearts, we still feel the difference between our old village and this new one. The picture of that village now resides in our dreams. We will never forget it. But if we tell the new generation about it, they may not believe us. We have not taken or preserved any photographs of our village. If we had, we would have shown them to our children and said, 'Here, see this is our village. Here we used to play. Here is our house. Here the river ran with the sweet sound of flowing water. In future, we can only show it to our children in the form of stories. But as long as we live, we will see our land with our eyes and also our village Nimgavhan.

NOTES

[1]While Nimgavhan accepted resettlement in 2004, a large number of families continued to stay in the partially submerged village of Jalsindhi in M.P.

[2]*Laha* is the system of collective labour in adivasi society based not on monetary wages but on the principle of exchanging labour for labour.

[3]Coarse grains traditionally grown in the region, including in the submergence villages, with many useful properties, one being that they could be stored for five to seven years or longer and would not rot, and hence would help tide over a drought year if corn or other crops failed.

[4]*Akhada* is a prayer-song sung collectively by large gatherings of adivasis through the night, and also the place where it is sung.

[5]Kevalsingh is referring to the rising waters of the dam entering his village and home.

[6]Also called *dak*, these are hourglass-shaped percussion instruments played when singing the gayana.

[7]A *Bodwa* is an adivasi shaman or priest-doctor who summons spirits for the purpose of healing, along with dispensing medicinal herbs.

[8]*Palya*, also *paliya* or *khambhi*, is usually a sacred stone marked with figures or inscriptions, often in memory of someone.

[9]Bawangaja, near Badwani in M.P., has a large statue carved out of a hill. That statue is worshiped as one of the Tirthankaras by the Jain community.

[10]After Vinoba Bhave's camp in Nimgavhan in 1952, Dagadu Sonavane was instrumental in helping Kevalsingh's uncles to pursue studies. This is covered in detail in Keshavbhau's interview.

[11]Kevalsingh's mother tongue is Pawri, which does not have a written script.

[12]When the waters rose to threatening levels, endangering lives, people offering satyagraha against the illegal submergence by refusing to move or leave their homes—like Kevalsingh's mother Pawalibai—were sometimes arrested and jailed by the police.

[13]Vaharu Sonavane, a senior Marxist adivasi leader of the Shramik Sangathana (a movement for the rights of the adivasis and the working class), is the founding member of Adivasi Ekta Parishad. A well-known poet, he raised the issue of representation of adivasis by non-adivasi leadership through his poem 'The Stage'. See: https://towardfreedom.org/story/archives/asia-archives/adivasi-movements-in-india-an-interview-with-poet-waharu-sonavane/ (accessed 16 March 2022).

[14]Kaluram Dodhade is the founding member of Bhoomi Sena, a movement for 'land to the tiller' that began in the early seventies in Maharashtra. See: http://www.ces.uc.pt/emancipa/voices/gen/kaluramdhodade.html (accessed 20 October 2021).

[15]The epidemic in which more than 100 children died due to gastroenteritis is detailed in Keshavbhau's interview.

[16]The distance between Nimgavhan in Maharashtra and Badwani in M.P. is around 100 kms.

[17]Songs played an important role in mobilising and organising people in the Narmada Valley. Songs written and sung by activists like Bhadraben Gamit, Kevalsingh Vasave and Amit Bhatnagar in particular became a rage in the NBA and enthused thousands.

[18]Nimad is a region in M.P. which includes the districts of Badwani, Khargone and Khandwa.

[19]Khemla Ajnaharia is a senior adivasi leader, a founding member of KMCS and a resident of Sondva, M.P.

[20]Arundhati Dhuru, a postgraduate from Tata Institute of Social Sciences and a firebrand activist of the NBA, played a significant role in building the movement in its formative years, particularly in Maharashtra and Gujarat. She was also a part of the Samarpit Dal—NBA's sacrificial squad. She lives in Lucknow and is an active member of the National Alliance of People's Movements (NAPM).

[21]Himanshu Thakkar, an engineer from IIT, Mumbai, and a full-time activist of the NBA, apart from mobilisation, played a key role in research and documentation as well as the media and campaign-related work of NBA. He is currently the coordinator of South Asia Network on Dams, Rivers & People; see: https://sandrp.in/ (accessed 23 October 2021).

[22]The NGNS was already in existence in M.P.; what Kevalsingh possibly means here is that it was not very active and, as he mentions above, only a few people assembled at Rajghat. For more on the NGNS, see note 76, pp. 137–138.

[23]Shankar Tadval, a senior adivasi leader of the KMCS, resides in Alirajpur, M.P. Shankar is a member of the Adivasi Ekta Parishad and is involved with forest rights and the issue of silicosis among the adivasis.

[24]These remote villages in M.P., inhabited by adivasis were officially non-existent as they were absent in the revenue records. These villages were not considered to be in the submergence zone of SSP and requiring resettlement.

[25]Manglya Pawra, an adivasi leader of NBA, is a great orator and mobiliser. He belongs to submergence village Bhadal, Maharashtra, and now resides in R&R site Chikli in Maharashtra.

[26]Like Kavant in Gujarat, Umrali in Alirajpur district, M.P. is a big market place for the adivasis.

[27]Dahi in Kukshi Taluka of M.P. is a market town for the adivasis of that region.

[28]Kailash Avasiya, from submergence village Bhilkedha, M.P. is a senior full-time adivasi activist of NBA. Kailash gave up opportunities of government jobs to continue work in the NBA. In the 2014 Lok Sabha elections, he contested as a candidate of the Aam Aadmi Party from the Khargone-Badwani constituency.

[29]The songs in mass programmes of the NBA were sung with such fervour that it electrified the atmosphere. Unfortunately, these are not recorded as they were sung spontaneously. However, glimpses of these songs can be had in the documentaries made on the movement.

[30]Representatives from 245 submergence villages of SSP falling in the three states of Maharashtra, M.P. and Gujarat as well as the 6 Kevadia Colony affected villages.

[31]Four activists including Kevalsingh, who were in Dhule attending a shibir, reached Roshmal town where the sarpanch was to be officially declared. The other three activists were Ajit, Jahangir and Milind Murugkar.

[32]Milind Murugkar is a food and agriculture policy analyst associated with Pragati Abhiyan, a developmental organisation

based in Nashik, Maharashtra. He is also a well-known columnist, an engineer and a supporter of NBA.

[33]NBA felt it necessary to focus on Akkalkuwa villages as they were closest to the dam and would be the first to face submergence.

[34]The nonstop rising of the dam wall before their eyes and the danger of imminent submergence put a constant psychological pressure on the people in the submergence villages of Akkalkuva to accept whatever poor rehabilitation was offered to them.

[35]The office of NBA located in Vadodara, Gujarat was ransacked by members of the Congress and the BJP in 1994 and documents were burnt.

[36]Surveys of 4,500 houses falling in the submergence area of SSP in the 33 villages of Maharashtra were carried out in great detail including the material used in the houses, cattle owned by the people, land holdings, trees, etc.

[37]Milind Kothavde, Pune, a full-time activist of NBA played a very important role in the submergence villages of Maharashtra, particularly at the time people were facing repression by the government.

[38]Shobha Wagh, an NBA activist who tragically drowned in the backwaters of the SSP, was a committed activist and greatly loved by the people.

[39]Largely a self-sustaining community, the adivasis in the submergence area did not have to go beyond the nearby market town for their needs. They had limited exposure to urban areas, just like people of urban areas have to forests. Therefore, the responsibility of escorting large numbers of people from remote forest villages for mass protests to metropolitan cities was a risky task.

[40]Mahesh Sharma, a senior activist of the NBA belongs to the submergence village Chikhalda, M.P. He played a key role in the valley during the phase of repression and submergence. He currently works with an NGO, Jan Swasthya Sahyog, at Ganiyari, Chhattisgarh.

[41]Ishwarbhai Prajapati an employee of the Physical Research Laboratory, Ahmedabad, was a senior activist with Lok Adhikar Sangh, Gujarat. Ishwarbhai played an important role in organising the people affected by the Kevadia Colony and the Narmada Canal in Gujarat during the early years of the NBA.

[42]Chittaroopa Palit (Silvy), a graduate from IRMA, Gujarat, has been a senior activist of the struggles of adivasis, peasants and landless people across the Narmada Valley since the 1980s, initially with KMCS and later with NBA. She continues to lead the NBA's struggle against other dams on the Narmada including the Maheshwar, Omkareshwar, Maan and Indirasagar dams in M.P. She has also been with the Aam Aadmi Party, M.P.

[43]The Mumbai–Agra National Highway was blocked on the bridge over the Narmada at Khalghat, in M.P. for thirty-six hours in 1990 by the NBA demanding a review of the SSP.

[44]The road block was withdrawn after Sunderlal Patwa, CM of M.P., promised that a review of SSP would be undertaken. However, the promise was never fulfilled, and NBA faced severe repression during Patwa's tenure as CM.

[45]Ali Kazmi's film *A Valley Rises* has extensively covered the Sangharsh Yatra in 1990–91.

[46]Nirmalbhai Patodi of submergence village Chikhalda in M.P. was a senior leader of NBA, and his role in building the NBA in M.P. along with other senior leaders like Maheshbhai Patidar of village Kundia remains unmatched. Unfortunately, he passed away young. He is survived by his wife Suman didi, also an active member of NBA, and their son Rajat.

[47]Bhadraben Gamit, an adivasi activist from South Gujarat, played an important role in mobilising the oustees of Kevadia Colony and the canal-affected villages, particularly women, in the early years of NBA. Her songs stirred the people of the valley to fight and she was popularly called the Lata Mangeshkar of NBA. She now lives in her village Songadh, Surat.

[48]The security around the dam site was so tight that a large number of police and security personnel were permanently deployed in and around Kevadia Colony. The Official Secrets Act was clamped adjacent to the dam site covering some of the submergence villages also. Section 144 was more or less permanently enforced in the area. It was difficult for the NBA activists to move freely and many a time, activists had to function by being underground.

[49]Bhagwanbhai Mukati of the submergence village Narmadanagar in M.P. is a senior activist of NBA. He has helped organise the project-affected people from all the three states including the people to be affected by other dams on the Narmada. Because of this he is well known among the people from Kevadia Colony right up to the Narmada Sagar dam.

[50]Kamala Yadav, popularly known as Kammujiji, of submergence village Chota Badada, Badwani district, M.P., is one of the pillars of the NBA. An effective speaker and excellent organiser, she has shouldered many responsibilities in the NBA, and has taken part in many fasts.

[51]The people opposed the government's clear felling of forest in the submergence zone of SSP like the women of the famous Chipko Movement in Uttarakhand who protected trees from being felled in their area in the 1970s.

[52]It was only to displace the people and clear-fell forests that roads were being built in the submergence villages. Till then no such amenities were provided. Naturally people opposed the coming of bulldozers along with large police contingents.

[53]It was routine for the state to flood the villages with *khaki* or uniformed police to instil fear in the minds of the affected people so that they would agree to leave the submergence villages.

[54]Kesubhai Tadvi's was the first house to fall in the SSP submergence zone in Manibeli. It was therefore very important for the government to evict him to set an example for the rest of the 45,000 PAFs in the 245 submergence villages to fall in line. Unprecedented force was therefore used to dismantle Kesubhai's house against his will.

[55]Kesubhai Tadvi's teenage daughters Kunta and Mangi were strong fighters of the NBA.

[56]Gumansingh Avasiya, a senior activist of NBA, belongs to the submergence village Pendra, M.P. Though severely affected by polio in both legs he remained a very active member of the NBA, carrying out diverse responsibilities. Guman was awarded the Zidd Puraskar by Dr Shriram Lagoo for his contribution to the movement.

[57]Vitthalbhai Tadvi of Manibeli along with the sarpanch Narayanbhai Tadvi, Jatarbhai, Natubhai Tadvi, Hiruben, Kavitaben, etc., spearheaded the resistance against SSP along with rest of the families in Manibeli. The people continue to live in Manibeli surrounded by the dam waters even today—over twenty years after the dam waters entered their village.

[58]There is no place or regard for indigenous knowledge among project authorities. People had lost faith in the government as it had stated that 101 villages would be submerged in the Bargi dam, one of the upstream dams, but when the Bargi Dam was filled, 161 villages submerged and so did 23 rehabilitation sites.

[59]Rama Mohariya and Rama Atya, both full-time NBA activists.

[60]The Narmada Water Disputes Tribunal (NWDT) award has listed in detail the provisions for R&R.

[61]Bhula Moti's house in Village Vadgam in Gujarat was the first house to be submerged in the Sardar Sarovar dam from among the 245 affected villages. It was difficult to swim against the tide in Gujarat where the pro-dam lobby was extremely powerful and supported by even NGOs and leading Gandhians. It was against this backdrop that Bhula Moti put up an extraordinary fight, resisting all inducement and intimidation, choosing to lose all his worldly possessions when the dam waters drowned his home. He was left with nothing except the clothes he was wearing. Bhula Moti was never provided any rehabilitation by the GoG.

[62]Manibeli in Maharashtra was the first village in the submergence zone of SSP on the left bank of the Narmada, while village Vadgam in Gujarat, was the first in the submergence zone of the dam on the right bank of the river. Manibeli was the main centre of the NBA and symbol of resistance to the dam as well as displacement. The powerful struggle in Manibeli drew worldwide attention and support. So it became imperative for the GoG to shift the oustee families of Manibeli, the backbone of the struggle, to resettlement sites, come what may, to be able to go ahead with the dam construction and also discredit the struggle. Besides, as Manibeli set an example for the rest of the 245 villages falling in the submergence zone of SSP to follow in its footsteps with the slogan, '*Koi Nahin Hatega, Bandh Nahin Banega*' (No One Shall Move, The Dam Shall Not Be Built), it became absolutely necessary for the government to crush the resistance at Manibeli. This is what Kevalsingh means when he says that the GoG carried out a campaign to remove/vacate Manibeli. There was a permanent police camp in the village, often with over 500 police, and it was government policy to flood the village with police to intimidate people on the one hand and put psychological pressure of the dam rising in front of their eyes on the other.

[63]Torch.

[64]Rehmat, a resident of the submergence village Chikhalda in M.P., is a senior activist of the NBA who set an example for other local youth of Nimad to take up full-time responsibilities of the NBA. Rehmat also managed the ashram of Baba Amte after he (Baba) left for Anandvan due to failing health. Rehmat currently works with Manthan Adhyayan Kendra, an organisation researching water and energy issues in Badwani, M.P.

[65]Sukhdev Yadav belongs to submergence village Pipri in M.P. He was a full-time activist of NBA for many years.

[66]Chogalal Dawar of submergence village Kundia in M.P. was a full-time activist of NBA along with many other adivasi youths from Kundia like Gendalal, Karansingh, Gopal, and Ashok who have carried out diverse roles in the NBA.

[67]Shashank Kela, a full-time activist of NBA as well as KMCS, is currently a writer and has authored the book, *A Rogue and Peasant Slave: Adivasi Resistance 1800-2000* (Navayana, 2012).

[68]The Jalsamarpan programme on 6 August 1993 was withdrawn after the government accepted NBA's demand for the review of the SSP. It took time for the news to reach the valley where there were no phones at that time.

[69]The determination of people of Manibeli and the magnitude of the loss of lands and homes due to the submergence has to be seen to

be believed. See: https://india.mongabay.com/2019/10/protesting-against-neglect-manibeli-village-in-the-narmada-valley-decides-to-boycott-maharashtra-polls/ (accessed 16 March 2022).

[70]There seems to have been a slip here. As per my knowledge, and as documented in Sanjay Sangvai's book *The River and Life: People's Struggle in the Narmada Valley* (Earthcare Books, 2000), the widespread submergence occurred in 1994, not 1993.

[71]The waters of the Narmada rose suddenly and the devastation was rapid. The presence of media at that time was very limited; therefore, there is not enough on record of the extent of loss the people of these villages in Akkalkuwa suffered or their struggle. Abhivyakti Media for Development, a Nashik-based organisation has extensively videographed the submergence that happened in the later years in the Akrani Taluka of Maharashtra.

[72]Manibeli was the core of the NBA struggle in the early years and was visited by thousands of supporters from all over the world. A small clay and wood home to coordinate the activities of the NBA in the village was named *Narmadaai*. Journalist Shailendra Yashwant gives an apt tribute to *Narmadaai* in an article in *Frontline* magazine: '...the hut that stood as a symbol of the courage of the downtrodden of the country.'

[73]Luharya Shankariya, a senior adivasi leader from the submergence village Jalsindhi, Alirajpur, M.P., allowed his home and fields to drown in the dam waters but refused to move out. *Drowned Out*, a film by Franny Armstrong, is based on his life and struggle; see: http://archive.org/details/WYCD20040929 (accessed 23 October 2021).

[74]Chief Minister of Madhya Pradesh.

[75]Twenty-four adivasi families of village Vadgam, the first of the 19 villages falling in the submergence zone of SSP, fled from the R&R site of Malu in Gujarat due to serious problems after being resettled there, and returned to Vadgam to join NBA. This was a great blow to the GoG and the pro-government/dam NGOs. Repressive measures were therefore adopted against these families, and it was only after a long struggle and court battle that the people were finally relocated again at Dharampuri R&R site in Dabhoi, Gujarat.

[76]'Durgaben' (name changed), who belonged to a remote submergence village in Gujarat, had no formal education and little exposure to the world outside. An extremely fearless woman, she defied the might of the state and refused to leave her village, becoming a symbol of resistance in Gujarat. The GoG subjected her to brutal repression. She was arrested on flimsy charges from her village after midnight by male policepersons and stripped and raped

several times on way to the police station. 'Durgaben' tragically ended her life due to the inhuman violation and humiliation she was put through.

[77]NBA also extended help to other movements, organisations and people when they were in crisis, for example, NBA carried out relief and rehabilitation work during the Latur earthquake in Maharashtra in 1993 and also after the earthquake in Gujarat in 2001.

[78]The protest in the submergence village of Anjanwara, in Alirajpur, M.P. against forcible survey, was also fired upon by the police and the village ransacked. Many adivasi activists were severely beaten and jailed. Families fled into the forest out of fear of police atrocities till outside intervention from civil society groups helped establish normalcy.

[79]Simantini Dhuru and Anand Patwardhan's film, *Narmada Diary*, won the Film Fare Award for best documentary in 1996.

[80]A large police camp was permanently stationed in Shoolpaneshwar village in Gujarat which was close to Manibeli.

[81]One of the main reasons why people who went missing could not find their way back was they were not used to the ways of large cities, and most adivasis did not know any language other than their own.

[82]Booker Prize winner, Arundhati Roy, a staunch supporter of NBA, gave a call for the Rally for the Valley, a programme where hundreds of people across the world came to the Narmada Valley to express their solidarity with the NBA. For her writing a critique of the Supreme Court judgement in the NBA case, she was declared guilty of contempt of court, fined and jailed for a day. Arundhati Roy's essay on the subject titled, 'The Greater Common Good', attracted many youths to the Narmada Valley.

[83]The oustees of the Bargi dam on the Narmada in M.P. have also been struggling for their rights as part of NBA. The Bargi dam was completed in 1989 but the oustees have not been resettled till date.

[84]Rajkumar Sinha, a senior activist of NBA has been at the forefront of the organisation of Bargi dam oustees and is based in Jabalpur, M.P. The Bargi Bandh Prabhavit Sangh has fought for R&R of Bargi oustees, for their rights to cultivate draw down lands of the dam, and for rights over fishing in the reservoir by forming a cooperative. There have been powerful struggles on the other large dams on the Narmada also.

[85]Although monsoon satyagraha was carried out in other villages also, the focus shifted from Manibeli in Akkalkuwa Taluka to Domkhedi in Akrani Taluka of Maharashtra as the dam wall kept rising and waters began to enter villages further in the valley.

Similarly, Jalsindhi was declared the satyagraha centre in M.P. from 1994 onward.

[86]Micro hydel project.

[87]A popular filmmaker from Bollywood, Mansoor Khan is the director of *Qayamat Se Qayamat Tak*. He is also an environmentalist and is the author of the book *The Third Curve* that questions the concept of unlimited growth. The NBA received support from many well-known artists associated with Hindi, Marathi as well as other regional cinema and the stage, prominent among them being Shabana Azmi, Nana Patekar, Sadashiv Amrapurkar, and Aamir Khan.

[88]The '*Doobenge, Par Hatenge Nahin*' strategy was carried out year after year by the people in villages facing submergence. Many times the police would come to arrest and drag people out of the rising waters, but many times they also ignored those who remained standing in water for hours.

[89]After large-scale submergence in the valley and loss of houses, lands and crops, NBA undertook relief work in the submergence villages in which food grains, tarpaulin, and other basic things required for survival were provided to the affected families.

[90]The houses of the adivasis, built with teak and bamboo were very valuable. Due to large-scale tree felling, and submergence that destroyed homes and forests, it became difficult to rebuild houses again and again after repeated submergence.

[91]Narmada, which turned into a reservoir, became dangerous for cattle and human beings to approach as heavy deposits of silt accumulated on its bank. With the change in the river ecology, crocodiles became aggressive and began attacking and killing domestic animals as well as human beings. The stagnant water of the reservoir also became non-potable. The Narmada River which was once revered by the people as their mother had turned into a bane.

[92]The people of the valley resisted the submergence by the dam with the slogan, 'No One Shall Move, The Dam Shall Not Be Built', and allowed their worldly possessions to drown as a mark of protest. The submergence upon the people was brought on by the governments without offering all the facilities as laid down by the NWDT for proper rehabilitation and resettlement. The people challenged this illegal submergence and demanded compensation from the government for the loss they suffered. For claiming damages due to the submergence, panchnama (record with due process with witnesses) of every household had to be carried out.

[93]In many cases in Gujarat, the land given to the oustees remained encumbered with the loans drawn by the original owners against that land.

[94]People brew alcohol from the mahua flowers.

[95]As there is no river in Vadchhil R&R site, fish from the river Narmada which was one of the major sources of food is completely absent here. Similarly, people were involved in raising chickens in the original villages, but in the densely populated less resource-filled R&R sites, the survival rate of chicken has gone down drastically. As there are no grazing lands at the R&R sites, the cattle population too has dwindled. All this has affected the PAPs adversely.

[96]Suhas Kolhekar, a senior activist of the NBA, is a post-doctoral researcher in Molecular Virology from the USA. On her return to India, she joined the National Institute of Virology, Pune and also worked as a teaching associate at the Department of Biotechnology, Pune University, for a year. She eventually gave up her job to work as an activist.

[97]At that time, the GoG had not got permission to install the gates and raise the height of the dam to a full 138 metres from its then height of 121 metres due to noncompliance of rehabilitation conditionality. However, in 2014, almost immediately after Narendra Modi became PM, he granted permission to install the gates and raise the dam height to 138 metres.

[98]While villages falling in the submergence zone have a right to rehabilitation, those that get surrounded by water, become islands and get cut off had no right to R&R.

[99]Nandini Oza, an activist of NBA, worked mainly among the people affected in Gujarat and M.P. She was also involved in NBA's campaigning in the drought-prone areas of Gujarat that supposedly fell in the command area of the project. Later, in order that the people's contribution in the Narmada struggle be recognised, she has been documenting the oral history of the struggle of the people of the Narmada Valley. This book is a part of her work with the people's oral history.

[100]Shripad Dharmadhikary, an engineer from IIT, Mumbai, one of the senior activists of the NBA, was involved in the work of organisation building and mobilising the people of the Narmada Valley from NBA's formative years. He was involved in the Supreme Court case filed by the NBA, the national and international campaign of the NBA, and in the work of documentation as well as research and analysis of the various issues put forth by the NBA before several committees including the Morse committee, the Jayant Patil committee, etc. He is the founding member of Manthan Adhyayan Kendra, a centre established to research, analyse and monitor water and energy issues. Shripad has authored many studies including one on the Bhakra dam named 'Unravelling Bhakra'. See: http://www.manthan-india.org/ (accessed 24 November 2021).

[101]Sanjay Sangvai, a journalist and a senior activist of the NBA sadly passed away in the year 2007. He played a key role in the NBA, particularly in its media and publication related work and the work of political mobilisation. His book *The River and Life* is referred to earlier (in note 70, p. 267).

[102]Alok Agrawal, a graduate engineer from IIT, Kharagpur, is one of the senior leaders of NBA. Having been at the forefront of the struggle around SSP, Alok currently leads the struggles on the other dams on Narmada including the Maheshwar, Omkareshwar, Maan and Indirasagar dams in M.P. Alok has also been with the Aam Aadmi Party, M.P.

[103]Joe Athialy, a full-time activist of NBA with diverse responsibilities, played a crucial role in NBA's national campaign. Thereafter he worked with Amnesty International and with Bank Information Centre, New Delhi. Currently, Joe is Executive Director of the Centre for Financial Accountability.

[104]Bija Jugliya actually travelled to Norway, and not to the USA.

[105]Champalal Avasiya from the submergence village Pendra has been a full-time activist of the NBA.

[106]Ashish Mandloi, a dam oustee and a firebrand activist of the NBA, was managing its activities from its Badwani office at the time of this interview; but sadly he passed away in 2010 at a young age. Ashish played a key role in exposing the scam in R&R in M.P., which lead to the appointment of the Justice Jha Commission and stoppage of the dam work for several years. The NBA office in Badwani is named after him.

[107]Former PM of India.

[108]Then CM of Maharashtra.

[109]Then home minister of Maharashtra.

[110]Mohanbhai Patidar, a senior NBA leader, belongs to submergence village Bhavaria, M.P., and continues to play an important role in the NBA. His wife Jankibhabhi and sister Bhagvatiben Patidar have been important women activists of the NBA.

[111]Batesingh Guruji and Girdhar Guruji, two senior teachers of Narmada Jeevan Shala, coordinate the activities of the schools. Their contribution to the Jeevan Shalas has been extraordinary.

[112]Adivasi children have been exceptionally good at sports such as running and archery, and some students from the Jeevan Shalas have reached the state and national levels in sports.

[113]Prof. Krishna Kumar, ex-Director NCERT, has been an NBA supporter.

[114]Eklavya, a well-known organisation in M.P. propagates creative educational methods for children.

[115]Aksharnandan is a progressive school in Pune that gives importance to alternative methods of teaching.

[116]As people got displaced and were moved to the rehabilitation sites, so also were the Jeevan Shalas started by the NBA in the submergence villages shifted to the rehabilitation sites and these continue to be run by the NBA.

[117]A 'Walk and Talk' shibir is a learn-while-traveling workshop.

[118]ST bus means a state transport bus which was hired for a special purpose for the Jeevan Shala trip.

[119]Senior activist and leader of NAPM, Suniti S. R. is a member of the NBA support group, Pune. Hiramanbhai Jadhav has been a very active member of the Malegaon support group of the NBA. Geetanjali Chavan, a full-time NBA activist, played an important role, particularly during the large-scale submergence of villages in Maharashtra, and continues to be active in the NBA. Rohan Joshi was also a full-time NBA activist.

[120]Baba Amte.

[121]*Mavashi*s and *kamathi*s look after the lodging and boarding of the students in the Jeevan Shalas.

[122]Siyaram (Sidiya) Singa Padvi of submergence village Danel, a student of Jeevan Shala and activist of NBA.

[123]NBA activist, late Shobha Wagh, referred to earlier.

[124]Oustees of Ukai dam in Gujarat, built many decades ago, have not been resettled fully yet.

[125]Filmmaker Simantini Dhuru.

[126]A film named *Laha* based on the collective labour system of the adivasis in the Narmada Valley, made by well-known film maker Sumitra Bhave and colleagues.

[127]Gods and goddesses.

[128]While the top leadership of the NBA along with NAPM had launched a political party, People's Political Front in 2004 (see: https://timesofindia.indiatimes.com/india/Medha-Patkars-party-to-contest-elections/articleshow/568873.cms [accessed 23 November 2021]), it was only in 2014 that some leaders of the NBA, including Medha Patkar, contested Lok Sabha elections as Aam Aadmi Party candidates (see: https://scroll.in/article/724118/why-narmada-bachao-movement-is-paying-the-price-for-the-fractures-in-aam-aadmi-party [accessed 23 November 2021]).

[129]PAPs are pressurised to opt for a cash compensation package and give up their right to get agricultural lands in lieu of land lost in the SSP.

[130]Letter written by Kevalsingh that elaborated the points of contention in the running of the Jeevan Shalas.

[131]As the dam height kept increasing, even houses that were shifted to higher places got submerged. So many families had to face the repeated submergence of their houses, some even thrice, and suffered extensive damages in terms of household goods, building material, wood, etc.

[132]The majority judgement of the Supreme Court in 2000 clearly stated that increase in dam height beyond 90 metres, the height at the time, would be, '...only *pari passu* with the implementation of the relief and rehabilitation measures and on the clearance by the Relief and Rehabilitation Subgroup (of the NCA).'

[133]Mangiben and Vitthalbhai Tadvi belong to village Manibeli.

[134]Adivasi leaders/activists like Kevalsingh gave the first preference for selection of land being allocated by the state for R&R to the other people of their village. So the leaders received poor quality land that was left over at the end. Had Kevalsingh chosen the land first, before others, he would have received better land with irrigation.

[135]A *mavashi* or maternal aunt is the mother's sister and is considered a close family member.